Cultural Translation and Postcolonial Poetry

Also by Ashok Bery

COMPARING POSTCOLONIAL LITERATURES: Dislocations (*co-edited with Patricia Murray*)

Cultural Translation and Postcolonial Poetry

Ashok Bery

First published 2007 by
PALGRAVE MACMILLAN
Houndmills, Basingstoke, Hampshire RG21 6XS and
175 Fifth Avenue, New York, N.Y. 10010
Companies and representatives throughout the world

PALGRAVE MACMILLAN is the global academic imprint of the Palgrave Macmillan division of St. Martin's Press, LLC and of Palgrave Macmillan Ltd. Macmillan® is a registered trademark in the United States, United Kingdom and other countries. Palgrave is a registered trademark in the European Union and other countries.

ISBN-13: 978–1–4039–3310–2   hardback
ISBN-10: 1–4039–3310–3   hardback

This book is printed on paper suitable for recycling and made from fully managed and sustained forest sources. Logging, pulping and manufacturing processes are expected to conform to the environmental regulations of the country of origin.

A catalogue record for this book is available from the British Library.

A catalog record for this book is available from the Library of Congress.

10   9   8   7   6   5   4   3   2   1
16   15   14   13   12   11   10   09   08   07

Printed and bound in Great Britain by
CPI Antony Rowe, Chippenham and Eastbourne

Contents

Acknowledgements

The writing of this book was greatly helped by a Research Leave award from the Arts and Humanities Research Council. I am also grateful for an Overseas Conference Grant from the British Academy, which enabled me to present part of the Louis MacNeice chapter at the triennial conference of the Association for Commonwealth Literature and Language Studies in Hyderabad during the summer of 2004.

Some portions of this book have been read and commented on by Lyn Innes, Harish Trivedi, Arvind Krishna Mehrotra and Patricia Murray; I am grateful to them for their comments and suggestions. I am also grateful to the anonymous reader for Palgrave Macmillan, whose comments helped me to clarify what I had actually done rather than what I thought I had been doing. The responsibility for any remaining errors is, of course, entirely mine. Parts of the chapter on A. K. Ramanujan have been adapted from my essay '"Reflexive Worlds": The Indias of A. K. Ramanujan', which appeared in *Alternative Indias: Writing, Nation and Communalism*, ed. Peter Morey and Alex Tickell (Amsterdam: Rodopi, 2005), pp. 115–39. I am grateful to the publishers for permission to use that material here.

Copyright Acknowledgements

Introduction

The bulk of literary criticism in the field of Anglophone postcolonialism is devoted to fiction. Although a number of individual poets such as Derek Walcott, Les Murray and Seamus Heaney have been the subjects of many books and articles, poetry has been relatively neglected. In particular, there have been few attempts to consider postcolonial poetry within conceptual frameworks which will allow comparisons across national and cultural boundaries.[1]

In this book, I use the idea of cultural translation to look at Anglophone postcolonial poetry from a comparative perspective. The first chapter explores this concept in more detail and subsequent chapters apply some of the issues raised in the first chapter to poets working out of and writing about a variety of locations – Ireland, India, Australia and the Caribbean. All the writers I discuss are in some sense involved in acts of translation. In a number of cases – Louis MacNeice, A. K. Ramanujan and Seamus Heaney – this is true in the most literal sense: all of them have produced a substantial number of distinguished translations from other languages into English. My main concern in relation to these writers, however, has not been with their actual translations (apart from Heaney's *Beowulf*), but with their own poetry. The other poets' connections with translation are of a looser nature, as in Walcott's reworking of Homer, or Murray's engagement with Aboriginal cultures and poetic models. In the case of Judith Wright, whose poetry includes neither interlingual translations nor the kind of reworking of poetic models undertaken by Murray and Walcott, I shall be concerned mainly with how she negotiates the relationship between Aboriginal and white settler populations.

The question of whether such an approach plays too freely with the notion of translation is one that I shall take up in the first chapter. In the rest of this introduction I want to say a few words about other aspects of the structure, scope, aims and methods of the book, so as to clarify what I have and have not attempted to do. After the first chapter, the book falls into two informal parts, each composed of three poets. Cultural translation is a process that takes place on both sides of the colonial divide, as people attempt to make sense of other ways of life (or, of course, largely fails to take place, if one denies that the other cultures make any reasonable, coherent or valuable sense).[2] Mary Louise Pratt, in discussing a related concept, transculturation, notes that it is 'used ... to describe how subordinated or marginal groups select and invent from materials transmitted to them by a dominant or metropolitan culture'. There is, however, another aspect of the phenomenon, which, in her words, is 'more heretical ...: with respect to representation, how does one speak of transculturation from the colonies to the metropolis?'[3] In the first part of this book, I address a version of this question by looking at three writers whose cultural, poetic or ancestral affiliations lean towards the metropolitan culture of Britain (these are, of course, matters of degree only rather than kind), but whose affiliations of location and birth raise questions about the hegemony of that metropolitan culture. One outcome of this tension is what I describe a little later on in this introduction as a concern with anxieties of definition.

The first two writers whom I discuss, the Australians Judith Wright and Les Murray, exhibit contrasting approaches to cultural translation. Wright, as I demonstrate in the chapter on her work, was strongly conscious of the wrongs that European settlers – who included her own ancestors – perpetrated on the indigenous people of Australia, and of the incommensurability between Aboriginal and white settler cultures (the outcome being a feeling that translation is impossible). These feelings, I argue, lead her to the borders of silence. Les Murray, who positions himself culturally as a European (while also insisting on the existence of a distinctive and 'authentic' Australian identity), takes a different stance, contending that a fusion of Aboriginal and European cultures is possible (translation is easy). However, I suggest, the actual poetic practice of these two writers qualifies and complicates both stances. The fourth chapter takes a short step back in time to Louis MacNeice, whose work, I think, falls somewhere in between these two, moving from what looks like a classic Orientalism, in Said's sense, which defines the East as Europe's other, to a more complex, translational sense of the relationship between West and East. In the course of this movement, MacNeice's poetry begins to show some of the creative and transformative possibilities of translation.

The inclusion of MacNeice in a book on postcolonialism may seem unusual, and I will comment more on this in the relevant chapter. For now, I think it sufficient to say that if MacNeice has not (to my knowledge) been discussed within the rubric of postcolonialism, that is no reason for not attempting to do so here. The conflicts of allegiance evident in his work have close affinities with conflicts in the work of writers who are more readily conceived of as postcolonial. While the readings of his work by Irish poets and critics – some of which I refer to in the relevant chapter – may not deploy a postcolonial vocabulary, the questions they raise concerning his location between Ireland and England (amongst other topics) have parallels in many other places and cultures; consequently, postcolonial perspectives have much to offer in a reading of his poetry.

The second part of the book discusses three poets – Seamus Heaney, A. K. Ramanujan and Derek Walcott – who are, as I see it, located culturally or ethnically more on the other side of what I have called the colonial divide. Heaney, a Northern Irish Catholic of rural origins in a dominantly Protestant part of Ireland, forms an interesting comparison with MacNeice, also born in northern Ireland, but with very different social and cultural roots: he was the son of a Church of Ireland clergyman who eventually became a bishop, and had a typically English upper-middle-class education. MacNeice, as I have said, saw his allegiances as divided between Ireland and England/Britain. Heaney's ambivalence is much sharper, as in the famous 'Open Letter' objecting to his inclusion in the 1980s Penguin anthology of British poetry edited by Andrew Motion and Blake Morrison.[4] Indeed, 'ambivalence' is an understated way of describing someone who speaks of himself as 'coerced' in relation to 'living in a northern Ireland that insisted that it – and I – was British'.[5]

Heaney is more deeply (or at least overtly) concerned than MacNeice about the loss or attenuation of the Irish language and Irish culture, as poems such as 'Traditions' and 'a New Song' (both in the 1972 volume *Wintering Out*) or the parable poem 'From the Canton of Expectation' (in *The Haw Lantern*, 1987) attest. In various ways, he attempts to re-connect with those cultural traditions. In these aspects of his work, he has obvious affinities with writers from other parts of the world, such as Ngugi wa Thiong'o, who have spoken of similar concerns.[6] Yet, for Heaney, any temptations to nostalgia and rancour over these losses are counter-pointed and countermanded by, amongst other things, a continuing engagement with English literary traditions as well as with European culture more broadly, as is evident in the impact on him of Dante and Eastern European poetry.

As MacNeice can, from one point of view, be located between Murray and Wright, so, too, can Heaney be positioned between Ramanujan and Walcott. In the way he draws on the resources of English and wider European models, he has strong affiliations with Walcott. On the other hand, his continuing engagement with indigenous traditions links him to Ramanujan. Although Ramanujan spent the majority of his working life in the United States, his work is rooted in Indian languages and cultural traditions, particularly the South Indian ones into which he was born (which is not to suggest that he does not also engage with European and other non-Indian traditions). For Walcott, the situation has been somewhat different; because of the history of the Caribbean, he necessarily writes out of more fragmented cultural locations, forging something for himself out of the disparate pieces I discuss in the chapter on *Omeros*. My discussion of this second group of writers is intended to explore different ways in which cultural translation might work creatively in different contexts with different sets of poetic and cultural resources to hand.

In thinking about the relationship between the first and second group of poets, I have found useful a distinction made by Seamus Heaney in the essay from which I quoted earlier. That essay, an exploration of the complex cultural affiliations of the Irish poet, differentiates between the terms 'other' and 'through-other', the latter a Hiberno-English word which Heaney defines as 'physically untidy or mentally confused' (it echoes an Irish expression meaning 'things mixed up among themselves').[7] Although such definitions may initially seem somewhat negative, Heaney's view is, on the whole, closer to the definition of 'through-otherness' in Terence Dolan's *Dictionary of Hiberno-English*: 'a comfortable state of untidiness'.[8] The state may not always be as comfortable as this suggests; nevertheless the creative mixing of identities which Heaney is discussing is certainly a contrast to self-definitions which work through contrast and exclusion. Commenting on the use of the term 'other' in postcolonial criticism and cultural studies, Heaney suggests that perhaps now is the time of the through-other.[9] This implies that we should move – or perhaps have already moved – beyond a defensive state in which our concern is with establishing a sense of our own cultural or national identity as an entity distinct from others. The time of through-otherness is a time of mixing. Broadly speaking, the first group of poets discussed in this book is more heavily concerned with considerations of otherness, the second, in one way or another, more with through-otherness. Another way to put it is to say that this second group is less inhibited by the anxieties of cultural definition which were part of earlier phases of the postcolonial experience, and are still felt by many today, although perhaps more by critics than by poets.

One of the implications of my assumption that the field of study has moved, or should move, beyond those anxieties of definition is that the term 'postcolonial' does not function as what Peter Hulme describes as a 'badge of merit'.[10] The approach Hulme criticizes often leads to what Bart Moore-Gilbert describes as a kind of perverse 'beauty contest in which the competitors are made to press their claims to have been the most oppressed colonial subjects'. Moore-Gilbert finds this attitude 'invidious and distasteful', and this is a view with which I concur.[11] It is not possible to say that some postcolonial places are in some sense *more* postcolonial than others. There are different ways of experiencing postcoloniality – diasporic, migratory, indigenous, settler, non-settler and so on.

In this spirit, I have not been overly concerned with providing representative coverage of postcolonial cultures and poetries. Significant regions of the postcolonial world, such as Africa, have not been dealt with here. African poets such as Soyinka, Okigbo and Okot p'Bitek have of course made significant contributions to poetry, as indeed have Canadian or New Zealand poets. The postcolonial field is, however, a vast and constantly expanding one and it is clearly not possible to include all of them in a selective study such as this. In my choice of poets here I have, consequently, been guided by my own current interests and by the kind of map I have drawn of this book rather than by any attempts to be somehow representative or comprehensive. While this may lead to certain kinds of omissions, there are for me compensating gains in the ability to prepare the ground for comparisons such as those between Wright and Murray or MacNeice and Heaney.

Something should also be said here about my overall approach and methods. After the first chapter, in which I engage with a number of significant contributions to postcolonial translation theory, my concern has been primarily to offer readings of the poets I have selected for discussion rather than to develop, or engage continuously with, postcolonial theories. Nevertheless, as the preceding paragraphs indicate, the themes of the book touch on many significant topics in postcolonialism. Prominent among these are hybridity, creolization, indigeneity and the question of the 'first peoples'. Indeed my central term 'translation' has become ubiquitous in postcolonial studies, taking on a variety of inflections, from the issues of cultural difference discussed by Homi Bhabha to metaphors for migration and other phenomena.[12] My own approach to the term in the first chapter through the perspectives of translation theory and ethnography will, I hope, help to add other dimensions to the ways in which the term is used.

1
Cultural Translation

Many words have been expended on defining, defending and criticizing the term 'postcolonial' used in the title of this book.[1] I do not want at this point to add very much to them apart from saying that I use it here as a flag of convenience, since, whatever the pros and cons of the term might be, it does at least have the minimum virtue of identifying for readers one of the areas within which this book is set.

More immediately pertinent to my aims in this book is the term 'translation', which I use to approach the poets whom this book discusses. The word will be used in a variety of senses which have become current in contemporary translation theory and postcolonial studies. In some cases, I shall be concerned with the most obvious sense – translations of texts from one language to another, such as Seamus Heaney's *Beowulf*, which I discuss in a later chapter (Old English and Modern English constituting different languages for my purpose). But I will also be using the word in more extended senses. One can speak of Derek Walcott's *Omeros* as constituting a 'translation', even though it is not a translation of Homer in the way that the versions by Robert Fitzgerald or Robert Fagles are. And in a still wider sense, one can speak of cultural translation, as the ethnographers I discuss later on do. There are several ways in which cultural translation can be understood, some guided by colonialist agendas, others not. Christian missionary enterprises during the colonial era were works of translation, since they were attempts to 'translate' non-Christians into a different way of conceiving of themselves and the world.[2] But in this broad sense, any attempt to understand the conceptual schemes of another culture – even when the cultures in question are more or less equal in terms of cultural, political and economic power – involves translation. To interpret the term 'translation' in these extended ways is to run the risk of making it unacceptably vague, and I will return to this problem at the end of the chapter and in the conclusion to the book.

These broad uses of the term are possible, even inevitable, because the concept of translation relates closely to some complex areas of debate – the notion of difference and the relationship between different cultures and languages. In what one might call the 'mainstream' of postcolonial theory, ideas of difference and translation – cultural translation in particular – take their bearings mostly from the work of Homi Bhabha.[3] There are undeniably points of contact between the ideas developed in this book and Bhabha's discussions of interstititiality, in-betweenness and the creative 'Third Space'. My own approach, however, draws on different sources, particularly translation studies and ethnography. Postcolonial theory has engaged with ethnographers such as James Clifford, Talal Asad and Clifford Geertz, but the mainstream referred to above has had little contact with postcolonial translation studies, although there is a growing body of work on the subject.[4]

The significance of these areas of study for my purposes is that in both of them there has been considerable methodological discussion of the different ways in which one language or culture can be related to, or transferred into, another, and of the problems with various approaches. Since interlingual translation is, among other things, a practical activity, it is imbued with a sense of process and technique. Similarly, in recent years, many anthropologists have been examining the problems of *writing* anthropology and of how relationships between observer and observed can have an impact on this. However illuminating the work of Bhabha and others may be, it tends to operate on an abstract theoretical and conceptual level without this sense of methodological process. Consequently, translation studies and anthropology have the potential to provide more specific points of entry for my main purpose here, which is to read poets and poems rather than specifically to make a contribution to postcolonial translation theory. In the remainder of this chapter, I shall focus primarily on certain issues that arise in discussions of cultural difference and translation and on the perspectives that postcolonial translation theory and ethnography bring to bear on these subjects.

In translation theory, it is now widely accepted that questions of difference and equivalence cannot simply be confined narrowly to language, but that they are inseparable from, and embedded in, wider issues of cultural difference; and, particularly in feminist and postcolonial perspectives on translation, there is an awareness that these issues in turn need to be related to power differentials between nations, languages and cultures.[5] It is when one tries to move beyond such generalities, however, that the difficult questions begin to emerge. A sample of these questions might include the following: How, indeed, does one step beyond the bounds of one's own language or culture to understand another language or culture? How do we find equivalents between one language and another? Indeed, is equivalence possible? Are we not bound to impose our own 'alien' perspectives on the cultures we are trying to understand, the languages we are trying to translate? Do we not distort them in the very act of translation?

I will use as a convenient point of entry into such questions the model put forward in George Steiner's influential work *After Babel* (first published in 1975). This can be criticized on a number of grounds, some of which I touch on later, but it is, nevertheless, helpful as an initial way of orienting oneself in the area.[6] The 'hermeneutic motion', as Steiner calls this model, breaks down the process of translation into four stages – trust, aggression, incorporation and restitution. Trust, in Steiner's words, consists of 'an investment of belief, underwritten by previous experience but epistemologically exposed and psychologically hazardous, in the meaningfulness, in the "seriousness" of the facing or, strictly speaking, adverse text'.[7]

The translator, then, moves towards the text to be translated; however, as Steiner's word 'adverse' suggests, that text resists him or her, proves intractable in various degrees and may even be actively hostile. The encounter with the other is 'exposed' and fraught with danger, as are all encounters with the strange and unfamiliar. The second stage in the process, aggression, is 'incursive and extractive': the translator 'invades, extracts and brings home'. In the third stage, incorporation, meaning and form are imported into the 'native semantic field' of the translator, a process which can 'potentially dislocate or relocate the whole of the native structure'. The final stage, restitution, involves something being returned to the source language text. This is a restoration of balance, an 'enactment of reciprocity', a process of 'exchange and restored parity'.[8] The aggressive act of translation is followed at some stage by reparation, so that restitution is on one level a mode of atonement for the act of linguistic invasion and aggression, a palliative for the guilt of altering a text (most of my remarks here apply largely to literary, rather than, say, technical, translations). In describing restitution, Steiner pursues the imperialistic tenor and implications of his terminology:

> We encircle and invade cognitively. We come home laden, thus again off-balance, having caused disequilibrium throughout the system by

taking away from 'the other' and by adding, though possibly with ambiguous consequence, to our own. The system is now off-tilt. The hermeneutic act must compensate. If it is to be authentic, it must mediate into exchange and restored parity.[9]

Restitution can take various forms. For instance, the very act of selecting a particular text to translate operates as a signal that it is considered to have some value; it is thought that the text will add to the language and culture into which it is being translated.[10] Furthermore, the 'process of translation, like all modes of focused understanding, will detail, illumine, and generally body forth its object'. A translation is also an interpretation and criticism – in some ways, a more rigorous interpretation and criticism than occurs in literary study. Different translations in different eras, for instance, can bring out different aspects of a text. A translation can also 'provide the original with a persistence and geographical-cultural range of survival which it would otherwise lack'.[11] Steiner locates an important dimension of restitution in a term that has a long history in European discussions of translation: the notion of 'fidelity'.

> Fidelity is not literalism or any technical device for rendering 'spirit'. ... The translator, the exegetist, the reader is *faithful to* his text, makes his response responsible, only when he endeavours to restore the balance of forces, of integral presence, which his appropriative comprehension has disrupted.[12]

Although total equity and total restitution are never achieved, 'the ideal', says Steiner, 'makes explicit the demand for equity in the hermeneutic process'. In Steiner's analysis, a failure of equity can occur in two broad ways – through a diminution of the source text, or, more rarely, through an enhancement of it, in which a 'translator produces a piece of work which surpasses the original in stylistic quality or in emotional scope'.[13]

However, although Steiner spends considerable time on the notion of equity, and despite the terminology of invasion and aggression, he has little, if anything, to say about the kinds of radical inequity in translation which arise from power differentials between cultures, nations, ethnic groups, classes, genders and languages. This lacuna no doubt has something to do with background and education. His cultural traditions are, as he says, those of 'Central European and Judaic humanism'.[14] Almost all his examples are European ones, so that power differentials do not appear as starkly as they do in colonial and postcolonial contexts. Nevertheless, in its use of terms such as 'invade', 'aggression', 'incorporation', 'extract' and 'bring home', Steiner's analysis has obvious political – specifically imperial – connotations, although such implications have a long history in European accounts of translation. Steiner's terminology, like that of those who precede him, at least has the merit of confronting us openly with the fact that *all* translation is in some sense invasive, manipulative and, if you will, imperialistic; it will not leave the source text as it originally found it.

After Babel has, in fact, a rather broad view of translation as something which operates not only between speakers of different languages, but also, for instance, between two localities within the same language community or even between two individuals. The process of translation also applies to the way we 'read' the past and utterances from the past. As Steiner puts it: 'No two historical epochs, no two social classes, no two localities use words and syntax to signify exactly the same things, to send identical signals of valuation and inference. Neither do two human beings.'[15] Such a conception is scarcely original to Steiner. One of the important reference points in translation theory, Friedrich Schleiermacher's essay 'On the Different Methods of Translating' (1813), opens with a discussion of the idea of translation as something applicable within one language in relation to different dialects, social groups and even individuals, before narrowing the scope of the discussion to translation between different languages:

> For not only do the dialects of the different clans that make up a people, and the different ways a language or dialect develops in different centuries, already constitute different languages in a stricter sense, between which it is often enough necessary to translate; even contemporaries who share a dialect but belong to different classes that rarely come together in social intercourse and diverge substantially in their education are commonly unable to communicate save through a similar mediation.[16]

This broad conception of translation is, of course, no more than an extension of the principle that translation is a way of trying to negotiate difference. Yet, as soon as one starts to invoke differences of social class as barriers across which translation must occur, one is beginning to be involved in differentials of power. Although neither Schleiermacher nor Steiner takes up this issue, it is nevertheless inherent in what they are saying. The dimension of power which permeates

Steiner's terminology has been present in explicit or implicit forms for centuries. Famous examples occur in John Florio's prefatory material to his translation (1603) of Montaigne's essays. In the 'Epistle Dedicatory', for instance, he refers to the translation as a 'defective edition' on the grounds that 'all translations are reputed females, delivered at second hand', and in 'To the Courteous Reader', he links translation to usurpation: 'What do the best then, but glean after others' harvest? borrow their colours, inherit their possessions? What do they but translate? perhaps, usurp?'.[17]

Much recent discussion of translation focuses more explicitly on the aggression and imbalance of power which exists and has existed in so many situations where translation is involved. To take the issue further, and in a direction which may prove fruitful for my own concerns here, it will be necessary to draw on these kinds of analyses. One way to start engaging with such issues is through an important debate in contemporary translation theory – that between the strategies of translation known by the terms 'foreignizing' and 'domesticating', which are neatly summed up by Schleiermacher, who is one of the main modern sources of this distinction: 'Either the translator leaves the author in peace as much as possible and moves the reader toward him; or he leaves the reader in peace as much as possible and moves the writer toward him.'[18] In another classic of translation theory, 'The Task of the Translator' (1923), Walter Benjamin quotes Rudolf Pannwitz to make the same point: 'Our translations, even the best ones, proceed from a wrong premise. They want to turn Hindi, Greek, English into German instead of turning German into Hindi, Greek, English.'[19]

'Domesticating' strategies involve an assimilation of the translated work into the idioms and traditions of the target language and its culture. This is associated with a 'sense-for-sense' approach in which the strategy is to strive for a translation that will, in Lawrence Venuti's words, 'work as a literary text in its own right, exerting its force within native traditions'. This kind of translation is 'strongly domesticating, assimilating foreign literatures to the linguistic and cultural values of the receiving situation'.[20] An example of this is Donald Davie's comment on how to judge translations: 'If what you have before you, offering itself as the translation of a poem, does not hang together as an English poem should, then you know that what you have before you is a mistranslation.'[21] 'Foreignizing' modes, in contrast, allow the otherness of the translated text to come through, and in doing so they make the reader aware of the distances that exist between their own culture and that from which the original comes. This is associated with a 'word-for-word' approach, one which, in Schleiermacher's words, 'adheres to the turns and figures of the original'.[22]

Domesticating strategies are often seen as ideological tools which deny or suppress difference, feeding the prejudices which a reader might bring to a text and reinforcing the hegemony of the translating culture (the analysis is predicated on the assumption that this is the 'stronger' one, and that it is usually European or North American). In Lawrence Venuti's words:

> A fluent strategy performs a labor of acculturation which domesti-cates the foreign text, making it intelligible and even familiar to the target-language reader, providing him or her with the narcissistic experience of recognizing his or her culture in a cultural other, enact-ing an imperialism that extends the dominion of transparency with other ideological discourses over a different culture.[23]

This criticism of domestication is prominent in postcolonial discus-sions of translation, such as Eric Cheyfitz's argument that that European colonizers in North America 'translated' the relationship between native Americans and the land into European terms so that they could then lay claim to it. Because the European term and idea 'property' did not seem to be shared by the indigenous population, the settlers could then say that, like animals, the native peoples lived in, but did not own, the land, since they did not cultivate it or fence it off:

> The European process of translation ... attempted to displace ... Native Americans into the realm of the proper, into that place where the relation between *property* and *identity* is inviolable, not so these Americans could possess the proper but so that having been trans-lated into it they could be dispossessed of it (of what, that is, they never possessed) and relegated to the territory of the figurative. *A Good Speed to Virginia* (1609) ... focuses one form of this displacement for us: 'Savages have no particular propertie in any part or parcel of that countrey, but only a generall residencie there, as wild beasts have in the forests.' Not to have 'propertie,' then, is to lose, from a European perspective, a significant part of one's humanness. No other *legitimate* mode of relation to the land – no other mode of identity – is imagined in the preceding passage.[24]

Such criticisms of domestication have led many to see 'foreignizing' approaches as more appropriate, more ethical and more engaged with difference and otherness, particularly in cases where there are considerable power differentials.

This distinction between 'foreignizing' and 'domesticating' is a useful way of mapping strategies of translation, if one treats them as constituting the two poles of a continuum, rather than mutually exclusive alternatives; and in practice what most translation theorists do is, as Anthony Pym suggests, to 'accept clines going from one pole to another, with a whole series of middling strategies'. However, Pym argues, the 'basic binarism remains anyway, not just in the mode of thought but more importantly in the generalized refusal to consider the translator, or the place of the translator, as a viable third term'.[25] Pym's argument, as I understand it, is that Schleiermacher's strict binarism in fact ends by reinforcing the mutually exclusionary demarcation between what is considered foreign and what is considered native to one's own culture. By allowing only a movement inwards towards the native culture *or* only a movement outwards towards the foreign culture, Schleiermacher excludes the intercultural place where the translator stands, the middle ground of hybridity. Take an example from two languages with which I am familiar. Here is a simple Hindi sentence: 'vah saṛak ke pās khaṛī thī' ('She was standing near the road'). If I were to translate the Hindi into English, trying as far as I could to follow the twists and turns of the original in a strict word-for-word version, I would have to write 'She road near standing was'. Apart from the aesthetic and pragmatic point that a whole book translated in this style would rapidly become intolerable, there are other considerations which go beyond questions of readability and take us into the realms of principle. In Hindi, the pronoun 'vah', which I have translated 'she', does not by itself specify gender; that job is done by the inflection of the adjective (kharī) and verb (thī). To incorporate this effect – the delaying of the person's gender – in the English version, one might render the original: 'Someone was standing near the road. She ...'; but then that would be a more radical transformation. This means that even the apparently foreignizing translation offered has already begun the process of domesticating; the translation does not strictly convey the contours of the Hindi, since the gender of the person being referred to would not be apparent from the first word in the sentence in Hindi as it is in English; it would only be ascertained towards the end of the sentence. And this might be a crucial difference in the effect and impact of the two versions (for instance, the writer of the Hindi sentence might, for some reason, be trying to delay the disclosure of the identity and gender of the person being indicated). In other words, even in trying to foreignize as much as one can, one is inevitably drawn to domesticate, and the strict demarcation between the two begins to break down because of the grammatical differences between the two languages.[26]

While, clearly, one can veer more or less towards one or the other, any translation will involve both. This might seem something of a truism, but I think that once there has been a breach of this sort in the dualism, once one has opened the door to a mixture of modes, then rather than deciding matters on a theoretical or ideological level alone, the question has to be negotiated each time, taking into account the text to be translated, the nature of the source language, what Pym describes as the 'place of the translator' and what an earlier age would have called the 'genius' of the language into which the text is being translated. This last idea opens the door to that almost forgotten concept in literary studies – value, and specifically the quality of the work *in its translated form*. In an Open University coursebook on poetry in translation, Donald Davie quotes Dante Gabriel Rossetti on the significance of value in a translation: 'The life-blood of rhymed translation is this, – that a good poem shall not be turned into a bad one. The only true motive for putting poetry into a fresh language must be to endow a fresh nation, as far as possible, with one more possession of beauty.'[27] As I noted earlier, Davie does, it is true, go on to offer a fully assimilative view of translation:

> A verse translation into English must be considered, first of all, *as an English poem*. … the first and minimal requirement of the translation of a foreign poem (one which many translators fail to meet) is that a poem be turned into *a poem*. If what you have before you, offering itself as the translation of a poem, does not hang together as an English poem should, then you know that what you have before you is a mistranslation.[28]

While there are certainly overstatements here and in Rossetti's remark, there is also a salutary emphasis on the literary quality of the translations, rather than its pedagogic or ideological value alone.

The opposition between foreignizing and domestication, I have been suggesting, poses the question in a misleading way, because in approaching other languages or cultures, we do not do so as *tabulae rasae*. In what Pym describes as the 'place of the translator' of my (admittedly modest) Hindi sentence, I am already approaching the Hindi through the grammatical and other filters of English (as I would approach English through those of Hindi if I were doing the translation the other way round). I am already in between the two. And this case is a general one; any foreign language or culture is already domesticated, simply because our approach to it is necessarily filtered through our own linguistic and cultural apparatus. What we are seeing is already positioned in a messy middle ground. This point can be extended by drawing on both ethnography and postcolonial approaches to translation. I want to approach it first by the ethnographic route, making use of classic discussions of cultural translation by Godfrey Lienhardt and Clifford Geertz.

Lienhardt's essay 'Modes of Thought' discusses the problem of understanding a 'remote' culture's ways of 'apprehending reality' as a question of translation:

> We mediate between their habits of thought ... and those of our own society; in doing so, it is not finally some mysterious 'primitive philosophy' that we are exploring, but the further potentialities of our own thought and language.
>
> The problem of describing to others how members of a remote tribe think then begins to appear largely as one of translation, of making the coherence primitive thought has in the languages it really lives in, as clear as possible in our own.[29]

These further potentialities are developed because, if 'we try to contain the thought of a primitive society in our language and categories, without also modifying these in order to receive it, ... it begins in part to lose the sense it seemed to have'. This modification can only be done by giving a 'temporary assent' to other ways of thinking, by a 'suspension of criticism', a willingness to 'entertain them in the mind, without at once trying to rationalize them to fit into a place ... already prepared for other, more familiar, ideas'.[30] And in this suspended place, our own categories and language infuse into and are infused by the other ones. There are aspects of Lienhardt's terminology which perhaps make contemporary readers uncomfortable, and it may be, as Tejaswini Niranjana argues, that his essay 'constructs an inner hierarchy: primitive thought needs to be translated into modern, for it is that which is not yet modern'.[31] Nevertheless, I don't think these considerations invalidate his description of the *processes* involved in dealing with another culture (or language).

Geertz, similarly, in his essay 'Found in Translation', suggests that our knowledge of other cultures steers a path between two different positions: 'we can never apprehend another people's or another period's imagination neatly, as though it were our own'. But this doesn't mean that 'we can ... never genuinely apprehend it at all. ... We can apprehend it well enough, at least as well as we apprehend anything else not properly ours, but we do so not by looking *behind* the interfering glosses that connect us to it but *through* them'.[32] We cannot simply get rid of the interfering glosses of our culture, which operate in and through our signifying systems, including, particularly, language. Anthropological understanding, then, involves a negotiation between two sets of signifying systems, those of the observer and those of the observed, the latter being necessarily filtered through the former. Another Geertz essay, '"From the Native's Point of View"', argues that such understanding does not need extra capacities for 'ego effacement and fellow feeling'. Instead, Geertz concludes:

> Whatever accurate or half-accurate sense one gets of what one's informants are, as the phrase goes, really like ... comes from the ability to construe their modes of expression, what I would call their symbol systems. ... Understanding the form and pressure of, to use the dangerous word one more time, natives' inner lives is more like grasping a proverb, catching an allusion, seeing a joke or, as I have suggested, reading a poem than it is like achieving communion.[33]

Both Lienhardt and Geertz are, to return to the terms of translation theory, involved in the inevitable but messy middle ground where foreignization and domestication meet. These anthropological contributions, then, also qualify and question any sharp and stable separation between the two sides involved in the process, between foreignization and domestication.

Although the insights in Lienhardt's and Geertz's essays have considerable validity, the analysis needs to be qualified by observing that neither really engages with the imbalances of power which mark much anthropological observation and linguistic translation.[34] However, postcolonial approaches to translation, which are generally conscious of power differentials, arrive at similar conclusions. Samia Mehrez, for instance, examining the phenomenon of the Francophone text in North Africa, suggests that they call into question the traditional demarcation between 'source' and 'target' languages:

> These postcolonial texts ... have succeeded in forging a new language that defies the very notion of a 'foreign' text that can be readily translatable into another language. With this literature we can no longer merely concern ourselves with conventional notions of linguistic equivalence, or ideas of loss and gain which have long been

a consideration in translation theory. For these texts written by post-colonial bilingual subjects create a language 'in between' and there-fore come to occupy a space 'in between.'[35]

Lienhardt and Mehrez explicitly, and Geertz more implicitly, are touching on *creative* uses of the process of translation. It is these aspects I now wish to pursue, drawing in more detail on issues raised by trans-lation in postcolonial contexts. The positions taken by postcolonial dis-cussions of translation range from Eric Cheyfitz's pessimistic view of the encroachments and invasiveness of translation to the more hopeful ver-sions of Vicente Rafael. In Cheyfitz's analysis, I noted earlier, the colo-nizers imposed their 'language' (their notion of property, for instance) on the native peoples of North America, and, by translating the Indians in this way, established their own dominion and destroyed a way of life. This leads him to a stance of extreme suspicion. Thus, after quoting a passage from Lévi-Stauss's *Tristes Tropiques* which discusses the possi-bility of '*using* all societies – without adopting features from anyone of them – to elucidate principles of social life that we can apply in reforming our own customs and *not those of foreign societies*', Cheyfitz comments:

> The issue of getting to know other societies better is deeply prob-lematic, dependent as it is on the problems of translation that I am trying to make excruciating. And the issue of 'using' other societies to reform our own even if in this process we somehow never use them, bothers me. But that is probably because 'use' in this context is the honest word. Even if we were to disavow the attempt to make other societies into our property, vowing only to get to know them better in order to reform the institution of property in our own, we would remember, as Lévi-Strauss does, that the history of this knowl-edge, the history of anthropology, cannot be separated from the his-tory of the West's appropriation of these societies.[36]

Of course the history of anthropology is bound up with 'the history of the West's appropriation of these societies', but to reject *all* translation on those grounds seems a counsel of despair, not least because of the parochial assumption that all of it is done at the instigation of what as shorthand I shall call 'Europe', and that knowledge of other societies is an exclusively European occupation and preoccupation. The logical out-come of Cheyfitz's view may well be, as Douglas Robinson claims, that since all translation appropriates and uses the other, the only alternative is 'non-translation'; that is, one must 'immerse oneself in a foreign culture without colonizing it, ... open yourself up to the "mysteries" of an alien culture without necessarily trying to render what you learn into English, the tainted language of the colonizers'.[37] And one might ask, why stop with translation between languages? All translation is a use and appropriation, all translation involves hegemonic relationships; consequently all translation is ethically compromised, including intracultural translation, such as that between the past and the present. And if, as Octavio Paz argues, 'the world' is both 'presented to us as a collection of similarities' and 'as a growing heap of texts, each slightly different from the one that came before it: translations of translations of translations', so that culture is, in effect, translation, then Cheyfitz's view dooms us to silence and stasis.[38]

All translation involves 'using' or appropriating other societies, as Steiner's terminology of invasion and aggression acknowledges. It is not the issue of 'getting to know other societies better', of 'using' them per se that is problematic; it is a question of *how* one uses them and gets to know them. In his postcolonial zeal, Cheyfitz seems to underestimate the significance of this. For Cheyfitz, the process of translation – particularly as regards the notion of 'property' – became a tool of imperialism, since the natives were 'translated' into European notions of property in order that they could 'legitimately' (in the European view) be dispossessed (as it turns out, in Cheyfitz, of something they didn't possess, because their relationship to the land didn't hinge on the idea of possession). Although this indeed appears to have happened, it is not, in principle, the only outcome.

Adjustments and counter-adjustments certainly have to take place on both sides; but is it adequate simply to dismiss these as *only* the appropriation of one culture by another? Colonized societies may be translated in large part in the service of colonialism, and this involves cultural violence and distortion; but also, often enough, the colonized society is seen by some to have qualities needed by at least sections of the colonizing society. Thus, the Romantic era's 'translation' of the East by Shelley, Coleridge, Byron, Southey and others was also seen as supplying corrective dimensions within European culture. The same might be said of, say, the late nineteenth-century engagement with Indian religions by institutions such as the Pali Text Society and writers such as Yeats. These can be described as 'uses' of colonized societies and as Orientalist in Said's sense, but to stop there is wholly inadequate, since at the same time they also display one of the important impulses which underlie the act of translation: an extension of the intellectual, spiritual, emotional and linguistic resources available to the society which is doing the translating (as indicated by Lienhardt and Lévi-Strauss in the passages discussed above). And if we move beyond the parochial assumption that all translation involves 'Europe', we can see other positive uses of it, some of them spectacularly creative. One example would be the translation of Indian religious and cultural traditions and texts into Tibetan, where, interacting with indigenous traditions, they became the singular and influential way of looking at the world and at spirituality that is known as Tibetan Buddhism.

In the counter-examples I have adduced, translations do indeed add something to the target culture, and don't simply appropriate the source culture. And this is true also of translations by the colonized society. The very Indian novels in English that many postcolonial critics value and spend their time analysing, teaching and discussing – not to speak of the many Indian novels in other languages – depend, after all, for some of their possibilities on the encounter between Indian and European cultures. Thus O. Chandumenon, the nineteenth-century writer of *Indulekha* (1889), which is generally held to be the first novel written in the South Indian language Malayalam, describes his book as an attempt to convey to friends the flavour of the English novels he was reading.[39] When the novel form was adopted in late nineteenth- and early twentieth-century India it came under the influence of native narrative traditions, and something different emerged.[40]

Another way of putting these points is to say that Cheyfitz's analysis portrays the translator (in his example, the British) as active and the translated (Native Americans) as passive. For Cheyfitz, Douglas Robinson argues, the former are the 'doers, the thinkers, the translators, the takers', the latter are the 'done-to, the thought-about, the translated, the bereft'.[41] It is important to remember that, despite the imbalances of power, there is a two-way (at least) process involved. As has often been argued in connection with Edward Said's *Orientalism*, the receiving culture, even a weaker one, is not simply and entirely imposed on; Geertz's 'interfering glosses' work for the weaker culture too, so that a creative process can and often does come into play. The translated are translating even as they are being translated. To see the fuller picture, we also need to look at things from the point of view of the colonized. For a number of reasons, the translation carried out on them does not occur in a smooth and unproblematic way. One is resistance (active or passive) and opposition to the act of translation (for instance, the failure of Christian missionary work to make much progress in India). But this resistance also occurs through the way in which the version of the self being offered is altered and adapted in the very process of reception. An example of this process is discussed extensively in Vicente Rafael's *Constructing Colonialism*, which analyses the impact of Christianity in the Philippines, and suggests that the way translation operated in the reception of Christianity by Tagalog society opened up the possibility of a partial evasion of colonial hegemony. What Rafael calls 'mistranslations' occurred on both side of this encounter:

> Conversion in early Tagalog colonial society was predicated on translation; yet Spaniards' and the Tagalogs' notions and practices of translation differed to the degree that the relative position of one to the other remained ambiguously defined. Christian conversion and colonial rule emerged through what appeared to be a series of mistranslations. ... Each group read into the other's language and behavior possibilities that the original speakers had not intended or foreseen. For the Spaniards, translation was always a matter of reducing the native language and culture to accessible objects for and subjects of divine and imperial intervention. For the Tagalogs, translation was a process less of internalizing colonial-Christian conventions than of evading their totalizing grip by repeatedly marking the differences between their language and interests and those of the Spaniards.[42]

The cultures that are being translated modify and adapt the versions of their translated selves that are offered to them. In this way, translation can extend the resources available to a society and enable it to find new ways of dealing with or representing their own and other cultures, while at the same time resisting the simple imposition of the other culture, which is, as I said earlier, being filtered through their linguistic and cultural apparatus.

A similar conclusion can be derived from the remarkable views of translation as cannibalism developed by the Brazilians Haroldo and Augusto de Campos from the modernist Oswald de Andrade's *Manifesto Anthopófago* of 1928, in which de Andrade reconsiders the case of the cannibalistic devouring of a Portuguese bishop by the Tupi Indians in 1554.[43] The manifesto is a fragmented modernist text which puts forward the notion of cannibalism not as a taboo but as a source of strength, a 'vaccine', which counters European ideologies, including the separation between spirit and body:

> The spirit refuses to conceive spirit without body. Anthropomorphism. Necessity of cannibalistic vaccine. For proper balance against the religions of the meridian. And exterior inquisitions.

We had the right codification of vengeance. The codified science of Magic. Cannibalism. For the permanent transformation of taboo into totem.[44]

For Haroldo de Campos, cannibalism was a 'critical devouring of the universal cultural heritage, formulated not from the insipid, resigned perspective of the "noble savage" ... but from the point of view of the "bad savage", the cannibal'. This, for de Campos, meant 'transculturation, or, better, a "transvalorization"', an act of 'appropriation ... expropriation, de-hierarchization, deconstruction'. He goes on:

> We could say that it deserves to be eaten, devoured. With this clarification and specification: the cannibal was a polemicist (from the Greek polemos, meaning struggle or combat) but he was also an 'anthologist': he devoured only the enemies he considered strong, to take from them the marrow and protein to fortify and renew his own natural energies.[45]

Elsewhere, de Campos writes: 'Translation as transfusion. Of blood. Ironically, we could talk of vampirization, thinking now of the translator's nourishment.'[46] One of the implications of this view, Else Vieira comments, is that 'if, in the cannibalist philosophy, translation becomes a two-way flow, the very terminology "source" and "target" becomes depleted. By the same token, the power relation between source and target, superior/inferior ceases to exist.'[47]

These remarks on the creative possibilities of translation are not intended to justify or mitigate the physical and cultural violence of colonialism, but merely to reiterate that translation can be a contributory source to an extension and negotiation of identity. I shall be concerned in this book mostly, although not exclusively, with these creative possibilities, as well as with the way in which what is being translated resists the process. It is with this subject of resistance that I want to round off the chapter.

It is easy to make the term 'translation' so protean and so metaphorical that it is increasingly drained of specificity, and a number of people have expressed unease about extended uses of the term. Harish Trivedi, for one, has criticized the whole idea of cultural translation as it is used in postcolonial studies by Homi Bhabha and others. For Trivedi, the use of the term 'translation' in a monolingual 'non-textual non-linguistic sense' to mean 'the process and condition of human migrancy', is an act of 'usurpation' and a threat to 'bilingual bicultural ground'.[48] Although only two of the poets I discuss in this book – Heaney and Ramanujan – are considered in contexts involving more than one language, Trivedi's view is one with which I have a great deal of sympathy. However, what I have tried to keep in mind throughout is something that is an important aspect of interlingual translation: what George Steiner calls the 'resistant particularity of the "other"', which he feels is something that all 'great translation' must convey.[49] In this connection, I find Prasenjit Gupta's distinction between 'surface' and 'deep' resistance helpful. Surface resistance, the kind that is apparent in 'foreignizing' translation, is marked by word-choice, syntax and other such means. This, however, runs the risk that the reader may be, in Gupta's phrase, 'awkwarded out'. Deep resistance, on the other hand, need not involve such obvious grammatical signs; instead, what is important is the marking of 'another culture's deeply different beliefs, the signification of a new world-view'.[50] The two types of resistance are connected, of course, since deep resistance must be manifested in language (as well as in other signifying systems). And it is likely that truly deep resistance can only exist if the languages involved are also different. Thus the difference between, say, Anglophone Americans and the British is not as sharp as that between the latter and Australian Aborigines or speakers of Tamil (to take two examples from subsequent chapters). Nevertheless, my contention here is that even when the writer involved (say Judith Wright) is working in a monolingual context, it is possible that the symptoms of deep resistance can be seen. My intention, therefore, has been to restrict the term 'translation' to various versions of the kind of process that Geertz, for instance, points to, that structure of similarity-in-difference and difference-in-similarity which he sees as characteristic of cultural translation. Interlingual translation is one, but not the only, example of this structure. However, although I have tried to limit my use of the term in this way, it remains possible, of course, that I may in practice have stepped beyond such a usage.

As I have asserted earlier, my main concerns and interests are not with postcolonial or translation theory, or with carving out a consistent theoretical position on the matters discussed above. Although not all the aspects of translation discussed in this chapter will be developed in later parts of this book, what I have tried to do is to raise a number of issues and perspectives which will, I hope, provide productive points of entry into the language and poetry of the writers I discuss in the chapters that follow.

2
Songlines: Judith Wright and Belonging

Two interlinked concerns have repeatedly pressed themselves on the attention of writers and commentators who have discussed the nature of Australian identities: one is the relationship between the Aborigines and white Australians, and the other is the meanings of the Australian landscape. These subjects are certainly of some importance in this chapter and the next: the Australian writers discussed here, Judith Wright and Les Murray, have been consistently preoccupied with both topics, in their prose as well as their poetry. They are also significant in relation to the idea of cultural translation which animates this book.

For the Aboriginal peoples, the land has always been a central part of their consciousness, spirituality and way of life, and as we have become increasingly aware of this, our sense of the contrast between it and the desacralized post-Enlightenment European attitudes which the settlers brought with them has sharpened. The inter-racial relationship is something which has been forced on the Aborigines, and to which they have had to accommodate themselves in mostly tragic ways, and from a position of extreme disadvantage.

Both landscape and race are also embedded in the historical consciousness of the white settler populations and in their attempts to learn to belong to what was for them a new and very strange country. The reasons for this go back to the first settlements towards the end of the eighteenth century. As Stuart Macintyre puts it in his recent history of Australia:

> The desire for a binding national past that would connect the people to the land was frustrated by the feeling of rootlessness, of novelty without depth. The longing for belonging to an indigenous culture

was denied by the original usurpation. A history of colonisation yielded to a realisation of invasion.[1]

The longing Macintyre speaks of here, the desire to be connected to the place, is inextricably intertwined with the historical memory and inherited guilt of the usurpation.

This connection and this guilt were constant features of Judith Wright's prose and poetry. In the introduction to her best-known critical work, *Preoccupations in Australian Poetry*, she invokes D. H. Lawrence's *Kangaroo* as a starting point:

> Lawrence. ... saw that something had gone out of the European consciousness, in this country, and that as yet nothing had taken its place. And he related this emptiness to the country itself. ... Lawrence saw ... the scar left by the struggle to conquer and waken, for our own purposes, a landscape that had survived on its own terms until the world's late days. Its only human inhabitants had been the aboriginals whom we dispossessed – who were bound to the land we took from them, by the indissoluble link of religion and totemic kinship, so that our intrusion on the land itself became a kind of bloodless murder, even where no actual murder took place.
>
> (*PAP*, pp. xvi–xvii)

Variations and transmutations of these themes, along with a stress on the importance of reparation, appear in her prose writings. In a short account of the historical events which form the subject of her poem 'Nigger's Leap, New England', she identifies 'two strands' which had become part of her, 'the love of the land we have invaded, and the guilt of the invasion', going on to add:

> It is a haunted country. We owe it repentance and such amends as we can make, and one last chance of making those amends is to keep as much of it as we can, in the closest state we can to its original beauty. It was not 'wilderness' to the people who lived by it and through it, but the source of their very life and spirit; and to those of them who somehow survived our invasion, it remains so. And for us, too, it can be a place where we find some kind of rest, joy, and even forgiveness.[2]

Here she focuses on reparation through conservation, a concern which was to become dominant in her last years.

Of the two concerns which I mentioned at the outset, it is the relationship to the land which has, historically, preoccupied the white settlers more than the relationship with the Aborigines. With a few exceptions, the latter was not a particularly worrying issue for most of the white population until well into the twentieth century. During the nineteenth century, the Australian landscape, because of its emptiness, difference and strangeness, was a threat to the very notion of identity and to 'at-homeness'; it negated the inherited civilization which the British brought with them. This point has been made by many over the last two centuries, but one of the most vivid and best-known expressions of it is a document which Wright discusses at length in her introduction to *Preoccupations in Australian Poetry*, Marcus Clarke's preface to an edition of Adam Lindsay Gordon's poems:

> The lonely horseman ... feels, despite his fortune, that the trim utilitarian civilisation which bred him shrinks into insignificance beside the contemptuous grandeur of forest and ranges coeval with an age in which European scientists have cradled his own race.[3]

The vast threat posed here to the 'lonely horseman' and his sense of himself, to the whole civilization from which he originates, is both a source of anxiety and an opening into 'grandeur', a grandeur no longer possible in his own culture, as the words 'trim utilitarian' suggest. Yet the contemptuousness of the grandeur again highlights the threat.

A page earlier in the preface, Clarke has suggested that meaning in landscape is a function of its enshrinement in the language, poetry and narrative of the past:

> In historic Europe, where every rood of ground is hallowed in legend and in song, the least imaginative can find food for sad and sweet reflection. ... Soothed, saddened, and cheered by turns, we partake of the varied moods which belong not so much to ourselves as to the dead men who, in old days, sung, suffered, or conquered in the scenes which we survey.[4]

'But this our native or adopted land has no past, no story. No poet speaks to us', he adds, an idea which, as we are now aware from our increasing knowledge of Aboriginal culture and philosophy, is an ethnocentric one, since, for the Aborigines, the land was deeply inscribed with meaning, stories and songs. It is a notion, though, which continued as a force in the white settler consciousness during the twentieth century, as we can see from another famous Australian text, A. D. Hope's poem 'Australia', with its reference to the country as being 'without songs, architecture, history'.[5] Even for those who are aware of and sympathetic to Aboriginal culture, of course, it continues to be a problem, because Aboriginal narratives cannot in any real sense be *their* stories, *their* past.

Yet, as other writers in other cultures – Whitman in the United States, Walcott in the Caribbean, for example – have suggested, this apparent lack of meaning is also an opportunity to make a new language, new stories. And this is what Clarke also sees:

> In Australia alone is to be found the Grotesque, the Weird, the *strange scribblings of nature learning how to write.* ... the dweller in the wilderness ... *learns the language of the barren and the uncouth, and can read the hieroglyphs of haggard gum-trees.* ... The phantasmagoria of that wild dreamland termed the Bush interprets itself, and the Poet of our desolation begins to comprehend why free Esau loved his heritage of desert sand better than all the bountiful richness of Egypt.[6]

The landscape, in which Clarke saw negativity and absence, is now taking on the potential for a positive meaning, if only the observer can learn to read it. It may be 'barren', 'uncouth' and like a child 'learning how to write', but there is also something else. Clearly, the implication is that by *learning* the new language of this strange new landscape, the poet will be able to *write* a new language, to create a new Australian poetry (as indeed Clarke has stated earlier when he says that Gordon's poems are 'something very like the beginnings of a national school of Australian poetry').[7]

The motif of writing meaning on the blank land has been a recurrent one in the history of Australian exploration, and it can be found in Wright's work as well.[8] In her essay 'The Upside-down Hut', as in the introduction to *Preoccupations in Australian Poetry*, she points to two main themes – exile and hope – which 'remain the inner argument of almost all important writing done here, however much they may be elaborated or disguised'.[9] One of the forms of hope is the inscription of meaning on Australia:

> It has been the outer equivalent of an inner reality – first, and persistently, the reality of exile; second, the reality of newness and unhistoried nakedness – the tabula rasa on which the European consciousness expected to write – something.[10]

Because the settlers saw emptiness, the demands of psychological and cultural survival, amongst other factors, required them to try and find meaning. The irony, as I have stressed above, is that presences and meanings already existed for the Aborginal inhabitants.

At this point, it seems appropriate to move on to the other main theme – the relationship between the white invaders and the Aboriginal inhabitants. As emblems and starting points, I want to invoke here two of Wright's prose books, *The Generations of Men* and *The Cry for the Dead*. The first of these primarily reconstructs the narrative of her ancestors, their attempts to settle themselves in, and lay claim to, Australia. Although the Aboriginal peoples play a role in this book, they exist largely on the fringes of the consciousness of Wright's forebears. *The Generations of Men* is based on diaries and reminiscences by her grandparents, but Wright later described it as a 'semi-novel' (*CD*, p. 3). It is not clear to what degree the accounts of what they thought and felt are actually and explicitly in those sources and to what extent they are extrapolations from them. In the circumstances, it may be justifiable to consider the book as being an amalgam of Wright's own feelings and those of her grandparents, perhaps a projection of herself on to them.

The Generations of Men expresses both a sense of achievement in what her settler forebears built in Australia, and an awareness of the cost of that achievement, mainly through an awareness of the hardship that those forebears experienced, but also in her speculative reconstructions of the feelings of the prior inhabitants. There is an intermittent sense that, while one way of life was being created, another was being destroyed. In describing the last train journey her grandfather Albert Andrew Wright makes before his death, she depicts him musing with some sympathy about the fate and feelings of the Aboriginal peoples, and trying to persuade himself that what the incoming settlers did was necessary:

How else, under that dominion, could they [the Aborigines] have been treated? he wondered now. What other solution could there have been of the problem they had presented by their very existence? With the land his people needed they had lived in the closest of ties, the most stationary of balances; losing it, as sooner or later it was inevitable they must do, they had only the alternatives of death or transformation in their very selves – to die, or to serve an idea utterly foreign to them, losing in that service all their own wisdom and traditions: and they had refused to serve.

Even Paddy, one of the survivors, one of the few who had achieved some kind of compromise, kept under his cheerful compliance a kind of obstinate pride of refusal. Deep in him, Albert sensed now a fatal wound that bled continually, a despair at the core.

(GM, pp. 154–5)

In *The Cry for the Dead*, on the other hand, she makes a more concerted and conscious effort to focus on the pain and suffering of the dispossession that Aboriginal peoples underwent. This book is an often harrowing account of the treatment of Aborigines by the white population, as the European migrants spread out in search of land. Amongst other things, Wright suggests the gulf of understanding between the two sides, the incompatibility of the interpretive schemes through and by which each viewed the other. As she repeatedly indicates, Aborigines were affected not only by the immediate material damage to such things as hunting grounds and sources of water, but also by encroachment on spiritual and ritual spaces, which left them unable to carry out necessary rites. The book ends with a melancholy image of the 'crumbling bones' of Aborigines in the caves of the Expedition Ranges: 'a few fading and eroding scratches and stains of old stencilled hands and figures may remain as the last memorials of the Wadja and their northern neighbours' (*CD*, p. 280). The Wadja and their neighbours have been as good as silenced, and even these fading scripts might as well not exist because there is no one to see them.

The title *Cry for the Dead* indicates a lament, of course (Wright describes in her introduction the Aboriginal ritual from which she derived the title), but it is also a cry on behalf of the dead. She is uncovering the silence of those who have disappeared into history; they could not speak for themselves then and cannot speak now. In that sense, as she points out, the dead of the title include *all* the silenced, all those marginalized in the historical record, white and Aborigine alike, although the latter suffered by far the brunt of the pain of white settlement. While speaking for the long-gone Aborigines is, rightfully, a task that belongs to their descendants, there is some expiation possible through the kind of task that Wright is carrying out in the book. As Adam Shoemaker points out in discussing the 'two major thematic streams of white Australian literature of the past fifty years which has dealt with Aborigines', Wright belongs to the 'school of concerned conscience (often motivated by guilt)'.[11]

The gulf of understanding I referred to earlier occurred because two world views were coming into collision. On more than one occasion, Wright has argued that Aboriginal and European attitudes were and are irreconcilable and incommensurable, in so far as there is no common scale of values by which to compare them. In her essay 'The Voice of the Aboriginals' (*BI*, pp. 151–62), she points out that the two cultures do not agree on 'assumptions about the ends of life and the way to live it' (p. 153). Aborigines 'have continued to insist on their difference, their separateness, against all white demands for "assimilation", and it seems they will go on doing this' (p. 161).

This incommensurability of attitudes applies with great force to the respective relationships to the land, as Wright stresses in her essay 'Landscape and Dreaming':

> For Aborigines, every part of the country they occupied, every mark and feature, was numinous with meaning. The spirit ancestors had made the country itself, in their travels, and fused each part of it into the 'Dreamtime' – a continuum of past, present, and future – that was also the unchangeable Law by which the Aborigines lived. The spirits remained in the land, passing on their essence through the births and rebirths of Aborigines themselves, and still present in the telling of their stories. ... The gulf between the Aboriginal way of seeing the landscape, and that of Europeans ... is clearly almost unbridgeable. ... In fact, this very word 'landscape' involves, from the beginning, an irreconcilable difference of viewpoint, and there seems no word in European languages to overcome the difficulty. It is a painter's term, implying an outside view, a separation, even a basis of criticism. We cannot set it against the reality of that earth-water-tree-spirit-human complex existing in spacetime, which is the Aboriginal world.[12]

Given the histories I have been discussing, what is to be an appropriate and just relationship between white and Aboriginal cultures, and hence an important component of a possible identity for Australia and Australians? One view is expressed by Bob Hodge and Vijay Mishra:

> Aboriginal people have been assigned the task by the majority of Australians of constructing the terms of a single Australian identity that resolves the opposition between Aborigines and Whites: the only identity that can constitute a secure basis for the legitimation of Australian society.[13]

However, this statement needs some investigation and qualification, particularly with regard to the word 'resolves'. Given the possibility of an incommensurability of values, what precisely can a resolution of the opposition consist of?

One of the questions I wish to highlight in this chapter (and the next on Les Murray) is whether the idea of translation might be a more appo-site way of thinking about this issue, since it is something which exists between rapprochement and an acknowledgement – even embedding – of difference. Is it possible to see in the notion of translation a valid and productive response to the general dilemmas of Australian identity dis-cussed above, to Wright's desire to honour both her ancestors and the devastating losses undergone by Aboriginal peoples? Is it possible, in other words, for translation to become both a way in which white set-tlers might learn to belong in a land where they and their ancestors have lived for just over 200 years now, and an acknowledgement of what their arrival and settlement did to the original inhabitants, who had been there for tens of thousands of years? However, is it possible for translation to take place in the context of Wright's assertion of injustice, incommensurability and radical difference? Translation requires at least some measure of commensurability, some overlap.

I will leave these questions aside for the moment, and return to them later. For the time being, I want to try and link the issue of Australian identities to a recurrent theme in some of the best recent criticism on Wright – negativity and positivity.[14] These have been approached mainly from psychological, spiritual or metaphysical perspectives. Paul Kane and Kevin Hart, for instance, invoke the *via negativa* and the con-cept of *kenosis* from Christian theology, as does David Brooks, who, although he sees negativity and absence, 'a disrobing of the mind', as crucial to Australian identity, spends much of his essay discussing how these themes relate to consciousness and ontology.[15] There are important insights in all three of these essays, and while I owe a great deal to them, I also want to extend them to carry a more political or cultural emphasis. One of my starting points is Kane's emphasis on silence and speech in Wright's poetry. For Kane, negativity is not in itself always purely negative, but often a necessary condition for the positive; discussing Wright's poem 'Blind Man's Song' (*CP*, pp. 67–8), with its statement: 'I have made silence speak; I found / for the night a sound', he points out that 'silence is the condition of possibility for speech and the condition to which all speech finally returns'.[16]

'Speech' I take, for the purposes of the present discussion, to be equiv-alent to language in all its manifestations, whether written or spoken, since for Wright the functions of language apply to both forms. An important document in investigating what these functions are for her is the essay of 1952, 'The Writer and the Crisis' (*BI*, pp. 165–79). The 'crisis'

to which the title refers is, most pressingly, a general cultural phenom-
enon of over-specialization, partial vision and the alienation of one
human being from another. The modern crisis manifests itself in lan-
guage, where there is an increasing 'gap between the event as it happens
to the individual, his immediate experience, and the words in which he
must express that event' (p. 172). This happens because language nec-
essarily freezes the living flux of experience into static concepts and
separates subject from object. Since, in her analysis, language is 'the vast
symbol of man's relationship to the universe ... the fundamental fact
which makes him man', the loss of 'vitality and meaning' (p. 175)
brought about by this crisis is a dehumanization which we must counter
by 'regaining a vital relationship with ourselves and our surroundings';
only in this way will we avoid 'becoming cogs in a mechanical process'
(p. 177). The solution is 'to reject the categories of the object and try to
open trapdoors to the inner man', in order to find 'a way to revitalize
language and the world'. It is through the 'poetic faculty' that this
renewal can occur (p. 178). The revitalization of language which Wright
discusses in this essay is both a way of renewing our sundered relation-
ship to the natural world and a means of achieving communion and
solidarity with others. Kane, like a number of other critics, emphasizes
Wright's connections with Romantic thinking, and the analysis set out
in her essay is clearly in a line of succession from such Romantic mani-
festos as Shelley's *Defence of Poetry* (which, indeed, she quotes towards
the end of the essay).[17] In the preface to *Because I Was Invited*, she asserts
that her preoccupation with conservation, with the preservation of nature
and landscape, is simply 'another aspect' of the concern with poetry and
language (p. vii). So, while 'The Writer and the Crisis' is describing a gen-
eral crisis and says nothing about Australia and Australian identities as
such, it has a clear applicability to these subjects too.

Although 'The Writer and the Crisis' dates from 1952, this preface to
Because I Was Invited (1975) stands by the ideas set out over two decades
earlier: 'I don't think ... that the intervening years have disproved my
argument' (p. xii). However, the evidence of her actual poems, even
early ones, is that language is in fact a rather precarious kind of medium
which is dogged by silence, often manifesting itself in rather vestigial
forms such as the 'broken chant' of 'Bora Ring' (*CP*, p. 8). In later years,
her doubts about the adequacy of language and poetry reduced her to
poetic silence, as is clear from an interview she gave in 1993:

> The fact of the matter is that the world is in such a bloody awful
> state that I cannot find words for it. The whole situation we've got-
> ten ourselves into is too immense, too insane as it were, for verse

to encompass ... I simply feel incapable of dealing poetically with what is happening now.[18]

At this point, I think it is possible to draw together the various aspects I have been discussing: language, landscape, Aboriginals and the white population. Although, as discussed earlier, for the white incomers the land was empty, for the Aboriginal peoples, it was saturated with a religious and mythological significance which was disrupted by the arrival of the Europeans: the 'complex network of living legend and bonds with place and time was shattered by the invasion of the whites and their taking over of the land' (*BI*, p. 151).

The 'network of living legends and bonds' delineates, amongst other things, the journeys of the creative Ancestors of the Dreaming, which, as Deborah Bird Rose explains, are 'celebrated in song, dance, story and ritual'. The Dreaming tracks – known also as 'strings' amongst the Yarralin people Rose lived with – 'fix country and people, demarcating human and geographical identity', and serve as both spatial and cognitive maps.[19] These notions have been publicized most prominently by the English writer Bruce Chatwin in the term 'songlines', but have been widely discussed by anthropologists and others.[20] Mudrooroo Nyongah provides a succinct definition:

> Song lines are the sound equivalents of the spacial journeys of the ancestors, the lines of which are found also inscribed in *Aboriginal* paintings and carvings. They detail the travels of the ancestors and each verse may be read in terms of the geographical features of the landscape. Encoded within them are the great ceremonies which reactivate the *Dreamtime* in the present.[21]

The network of narrative meaning which existed in the form of Aboriginal legend, mythology and spirituality was, however, completely closed to the earlier settlers – even if they had been interested in them, which is unlikely. As Australians learned more about Aboriginal philosophy over the course of the twentieth century, they became increasingly aware that the landscape was not a blank or a hieroglyph, but that there was already a language inscribed on what Marcus Clarke called the 'barren and uncouth' country. Writers such as the Jindyworobaks drew sustenance from this knowledge and proposed making Aboriginal culture the centre of an Australian identity. Although they can be criticized, not only for the quality of their writing (on the whole), but also for the artificiality of their overall project, their example became an important resource for some subsequent writers, including Wright and Les Murray.[22] But these two, along with their different forms of sympathy to the Aboriginal narratives, were also conscious of the narratives of their own ancestors, and Wright of an inherited guilt for what those ancestors had done to the land and to the Aborigines. The problem existed of somehow bringing these together.

Sound and language in various manifestations (songs, stories, speech and so on) make frequent appearances in Wright's poetry, early and late; and when I use any of these words and cognate ones in the discussion that follows, it is as a shorthand for the entire range of such manifestations. The main reason for this frequency of appearance is no doubt something like the Romantic model of language as a mode of healing I discussed earlier. But it may also be worthwhile asking whether there is a connection with the Aboriginal conceptions of song and songlines here. Although the parallel can only be a distant one, it should be noted that the idea of language as a remedy or cure, which we can find in Romantic thinking, is part of Aboriginal cultures too: 'The sickness is cured by singing', runs a line from an Aboriginal song.[23] Nevertheless, song serves, I think, *some* of the same functions as it has in Aboriginal culture (although it lacks the integral functions that it has in the networks of Aboriginal spirituality). In particular, it can be seen perhaps as a somewhat paler reflection of the way that Aboriginal song marks the livingness of the creative ancestors, the idea of the Dreaming as 'ever-present'.[24] As Deborah Bird Rose says, 'Dreaming is both a model for, and a celebration of, life as it is lived in the present'.[25]

For Wright song has a strong connection with life. Thus, in 'Lament for Passenger Pigeons' (*CP*, pp. 319–20), the extinction of this once-numerous bird, and the possibility of somehow giving it an alternative but non-physical life, are both metaphorized in terms of sound and song:

> We have not heard the bird. How reinvent
> that passenger, its million wings and hues,
>
> when we have lost the bird, the thing itself,
> the sheen of life on flashing long migrations?
> Might human musics hold it, could we hear?

The immediate answer to this last question is in the negative:

> Trapped in the fouling nests of time and space,
> we turn the music on; but it is man,
> and it is man who leans a deafening ear.

Not only do we not listen, we impose our own voices on what we might hear, as we impose ourselves on the planet and pollute it:

> The sirens sang us to the ends of sea,
>
> and changed to us; their voices were our own,
> jug jug to dirty ears in dirtied brine.

At the end of the poem, though, an alternative is posed:

> What is the being and the end of man?
> Blank surfaces reverb a human voice
> whose echo tells us that we choose to die:
>
> or else, against the blank of everything,
> to reinvent that passenger, that bird-
> siren-and-angel image we contain
> essential in a constelling word.
> To sing of Being, its escaping wing,
> to utter absence in a human chord
> and recreate the meaning as we sing.

The question 'what is the being and the end of man?' is answered with two alternatives – death or life – but the implicit balance seems to be on the side of the latter. I use the word 'balance' deliberately, since the length of this concluding stanza, coming after the tristichs of the rest of the poem, guides us to place more weight on the alternative offered here. 'To utter absence in a human chord / and recreate the meaning as we sing': this, I have been suggesting, is the role attributed to speech, in the wide sense sketched earlier, and hence to song, sound, narrative in Wright's work. Absence and presence are here folded into each other, as silence and speech are in Paul Kane's reading of Wright. In 'Lament for Passenger Pigeons', the recreation of the pigeon's meaning and Being by our own song is some kind of compensation – however inadequate – for the physical absence of the pigeon ('the thing itself'), and for the absence of its sound ('We have not heard the bird'). In some way it brings the bird back to life.

In another poem, 'Flame-Tree in a Quarry' (*CP*, p. 60), the scarlet flowers of this tree, still growing in a destroyed landscape, continue to live and to sing:

> Out of the torn earth's mouth
> comes the old cry of praise.

> Still is the song made flesh
> though the singer dies

Despite the destructiveness of human activity, there is also a suggestion here of continuity and perhaps even immortality through 'song': the cry is one that has been heard many times before ('old'), it continues to be heard ('still') and will always be heard ('still' again). The allusion to *John* 1: 14 ('And the Word was made flesh') reinforces the sense of immortality.[26]

In 'The Unnecessary Angel' (*CP*, pp. 291–2), song is explicitly linked to Australia and its settlement:

> Yes, we still can sing
> who reach this barren shore.
> But no note will sound
> as it did before.

The poem then seems to move away from the specific matter of Australia and to connect the fate of 'song' with a more general narrative of innocence and the loss of it, drawing on the Christian imagery of the Fall. At first, it would seem, song, which began in 'selfless innocence', was all-inclusive and adequate to its task:

> Every tone and key,
> every shade it learned
> that its limits held
> and its powers discerned:
>
> love and history,
> joy in earth and sun,
> its small chords embraced,
> joining all in one.

But the sin of pride, and the specific human crime of the crucifixion, which I presume is all crime, threaten to overpower song:

> But no note can come
> from the flesh's pride
> once the weapon's lodged
> in the bleeding side;

Despite this, song is still possible. 'We can still sing', the poem continues, with one proviso: that our words should not be taken for truth. And it concludes with a continuation of song, although it is a very different kind of song compared to the one with which the poem began

> Let the song be bare
> that was richly dressed.
> Sing with one reserve:
> Silence might be best.

Although 'The Unnecessary Angel' ends with the line 'Silence might be best', this is a reservation despite which the singer continues nonetheless to sing. I said earlier that the settlement of Australia apparently referred to in the first stanza seems to disappear and to be replaced by a more general narrative of innocence and guilt. But there is a possibility that it remains as a kind of reverberation in the poem, so that the invasion of Australia and the consequences of that, such as the dispossession of the Aborigines, are also, in the terms the poem uses, primal crimes like the crucifixion. Certainly the idea that the invasion needs expiation is present elsewhere in her work, as in the comment made in her essay on 'Nigger's Leap, New England', which I quoted towards the beginning of this chapter, where she described Australia as a 'haunted country' and argued that one form of reparation would be to try and conserve what remained of its natural beauty so that some forgiveness might be achieved. Is that, perhaps, why silence haunts song at the end of 'The Unnecessary Angel'?

Song in these poems is precariously poised on the edge of silence, disappearance and nothingness. This is a fairly widespread motif also in Wright's poems about both the white settlers and the Aborigines, early as well as late. Wright's memoir *The Generations of Men,* as I have suggested earlier, can be seen as, amongst other things, a construction of a narrative that will create 'bonds with place and time' – perhaps not as rooted in an entire way of life as the songlines or mythological tracks of Aboriginal culture, but bonds nonetheless. This project is exemplified in the epigraph to the book, a quotation from Blake's poem *Milton*: 'The Generations of Men run on in the tide of Time / But leave their destin'd lineaments permanent for ever'. The word 'lineament', it should be noted, derives from *lineare*, 'to trace lines'.

A number of Wright's early and most famous poems are preoccupied precisely with this effort to carry out the task of creating such lines, narratives and bonds. The bullock-driver of 'Bullocky' (*CP*, p. 17), for instance, combats the threat, loneliness and meaninglessness of the 'long straining journey' by constructing a 'mad apocalyptic dream' in which he is 'old Moses, and the slaves / his suffering and stubborn team'. In 'South of My Days' (*CP*, pp. 20–1), the 70-year-old Dan's yarns are described as 'a blanket against the winter'. The central sections of the poem are presented as Dan's own language and narratives, and each of the stories is a connection between people and places:

> Droving that year, Charleville to the Hunter,
> nineteen-one it was, and the drought beginning;
> sixty head left at the McIntyre, the mud round them
> hardened like iron; and the yellow boy died
> in the sulky ahead with the gear ...
>
> Or mustering up the Bogongs in the autumn
> when the blizzards came early. ...
>
> Or driving for Cobb's on the run
> up from Tamworth – Thunderbolt at the top of Hungry Hill,
> and I give him a wink.

These connections of story and place can be seen as attempts to give significance to the landscape through narrative, to imbue it with meaning, to sink roots in the land, as the concluding lines of the poem make clear:

> South of my days' circle
> I know it dark against the stars, the high lean country
> full of old stories that still go walking in my sleep.

Here Wright depicts the 'high lean country' from which the speaker is currently separated being reanimated by the 'old stories' which are 'walking', like living things: land, narrative and the human mind seem to become one (the country and the stories reappear in her dreams). This whole poem can be seen as an Australian equivalent of that hallowing of the ground 'in legend and in song', which Marcus Clarke found so pervasive in Europe, and which already existed, of course, for the Aboriginal inhabitants of Australia.

It has been argued that this poem claims a connection with Australia which is in some sense illegitimate. Jonathan White focuses specifically on the phrase 'my blood's country', which, he says, suggests not only a deep-seated connection with place, but also a sense of blood spilt for the land, and therefore a 'notion of appeasement of its harshnesses through sacrifice, leading to rightful possession'. Through their use in Australian schools, he argues, such poems 'served as a way of introducing a specific kind of appreciation of Australia' by establishing a 'sense of meaningful life-styles, made possible in an Australia variously won for its people through toil, adventure, and sacrifice'.[27]

It is true that the notion of sacrifice is a significant element in some of Wright's poetry;[28] and it is also true that the two poems I have been discussing do indeed try to link human beings to landscapes as a way of giving meaning to both. But there are also ironic currents at work within them. In 'South of My Days', for instance, the narrative of belonging is undermined by the hint that Dan's stories might be the futile ramblings of a garrulous old man who bores his audience: 'Wake, old man. This is winter, and the yarns are over. / No one is listening.' Wright herself later objected to the kind of reading of 'Bullocky' which makes it into a foundational Australian poem, eventually refusing to have it reprinted in anthologies because she felt that it was being made to serve 'as a kind of justification for the whole invasion of Australia'.[29] In her essay 'Some Problems of Being an Australian Poet' (*BI*, pp. 49–58), she adduces the 'long popularity' of 'Bullocky' as an example of the Australian tendency to demand that their poets should affirm 'Anglo-Australian identity', of the desire for 'assertions, not questions; celebrations, not criticisms' (p. 51). The bullocky's Mosaic narrative of his journey is questioned by its characterization as 'a mad apocalyptic dream'; and the 'shouted prayers and prophecies' he utters from his campfire at night have no audience but the 'steepled cone of night'. Indeed, in a later essay, 'Reading and Nationalism', although with reference not to these lines but to the last two stanzas of the poem, she complains that readers missed their tone; where she had seen them 'as a gently affectionate sendup of the Vision' of the pioneers, they were being read as 'a hyperbolic celebration of it'.[30]

The ironizing is unmissable in the late sequence about herself and her siblings, 'For a Pastoral Family' (*CP*, pp. 406–10). The first poem in the sequence begins by depicting the changes that have taken place as they have all grown old. Yet there remain 'luxuries' and consolations, amongst them the landscape and the 'pastoral silence'. At this point, however, the underside of all these enters the poem:

> These are owed
> to the forerunners, men and women
> who took over as if by right a century and a half
> in an ancient difficult bush. And after all

the previous owners put up little fight,
did not believe in ownership, and so were scarcely human.

Our people who gnawed at the fringe
of the edible leaf of this country
left you a margin of action, a rural security,
and left to me
what serves as a base for poetry,
a doubtful song that has a dying fall.

(p. 406)

The sense of rightful possession through sacrifice and endurance of hardship ('difficult bush') is, very obviously, countered later by heavy doses of irony. Although her brothers might have this feeling, it is clear that the speaker does not. And once the spectre of dispossession appears in the poem, it stays to haunt. The supposed heroism of the ancestors who settled the land is reduced to a pettier insect-like scale: all they did was to gnaw 'at the fringe / of the edible leaf of this country'. And what they handed on to the speaker was 'a doubtful song that has a dying fall'. The fact that the stanza containing this account of the inheritance follows the account of the usurpation of the original inhabitants would suggest that the silence is connected to the usurpation, as if all song and all poetry in Australia are now marked and permeated by the original crime, an idea which is countenanced in 'The Unnecessary Angel'.

In nearly all these cases where 'song' or other forms of language seem poised on the verge of disappearing into silence, whether because of what I have described as the original sin of usurpation, or because silence constitutes, more generally, what Paul Kane describes as 'the condition of possibility for speech and the condition to which all speech finally returns', the language does nevertheless survive, however haunted it may be.[31] In 'For a Pastoral Family', the song is 'doubtful', and has a 'dying fall', yet there is still a 'base for poetry'.

These points are also true for a number of the poems in which Wright deals more directly with the fate of the Aborigines and the impact of settlement on them: language survives, often precariously, yet it does survive, and also furthers some kind of survival for those to whom it refers. 'Old House' (*CP*, pp. 81–2) looks back to the days of Wright's great-great-grandfather as he set about creating somewhere to live. The Aborigines in a nearby camp made up songs about him and his family, thinking of the day when they would vanish (whether they looked forward in anticipation or merely saw it neutrally as an inevitable event in the passage of time is not clear):

> These were a dream, something strayed out of a dream.
> They would vanish down the river, but the river would flow on,
> under the river-oaks the river would flow on,
> winter and summer would burn the grass white
> or red like the red of the pale man's hair.
> In the camp by the river they made up those songs
> and my great-great-grandfather heard them with one part of his mind.

When the transient human beings are gone, the landscape will still exist. Although the Aborigines and the great-great-grandfather are no longer there, the river flows on as the Aborigines predicted – and so, just about, does song, although it is only a fragment held in the pepperina tree with which the poem began:

> And the trees and the creatures, all of them are gone.
> But the sad river, the silted river,
> under its dark banks the river flows on,
> the wind still blows and the river still flows.
> And the great broken tree, the dying pepperina,
> clutches in its hands the fragments of a song.

The song here is a fragment of continuity and memory, not only of Wright's family but also of the Aborigines. Again, in the well-known early poem 'Bora Ring' (*CP*, p. 8), the passing of the Aborigines is lamented as the vanishing of a ritual, the supplanting of one narrative by another:

> The song is gone; the dance
> is secret with the dancers in the earth,
> the ritual useless, and the tribal story
> lost in an alien tale.

The piling up of absences and negativity here, and the flat, enervated rhythm, create a feeling of apparent hopelessness about the disappearance of song, dance, ritual and tribal story; yet the landscape itself remains to sing and performs fragments of the vanished ritual, to continue, in however attenuated a fashion, the tribal story:

> Only the grass stands up
> to mark the dancing-ring: the apple-gums

> posture and mime a past corroboree,
> murmur a broken chant.

In 'Nigger's Leap, New England' (*CP*, pp. 15–16), a poem about the place where a group of Aborigines were driven to their deaths over a cliff, the victims are silenced:[32]

> Swallow the spine of range; be dark, O lonely air.
> Make a cold quilt across the bone and skull
> that screamed falling in flesh from the lipped cliff
> and then were silent, waiting for the flies.

The atrocity which this poem records is depicted almost as a primal crime lying at the root of, and undermining, all positives:

> Now must we measure
> our days by nights, our tropics by their poles,
> love by its end and all our speech by silence.
> See in these gulfs, how small the light of home.

The poem ends with a vision of virtually total destruction, as night sweeps across the landscape: 'Night floods us suddenly as history / that has sunk many islands in its good time.' Yet even in this apparently absolute darkness and negativity, it seems to me, something positive survives. It may be only a vestige, a trace, a faint sound, yet it is still there, I think, in this poem. In the first stanza, Wright has referred to the 'lipped cliff', and in the final stanza she returns to part of this image: 'Night lips the harsh / scarp of the tableland and cools its granite.' The reference of 'lipped' in the first of these is primarily to the edge of the cliff, and in the second, 'lips', I presume, seeks to capture a sense of the edge of darkness creeping over the tableland. But surely also the image of the mouth and, consequently, of speech is an undercurrent (or, perhaps more appositely, a reverberation) here. Is there, then, the possibility that although the Aborigines were silenced by being driven over the cliff, the cliff itself speaks of the massacre, since it marks the spot where the atrocity happened. Is it possible that the night is not just creeping but also speaking – or at least whispering? What, in this case, does it mean to 'measure / our days by nights, ... and all our speech by silence'? Perhaps that our speech must take the measure of silence, must contend with silence, and yet not fall totally silent itself? So while the original atrocity itself can never be undone, some (however inadequate) reparation can be made by remembering the victims and honouring their memory. There is a possible resonance here with the Aboriginal readings of landscapes; as a waterhole or a sandhill speaks of a mythological event, so the cliff speaks of the dead Aborigines.

In these poems, the past is transfigured into landscape and the flora and fauna which inhabit or once inhabited the landscape, and then landscape, flora and fauna, it appears, are turned into 'song', speech or some other sound. But these songs are fragments or vestiges or whispers. Is this then, perhaps, the way Wright accommodates the two competing impulses I referred to at the beginning as being operative in the case of white Australians: the need to belong and the consciousness of guilt? The land speaks, as it spoke and speaks much more eloquently for the Aborigines through their networks of mythical and narrative meaning. But it can only do so in broken fragments, 'dying falls', whispers and so on, since both the Aborigines and the white population are now fragments, the former because of the virtual destruction of their way of life, the latter because of their sense of belatedness and usurpation, or their still not fully-acknowledged historical memory of guilt (as illustrated, for instance, in the statements and actions of the current Liberal government of John Howard). Even where the object, event or person being commemorated is gone, unlike the flame-tree or the pepperina, there is a kind of victory in the survival of the memory, however saturated with sadness that memory might be. Victory and defeat, speech and silence are bound together. This is why silence always threatens to take over, at least in these poems.

Our sense of the dialectic of speech and silence in Wright's poetry grows more acute, I think, if we examine its connections with how nature is represented at various points in her poetic career. In some early poems, Wright appears to abolish – or at least want to abolish – the distinction between the human self and the landscape, and it could be argued that this is a way of claiming something like the Aboriginal relationship with it – the kind that Les Murray, for instance, seems to claim in the last line of his poem 'Thinking about Aboriginal Land Rights, I Visit the Farm I Will Not Inherit', where he turns himself into one of the creative ancestors of the Dreaming ('I go into the earth near the feed shed for thousands of years').[33] In 'South of My Days', as my discussion earlier indicated, the phrase 'my blood's country' could be read in such ways, and Jonathan White does precisely this. Indeed, many of the metaphors in the poem infuse and permeate the landscape with the human body: 'bony slopes wincing under the winter'; 'lean, hungry country'; 'the old roof cracks its joints'. The operation of metaphor fuses narrative, country and human subject into a unity, so that by the end 'the high lean country' is 'full of old stories that still go walking in my sleep'. The stories that old Dan tells here could be seen as versions of the mythological tracks of ancestors and others that Aborigines trace in the landscape. Yet, as I have already argued, there is a counterpointing and separating note in the poem, since 'no one is listening' to Dan's stories.

In 'For New England' (*CP*, pp. 22–3), a similar fusion occurs between human subject and natural objects, so that Wright's ancestral landscape in northern New South Wales permeates her, as she permeates it; but again something arises to separate her. In this poem, the fusion occurs not through metaphor but through a reflexivity which positions the speaker as both agent ('traveller', 'swimmer', 'gazer') and that which is acted on ('the ways I travel', 'mountain river', 'the land I stare on'):

> Many roads meet here
> in me, the traveller and the ways I travel.
> All the hills' gathered waters feed my seas
> who am the swimmer and the mountain river;
> and the long slopes' concurrence is my flesh
> who am the gazer and the land I stare on;
> and dogwood blooms within my winter blood,
> and orchards fruit in me and need no season.
> But sullenly the jealous bones recall
> what other earth is shaped and hoarded in them.

The last two lines, however, refer to her English inheritance, the land her ancestors came from. Thus the fusion of self and landscape which she stresses in the reflexive imagery of the preceding lines is qualified by the 'other earth' hoarded in her bones which separates her from the Australian earth (an idea that has been in operation from the first line of the poem, when she speaks of two different trees, sycamore and chestnut, as 'the homesick and the swarthy native', and later on finds in herself a 'double tree'). The word 'recall' seems not just to denote an act of remembering, but also something more – a calling back into the body, a *re-call*. And the sudden leap to Ulysses in the next verse-paragraph appears to reinforce this sense of separation:

> Where's home, Ulysses? Cuckolded by lewd time
> he never found again the girls he sailed from,
> but at his fireside met the islands waiting
> and died there, twice a stranger.

So do Wright and people like her resemble Ulysses in their homelessness; are they too strangers twice over – strangers to both Europe and Australia? Yet the last lines of the poem again veer towards fusion in a prayer or plea to the wind:

> Wind, blow through me
> till the nostalgic candles of laburnum
> fuse with the dogwood in a single flame
> to touch alight these sapless memories.
> Then will my land turn sweetly from the plough
> and all my pastures rise as green as spring.

Here again human objects and creations such as candles and fire fuse with natural objects such as laburnum and dogwood; memories become trees. Now, though, it seems to be a desire rather than the already achieved state that it was earlier in the poem. There is clearly a divided impulse here too, an acknowledgement of both belonging and non-belonging.

The sense of separation heightens in her late poems. I have already referred to Wright's poetic silence towards the end of her life as a symptom of despair about the state of the world, an acknowledgement of the inadequacy of language. There are prefigurings of this sense of inadequacy before that period, although it arises perhaps less out of despair than out of a sense that language (or at least the language at Wright's command) is inherently limited. Traces of this come through in the sequence of 'ghazals' called 'The Shadow of Fire' (in fact, they resemble the ghazal form only in consisting of couplets). The third poem in the sequence, 'Rockface' (*CP*, p. 420) is a meditation on the meanings of a 'split upstanding stone, like a gravestone', which is all that remains of a fallen cliff-face. The third couplet of the poem suggests that for the Aboriginal peoples of the area in the past, the rock had meaning and significance, at least partly because it had a name: 'In the days of the hunters with spears, this rock had a name. / Rightly they knew the ancestral powers of stone.' For those Aborigines, perhaps, with their connection to the sacred ('the ancestral powers of stone'), there was no separation between language and reality. The speaker, though, is faced with something huge, intractable, beyond language:

> Walking here in the dark my torch lights up
> something massive, motionless, that confronts me.

> I've no wish to chisel things into new shapes.
> The remnant of a mountain has its own meaning.

The last couplet here is susceptible to different interpretations. Is the renunciation of the desire to 'chisel things into new shapes' an awed, reverent acknowledgement of what Hopkins called the 'inscape' of the rock, a feeling that language is a distortion, as sculpting the rock would be an intrusion into what Wallace Stevens calls 'mere Being'? Or is it a wearier acknowledgement that things are beyond language and therefore that the task of chiselling them into new shapes, of writing poetry, must itself be renounced?

The next poem in the sequence, 'Summer' (*CP*, p. 421), continues this exploration of language and naming. In a reprise of 'Flame Tree in a Quarry', the speaker, returning to a now-abandoned mining area, sees the place struggling to 'heal itself after many wounds', as the flora and fauna return, regenerate themselves and build. 'I'll never know its inhabitants', the speaker acknowledges; and the reason for this seems to be indicated at the end of the poem: 'In a burned-out summer, I try to see without words / as they do. But I live through a web of language.' The unselfconscious creatures do not need language, but human beings do. The tone in these two lines seems regretful and rueful, with the last sentence's implication of being trapped in a sticky medium which she would rather be outside. There is less of a sense of awed reverence for the sheer otherness and ineffability of nature, although that may be somewhere in the background. In both of these examples, language is an impediment, and in both nature confronts the human being with its sheer otherness; the 'web of language' is an unsatisfactory medium. The fusion of human and non-human asserted or desired in the earlier poems is absent; no longer can the poet be both 'the gazer and the land I stare on'. The greater (Romantic) confidence in the powers of language that is asserted in 'The Writer and the Crisis' is absent in these late poems. Yet, as Rose Lucas and Lyn McCredden point out, the very act of writing the poems means that '"new shapes" are ... chiselled into the rockface of the external world'.[34]

In what sense can this dialectic of speech and silence be connected with translation? For the settlers, and for their descendants to some degree, learning to belong was always an act of cultural translation, a translation between Australia and Europe, between the landscapes and cultures they faced and the internalized landscapes and cultures they brought with them, or, in later generations, inherited. The process of imperial or colonial translation – clearly I am using the word 'translation' in a broad sense here – sought to overcome the resistance of otherness in a variety of ways, the most brutal of which was elimination through murder and genocide. But there were other, less openly violent ways which involved different methods of writing a meaning and a language on the indigenous peoples and their way of life (although, of course, this is a hopelessly inadequate way of referring to the destructiveness of the process). The policy of 'assimilation' is one example of this. The *terra nullius* principle is another. The idea that the land did not belong to anyone because there were no fixed settlements, and because the land was not cultivated, which the British government used to justify their taking possession of Australia is founded, amongst other things, on the notion that relationships to the land other than property are not real relationships at all (there is, of course, a similarity here with the case of the United States). The falsity of this assumption was recognized in the landmark *Mabo v. Queensland* case in the Australian High Court in 1992, when Justice Brennan stated:

> The common law of this country would perpetuate injustice if it were to continue to embrace the enlarged notion of terra nullius and to persist in characterizing the indigenous inhabitants of the Australian colonies as people too low in the scale of social organization to be acknowledged as possessing rights and interests in land.[35]

However, the attempted translation into European notions was and is resisted by the Aborigines, who, as Wright notes in words already quoted from 'The Voice of the Aboriginals', 'insist on their difference, their separateness, against all white demands for "assimilation"' (*BI*, p. 161).

The flora and fauna were different matters: for the early Europeans in particular, Australia was a place of oddities, a land which was 'upside-down, topsy-turvy', where natural laws were inverted.[36] They could neither be wiped out completely, nor assimilated. For white Australians to learn to belong, they had to both translate and allow themselves to be translated, in a sense. Yet, like the Aborigines, the place also resisted translation, a resistance which manifested itself in the realm of signification and meaning. The resistance of language is partly to do with the very medium itself. As T. S. Eliot says in those famous lines from 'Burnt Norton', words 'slip, slide, perish, / Decay with imprecision, will not stay in place'.[37] In the 'ghazals' of Wright discussed earlier, the resistance of language goes even further than this intractability and is connected with a desire to 'see without words' altogether.

This inherent resistance of language is also inescapable in translation, since any theory of translation must also be connected with a theory of language and languages. Although the idea of resistance in linguistic translation has a long history, it has become increasingly systematized and prominent in more recent discussions, where it has taken a number of forms. Steiner's discussion of the hermeneutic motion, as I pointed out in the first chapter, argues that in translation we should feel 'the resistant particularity of the "other"' and that 'great translation must carry with it the most precise sense possible ... of the barriers intact at the heart of understanding'.[38] In translation strategies which advocate 'foreignizing', the resistance of the other is often given a more political inflection than Steiner gives it. Thus Indira Karamcheti advocates a policy of 'opaque translation' in translating Aimé Césaire, 'refusing fluency' in order to 'guide the reader to question the easy codes of the exotic' (the exotic being a colonial or neo-colonial code).[39] These methods aim to convey some sense of the incommensurability of languages and cultures.

The methods of 'opaque translation' discussed by Karamcheti include silence, by which she means 'not-naming' and a 'refusal to translate' (for example, through a use of the words in the source text).[40] Silence has other, more metaphysical or mystical connections with translation as well. I want to draw here on some observations that George Steiner makes about the connections between translation, language and silence in two highly speculative but also stimulating chapters of *After Babel*, 'Language and Gnosis' and 'Word against Object'. Some of the ideas in these chapters resonate with Wright's poems and the issues I have been discussing here.

Ideas of silence and inherent untranslatability are never very far away in these chapters. The first of them centres on the question: why are there so many languages, when human beings are so similar biologically throughout the world? In the process of examining this, Steiner discusses Kabbalistic speculation and Christian mysticism, including the work of the seventeenth-century Catholic convert and mystic Angelus Silesius:

Angelus Silesius asserts that God has, from the beginning of time, uttered only a single word. In that single utterance all reality is contained. The cosmic Word cannot be found in any known tongue;

language after Babel cannot lead back to it. The bruit of human voices, so mysteriously diverse and mutually baffling, shuts out the sound of the Logos. There is no access except silence.[41]

Steiner sees Walter Benjamin's 'The Task of the Translator' as being in the line of 'gnostic reveries' such as this, although 'changed into model and metaphor'.[42] It is the notion of 'pure language' which links Benjamin to such currents of thought.

For Benjamin, translation is always on the edge of untranslatability, which is a kind of silence, since if there is such a thing as untranslatability, it means that speech is met by a lack of response. Yet at the same time, in a post-Babel world, translation is an absolutely necessary activity. As Steiner points out, language in general and the existence of multiple particular languages rescue us from imprisonment in the given world, since they allow us at least to conceive of other worlds and other possibilities, what Steiner calls 'alternities of being'; they allow us to imagine otherwise:

> Through language, we construct ... 'alternities of being'. To the extent that every individual speaker uses an idiolect, the problem of Babel is quite simply, that of human individuation. But different tongues give to the mechanism of 'alternity' a dynamic, transferable enactment. ... To a greater or lesser degree, every language offers its own reading of life. To move between languages, to translate, even within restrictions of totality, is to experience the almost bewildering bias of the human spirit towards freedom. If we were lodged inside a single 'language-skin' or amid very few languages, the inevitability of our organic subjection to death might well prove more suffocating than it is.[43]

Yet those 'alternities' are, finally, out of reach, as is the 'pure language' to which Benjamin links translation. Translation, in the telling word used by Benjamin's translator, can only 'intend':

> Unlike a work of literature, translation does not find itself in the center of the language forest but on the outside facing the wooded ridge; it calls into it without entering, aiming at that single spot where the echo is able to give, in its own language, the reverberation of the work in the alien one. Not only does the aim of translation differ from that of a literary work – it intends language as a whole, taking an individual work in an alien language as a point of departure – but it is a different effort altogether. ... For the great motif of integrating many tongues into one true language is at work.[44]

Benjamin describes this true or pure language in ways which make it almost impossible to distinguish from silence:

> In this pure language – which no longer means or expresses anything but is, as expressionless and creative Word, that which is meant in all languages – all information, all sense, and all intention finally encounter a stratum in which they are destined to be extinguished.[45]

This pure language, which no one has ever heard or will ever hear seems very much like Angelus Silesius's single cosmic Word which too no one has heard.

Translations are, in Benjamin's account, asymptotic approaches to that pure language which is beyond any specific language. They are therefore engaged in an ultimately impossible but absolutely necessary task. It seems to me that in his own idiom, he is expressing both the impossibility of translation (it always 'intends', but never reaches, the 'pure language') and the always present need and desire to go on trying, since to try is to approach what Steiner calls that 'alternity of being' without a sense of which we suffocate in ourselves, in the world of fact, in monoculturalism and in monolingualism.

Many of these speculations resonate with some of Wright's own ideas of language. In the poem 'To Hafiz of Shiraz' (*CP*, pp. 215–16), she probes the differences between her young and older poetic selves. The younger poet 'did not know the birds were described, / classified, observed, fixed in their proper localities' and thought that 'Each bird ... / ... was sole, new'. Similarly, 'any word that I heard ... / might ... open worlds on its hinge'. For the older poet, who knows, amongst other things, that 'each bird / is finally feathered and grown in the unbroken shell' (which I take to mean that she knows that each follows the inevitable 'laws' of nature), 'should the pen shake less in my hand?'. 'No', is the answer in the concluding stanza:

> Every path and life leads one way only,
> out of continual miracle, through creation's fable,
> over and over repeated but never understood,
> as every word leads back to the blinding original Word.

I am conscious that in paraphrasing like this, I am doing less than justice to this beautiful poem, in which metaphor, rhythm and meaning are tightly bound together. But here again is a view of language and creation which is asymptotic ('over and over repeated but never understood') and rather like Silesius ('every word leads back to the blinding original Word').

In Wright's poetry, speech, I am suggesting, is haunted by silence for a number of reasons: the language-defying nature of Australian landscapes; a guilt so intense that it verges on the negation of speech; a primal atrocity that makes those who would speak feel the inadequacy of language, so that, as in 'The Unnecessary Angel', 'silence might be best'; a consciousness of the destruction wrought on Aborigines and their cultures, which can now speak only in a 'broken chant' and in whispers (as in 'Bora Ring' and 'Nigger's Leap, New England'). And, in the late ghazals, there is a sense of language in principle being an unsatisfactory medium; the language which is our most powerful means of interpreting the world is also an enmeshing web, and the poet would rather try to do without words, thus undercutting the very basis of her art. Yet to go on writing is to go on trying, to go on having some kind of faith in language, even if all that can be produced is a cracked note.

Perhaps reparation for the primal crime or the bridging of the gap between invader and Aborigine, between European and landscape, is impossible. But that is no reason for not continually trying. This, perhaps, is what lies behind the dialectic of speech and silence in Wright's poetry. Language is one of the most important means available to us in our attempts to bridge the gap with other cultures and with nature. Yet Wright's attempted translations of silence into speech, Aboriginal and her own ancestral voices into her poems, landscape into meaning, are always haunted by a sense of the inadequacy of language. Silence in the various forms I have been examining is a manifestation of resistance to translation and signification. These tensions between speech and silence – consciousness of the necessity of speaking across the various gaps I have discussed and simultaneous awareness of the precariousness of speech – have, it seems to me, a kind of isomorphic or homologous relationship with the tensions of sameness and difference which permeate acts of cultural translation.

3
Fusion and Translation: Les Murray's Australia

Like Judith Wright, Les Murray has been concerned with Aboriginal peoples and with the Australian landscape; but his approach has been rather different from hers. There is less emphasis on the ravages which invasion brought to the Aborigines and he does not share Wright's sense of incommensurability between white and Aboriginal cultures. Instead, he is engaged with a project of creating 'fused' identities. Unlike her, he also claims a relationship with the land which is not different in kind from the Aboriginal relationship.[1] These differences between the two poets are in part generational, but they are also ideological, manifesting themselves in, for instance, Murray's partly self-created legend of himself as an embattled, independent man of the people, a 'vernacular' Australian confronting an intolerant, mean-spirited, snobbish urban elite full of the fashionable ideas of the 1960s and 1970s, such as multiculturalism, radical feminism and leftism.[2]

Ideas of division and fusion form a recurrent pattern in both his poetry and his prose. The nature of Australian identity, society and culture, the human self, poetry (aesthetics, more generally) and religion, amongst other subjects, are all discussed by means of this pattern, in which, typically, something is divided into opposed terms, which are then made to merge. Examples which I discuss include Athens and Boeotia; the urban and the rural; Narrowspeak and Wholespeak; reason, dream and the body; and Aborigines and whites (superseded by a dualism in which 'ordinary' white Australians and Aborigines together are contrasted with an oppressive neo-colonial white Establishment).[3] These often overlap with each other. In each case, the dominance of one term over the others in the division is seen as dangerous and one-sided, and the fusion, abolition or reconciliation of the two or more terms in the pattern is considered a desirable outcome. Murray refers to the structure of domination and subordination as 'relegation' and to the process of fusion as 'convergence'.[4]

In order to orient this chapter amongst these themes, I want to begin by looking at one example of the pattern in more detail. Murray's essay 'Embodiment and Incarnation' (*PT*, pp. 251–69) discusses, amongst other things, the nature of poetry and religion, arguing that a 'real poem' (or art more generally) fuses or integrates dream, reason and the body, the last of these through the 'materials in which a work is realized, and ... its somatic effect upon the beholder' (pp. 263–4). 'Properly integrated poetic discourse' is an example of what he calls 'Wholespeak', as opposed to a discourse 'based on the supposed primacy or indeed exclusive sovereignty of daylight reason', which is 'Narrowspeak' (p. 263).[5] In religion, the three dimensions of reason, dream and body are joined by a fourth, the Divine, so that 'to fusion we must now add the dimension which theology calls infusion' (p. 265). The analysis, as regards art at least, is repeated elsewhere in Murray's prose.[6] The fusion achieved in poetry is intense but evanescent; although we can return to it time and time again, we can't reside in it permanently: 'We can have it repeatedly, and each time timelessly, but we can't have it steadily. We are as it were not yet permitted to live there. And yet it is itself a quietly perpetual thing, this ordinary ecstasy' (p. 259). This 'ordinary ecstasy' is perhaps what he writes about in the poem 'Equanimity' (*NCP*, pp. 178–80), a state of mind which is 'Almost beneath notice, as attainable as gravity, ... / a continuous recovering moment' (*NCP*, p. 179). Paradoxically, although we have it, as these quotations suggest, continuously and perpetually, we also in some sense do not have it at all, since we can never have all of it: 'it lights us from the incommensurable / we sometimes glimpse'. Equanimity is 'Of infinite detailed extent / like God's attention. Where nothing is diminished by perspective' (p. 180). As I read these lines, perspective, rather like MacNeice's 'bridgeheads into reality', which I discuss in the next chapter, is a limitation without which human beings cannot live, but it is at the same time 'diminished', precisely because it has limits. In this reading, the poem expresses something like the oscillation between merger and separation which I have seen as characteristic of translation, an oscillation – to put it in religious terms – between immanence and transcendence.[7] In 'Equanimity', there is an unbridgeable or 'incommensurable' gulf between ordinary life and God, and yet in some sense God is always there.

Another example of the pattern, this time from a different realm of experience, the nature of Australian identity and culture, will lead more directly into some of the overarching themes of the present book. Although in his essay 'The Trade in Images' (*PT*, pp. 295–301), Murray

expresses impatience with too much 'making images of Australia', sug-
gesting that 'we have indulged gluttonously in mirror staring and navel
gazing' (p. 295), one of the most enduring concerns of his own work has
been precisely with images of Australia. His book *The Quality of Sprawl* –
subtitled *Thoughts about Australia* – gathers together earlier essays, two
of his finest poems ('The Quality of Sprawl' and 'The Dream of Wearing
Shorts Forever') and a new essay called 'The Preamble's Bottom Line': all
devoted to the subject.[8] In 'The Human-Hair Thread' (*PT*, pp. 71–99), he
discusses in detail his own negotiations with Aboriginal cultures and
Aboriginal elements in his poetry; here he aligns himself with the
Jindyworobaks, who, for him, 'represent a creolizing element in our cul-
ture' (p. 98). For readers of Murray's poetry, there is much of interest in
this essay, but at this point I want to pick out one passage in which he
discusses his intentions in writing his poem 'The Buladelah-Taree
Holiday Song Cycle':

> I realized it would be necessary to incorporate in it elements from all
> three main Australian cultures, Aboriginal, rural and urban. But I
> would arrange them in their order of distinctiveness, with the senior
> culture setting the tone and controlling the movement of the poem.
> What I was after was an enactment of a longed-for fusion of all three
> cultures, a fusion which, as yet perhaps, can only exist in art, or in
> blessed moments when power and ideology are absent.
>
> (p. 92)

Here again, we have the same pattern: division followed by an evanes-
cent fusion, which can be achieved only temporarily in 'blessed
moments'. It is true that later in the essay, he says: 'It would have been
treason to the facts of modern Australian life if all conflict, all edginess,
had been left out, and only a sugary picture of too-easy reconciliation
allowed to remain.' This comment, however, is made in relation to the
fact that his poem contains 'irony and social comment', unlike its
Aboriginal model (p. 94).

Murray's views on the convergence of cultures in Australia are con-
nected to the idea that Aborigines and poor rural white people actually
belong to a larger disadvantaged class, and this in its turn to the oppo-
sition between the Athenian and the Boeotian. In 'The Human-Hair
Thread', he says:

> The Aborigines were partly a people, partly a caste, partly a class,
> though really that last term is inaccurate: they were actually part of
> a larger class of the rural poor, and it is still often more useful to see

them in that light than in currently fashionable radical-racialist terms. We, my family, were in the same class ourselves.

(*PT*, p. 72)

The 'fashionable radical-racialist' element he singles out here is part of the ideological divide I discussed briefly earlier: what he sees as an urban orthodoxy which constantly belittles the poor and the supposedly unsophisticated. For Murray, the rural or Boeotian culture is seen as more 'truly' Australian, more egalitarian, more decolonized than the urban or Athenian culture, in particular the urban mandarinate, which is, in his view, hierarchical and still semi-colonized.[9] The poem 'Sydney and the Bush' (*NCP*, pp. 123–4), for instance, depicts briefly the history of Australia since the white arrival in terms of an initial community of interest (when 'there was no open ground') being superseded by oppressive ('a warders' shop') and patronizing ('Australians are sent up') attitudes:

> When Sydney rules without the Bush
> she is a warders' shop
> With heavy dancing overhead
> the music will not stop
>
> and when the drummers want a laugh
> Australians are sent up.
> When Sydney and the Bush meet now
> there is no common ground.

The ballad metre of this poem is itself an indication of his desire to assert solidarity with the 'common people'. The Boeotian, 'vernacular' identity which is denigrated and suppressed by intellectuals and the elite, is, for Murray, the more authentic, truly Australian identity:

This other republic, the one we have to discern, is inherent in our vernacular tradition, which is to say in that 'folk' Australia, part imaginary and part historical, which is the real matrix of any distinctiveness we possess as a nation, and which stands over against all of our establishments and colonial élites.

(*PT*, p. 46)

There are inconsistencies in Murray's thinking on these matters. His assimilation of the Aborigines into the rural poor and his dismissal of the 'fashionable radical-racialist' way of seeing them, quoted above, are instances of this. The particular passage in which he makes this statement follows directly on from a paragraph in which he furnishes examples of the most significant reason why Aborigines could not be assimilated with the rural white poor – race and racism. Here we are told about the 'ugly, contemptuous words' which were applied to the Aborigines, and about the 'six o'clock curfew ... imposed on Aborigines in Taree in those days' (p. 72). Another inconsistency is evident in his dismissal of those whom he opposes, or who oppose him, as proponents of 'ideology' and 'politics', terms which for Murray are synonymous with the radicalism of the 1970s. In his sequence of poems about returning to live in Bunyah (where he grew up), 'The Idyll Wheel' (*NCP*, pp. 281–301), he writes that 'society vanished into ideology' (p. 290). The use of 'ideology' in this way clearly assumes that the views he espouses are somehow 'natural' and free of the taints of ideology.[10] Furthermore, the longed-for fusion of which he speaks is a mirage as a practical proposition, however important and inescapable a part of human longing it might be.

The aspiration to fusion and the incorporation of Aborigines and poor whites into a single class can be related to two other concerns: the desire to move beyond an unending colonial guilt, and the claim that white Australians, especially rural white Australians, have what Philip Larkin in his poem 'Places, Loved Ones' called a 'proper ground', that they can belong unambiguously in Australia alongside the Aborigines.[11] And this in turn is a way of loosening the grip of the 'derivative' mandarinate and purging the country of its colonial hangover by breaking with the West. In his essay 'On Sitting Back and Thinking About Porter's Boeotia' (*PT*, pp. 56–65), he argues that

> not all of our culture derives from Europe, just as not all Australians are of European descent. Some, the black Australians, have been here for tens of thousands of years, and their culture is a Boeotian resource of immeasurable value for us all. Again, the idea of our deliberately remaining Boeotian is full of exciting possibilities. It would be something indeed, to break with Western culture by not taking, even now, the characteristic second step into alienation, into élitism and the relegation of all places except one or two urban centres to the sterile status of provincial no-man's-land largely deprived of any art or any creative self-confidence.
>
> (*PT*, p. 64)

The assimilation of the Aborigines into the wider rural class goes along with taking imaginative possession of the land. Thus, disputing a statement by David Malouf that Aborigines 'have possessed the land' in a way that more recent arrivals can't, Murray argues in 'The Human-Hair Thread':

> My contention is that of course 'we' can, and some of us do possess the land imaginatively in very much the Aboriginal way. We have recently been awed by the discovery that the Aborigines have been here for thirty or forty thousand years, or even longer, but I think too much is often made of this. Forty thousand years are not very different from a few hundred, if your culture has not, through genealogy, developed a sense of the progression of time and thus made history possible. Aboriginal 'history' is poetic, a matter of significant moments rather than of development. To make it historical in our sense requires an imposition of Western thinking.
>
> (*PT*, p. 95)

There seems to be a contradiction between the beginning and end of the passage. As Murray is aware, the Aboriginal possession of the land is bound up with many other parts of Aboriginal culture and spirituality. But the fact that the Aboriginal sense of time is different from the Western historical one undermines the claim that when it comes to the land, a few hundred years are more or less the same as 40,000. For the point is that an 'imposition of Western thinking' – historical thinking in this case – immediately makes the relationship to the land different; the Aboriginal relationship is simply incommensurable with Western historical thinking and ideas of progress. The Aboriginal world is, in the words of Judith Wright quoted in the previous chapter, an 'earth-water-tree-spirit-human complex existing in spacetime', and the Dreaming, which is bound up with that relationship, is simultaneously past and ever-present.[12] Murray's phrase 'an imposition of Western thinking' inevitably suggests a degree of violence, and the word 'imposition' implicitly acknowledges what many historians and political thinkers have suggested explicitly: that the Western historical sense can indeed be a kind of cultural violence bound up with imperialism.[13]

These uncertainties in Murray's relationship to Australia also manifest themselves in comments about the West. In the passage from 'The Human-Hair Thread' last quoted, when he speaks of imposing Western thinking he clearly identifies himself with the West. In the passage quoted before that, however, he speaks of drawing on the resources of Aboriginal culture in order to 'break with Western culture'. This uncertainty about his relationship to Europe and the West is evident also in what appear to be almost automatic references to himself as a 'Westerner' or a 'European'. Thus in an essay about a trip to India, he says: 'Like many Westerners heading for India for the first time, I experienced a deal of apprehension about the horrors of poverty I might see, and the guilts I might have to feel' (*PT*, p. 291). In 'Some Religious Stuff I Know About Australia' (*PT*, pp. 142–62), he writes: 'With the decline of the normative position of Christianity in the West, we now live in a sort of spiritual supermarket' (p. 155); here the implication is, clearly, that the decline is taking place in Australia as well and that 'we' are of the West too.

I make these points not in order to criticize Murray for any inconsistency, but to suggest that, although he speaks of fusion and an Aboriginal relationship to the land, his views can in fact be seen as manifestations of a divided relationship to Australia which is inevitable, given the particular history of the European in that country. What is implicit here is that 'we' both are and are not of the West. This might seem a self-evident truth; but the point is, as I shall argue in more detail later, that Murray effectively keeps the two sides of this truth insulated from each other.

That divided relationship to Australia is something I discussed in relation to Judith Wright and the ideas about 'Australia's double aspect', which she explores in the opening chapter of *Preoccupations in Australian Poetry*, the two sharply contrasting meanings Australia had for the European colonizers and settlers. On the one hand, it was a hostile and alien 'land of exile', with a landscape, flora and fauna that defied their expectations and what they considered 'normal'. On the other hand, it was for a few a potential Utopia, a place where 'something new could be made', where 'some kind of new relationship between men was mistily becoming possible' – a place where the European could learn to belong.[14] Clearly the former meaning would prevent identification with the environment, and reinforce a sense of being a Westerner or European stranded on a distant shore; the latter, in contrast would eventually lead to a new identification in which the settler could cut free of Europe.

I claimed earlier that the idea of fusion is something of a mirage. But Murray's hankering after it, along with his consciousness of division and his uncertainties about Australia and the West can, I would suggest, be interpreted within frameworks provided by the idea of translation. Translation cannot abolish barriers and transport us entirely into another culture; rather, it is a situation in which we partially (and this 'partially' can occur to varying extents) move into another culture or language from the basis of the cultures and languages to which we belong, and which constitute our own 'bridgeheads into reality', to quote Louis MacNeice again. In the two preceding chapters I have used the word 'dialectic', and it again seems readily applicable here. The oscillations between convergence and relegation, fusion and division, merger and separation are all inherent in the process of linguistic and cultural translation: they both bring together and separate.

To start relating these issues to Murray's poetry, I want to begin here with one of his best-known poems, the unrhymed sonnet 'Thinking About Aboriginal Land Rights, I Visit the Farm I Will Not Inherit' (*NCP*, p. 93). One of the backgrounds to the title of this poem is Murray's family history: Murray's father Cecil was disappointed in his hope of inheriting the family farm and, out of pride, rejected the chance to buy it when *his* father didn't will it to him.[15] The title also relates to Murray's idea that white people can have a relationship to the land not dissimilar to that of the Aborigines. In 'The Completed Australian', a book review from the 1970s, Murray reiterates this point and links it to the issue of Aboriginal land rights:

> Land rights for Aborigines involve a possibility of land rights for white people, too, and a blurring of conceptual apartheid between the two. If our crimes in the matter of land have been brutal, rapprochement and convergence are subtle; they need not be ignored on that account.[16]

In Murray's own description of the poem, what it does is to describe 'how the bush would reoccupy and obliterate our old farm, and how the potentials for such an obliteration lie everywhere in the landscape' (*PT*, p. 85). The poem begins with the speaker watching from a barn and noting the signs of human activity in the landscape: 'I see the only lines bearing / consistent strains are the straight ones: fence, house corner, / outermost furrows.' The human impact manifested in the straight lines is contrasted with the different shapes of nature: 'The drifts of grass coming and canes / are whorled and sod-bunching'; the lagoons have 'wind-lap outlines'. These closely observed details, which disturb the neatness of the human shapes imposed on nature, are precursors to the poem's concluding vision of the bush's obliterating activities:

> The ambient day-tides contain every mouldering and oil
> that the bush would need to come back right this day,
> not suddenly, but all down the farm slopes, the polished
>   shell barks
>
>   flaking, leaves noon-thin, with shale stones and orchids at foot
> and the creek a hung gallery again, and the bee trees unrobbed.

By sundown it is dense dusk, all the tracks closing in.
I go into the earth near the feed shed for thousands of years.

Taken on its own terms, this is a powerful, effective and moving poem. In the first five lines just quoted, the single sentence and the copious use of enjambement create a momentum and rhythm which enforce or reinforce a sense of inevitability in the idea of the bush taking over. And the authority of the two syntactically self-contained lines that conclude the poem reiterates this sense of inevitability about the processes depicted. The details of the poem, Murray has said, counteract 'a feeling of dispossession by talking about dimensions, intimacies, knowledge of the place which dispossession cannot touch'. This intimacy puts the speaker 'in a rather Aboriginal position, *vis-à-vis* the usurper', a point which is emphasized, according to Murray, by the last line, in which the speaker becomes 'in effect a totem ancestor' (*PT*, p. 85). But are the two situations the same? Are the intimacies with place known by Aborigines of the same kind as those Murray claims? Is Murray's dispossession like that of the Aborigines?

These questions were among the reasons why I used the qualification 'on its own terms'. Those terms themselves need some examination, beginning perhaps with the word 'inherit' in the title. Aborigines, too, traditionally inherit land from their predecessors, but this inheritance is not of a kind that involves property in the legal sense, something that can then be passed on to your particular descendants and, if need be, sold for cash. Murray has denied vehemently that white Australians only see their land as property, but that still doesn't amount to an equivalence between the two cultures.[17] Land, for Aborigines, does not and cannot belong to an individual; it is more in the nature of a trust. Doesn't this difference immediately undermine the claim to similarity which Murray makes here and elsewhere? The usurpation which occurred in Murray's case is not the same as the usurpation which Aborigines underwent. And similarly, the claim to have become 'in effect a totem ancestor' seems willed and extravagant, given Murray's awareness of the different senses of time that Europeans and Aborigines have. It is not Murray's feeling for the land that is in question here; rather, it is his claim that this feeling is *the same as* that of the Aborigines. This is not an issue of emotional intensity, but of the very nature of the relationship.

Further light might be shed on some of these points through a discussion of the most celebrated of Murray's 'Aboriginal' poems, 'The Buladelah-Taree Holiday Song Cycle' (*NCP*, pp. 137–46). As Murray indicated in a passage from his essay 'The Human-Hair Thread' which I quoted earlier, fusion is central to the way he sees this poem. In that essay, he also compared it to Aboriginal ways of belonging: 'The poem would necessarily celebrate my own spirit country, the one region I know well enough to dare comparison with the Arnhem Landers' (*PT*, pp. 92). Since this poem was based on an Aboriginal model, an exploration of some of the similarities and differences between Murray's poem and its model may help to elucidate ways in which European ways of possessing the land differ from Aboriginal ways, as manifested in these two poems at least. What Murray says of his aims in this poem – in a passage that I quoted earlier – is that he was aiming at 'a longed-for fusion' of rural, urban and Aboriginal cultures, 'a fusion which, as yet perhaps, can only exist in art, or in blessed moments when power and ideology are absent'. This '*enactment* ... of ... fusion', as Kevin Hart puts it, 'mysteriously integrates all aspects of the experience'.[18]

Although Murray wanted the 'senior' Aboriginal culture to set the tone, the actual subject and centre of the poem is a ritual of the white population, the annual holiday exodus of urban Australians to the countryside and the seaside. Each of the specific examples of the motivations that Murray gives for those who enact this annual ritual seems to express both a connection with the land and a simultaneous dissociation from it. These urban Australians are, Murray suggests, people who are

> going back to their ancestral places in a kind of unacknowledged spiritual walkabout, looking for their country in order to draw sustenance from it. Or newcomers looking for the real Australia. Or people going to seek unadmitted communion with the sea, with the bush and the mountains, recovering, in ways which might look tawdry to the moralising sophisticated eye, some fragments of ancient festivity and adventure.
>
> (*PT*, p. 92)

There seems to be some exaggeration and special pleading here, and possibly a wrenching of the annual holiday into a spiritual and religious meaning which the actual event may not bear ('spiritual walkabout', 'unadmitted communion'). It is true that Murray twice stresses a motivation which is not known to the people concerned (the walkabout is 'unacknowledged', and the communion is 'unadmitted'), but there is also a hint of unease in his awareness that the people's actions 'might look tawdry to the moralising sophisticated eye'. There may well be a degree of forcing onto the annual ritual a significance it does not possess.

Commenting on Bernard Smith's suggestion that the conception of Australian identity which places great emphasis on the landscape is a 'false consciousness', since in fact Australia is a heavily urbanized country (in the proportion of its population living in cities, rather than in terms of square miles), Bob Hodge and Vijay Mishra argue that 'one function of this contradiction is to legitimate the illegitimate'. The reason is that the 'prior rights of the Aboriginal peoples are the largest barrier to nonAborigines' sense of their right to be here'. Consequently, 'the new possessors must claim to know and love the land as much as those they dispossessed'. What does this amount to in practice, though? Hodge and Mishra note without comment: 'For contemporary Australians, tourism and the practices of leisure provide many opportunities to (re)create a national identity, compressed into week-ends and the four weeks of annual leave'.[19] To put it this way, to suggest that weekends and annual leave are sufficient to build a relationship to the land equivalent to that of the Aborigines, is itself to imply the thinness of the claim to possession which is being made by these 'contemporary Australians'. The same might be said of Murray's holiday visitors in his poem.

If the Aboriginal culture sets the tone for Murray, it is mainly through the fact that he models it on an Aboriginal precursor, the 'Song Cycle of the Moon-Bone', in the anthropologist R. M. Berndt's translation (which Murray includes in his *New Oxford Book of Australian Verse*).[20] This means that Murray's poem is a 'translation' (in a loose sense) of a translation (in the narrower linguistic sense). Adam Shoemaker wonders whether 'Berndt's role in the production of the English version of the text was more than that of a translator; that he was, in effect, also an editor and nearly a co-author'.[21] Murray himself acknowledges something like this when he describes the original as being 'in a sort of telegraphese verbal shorthand meant to be filled out by music and dance, rendered into long, syntactically complete lines by Professor Berndt' (*PT*, p. 90). The implication is that Murray's poem is several times removed from the original. Without a knowledge of the original language, it is, of course, impossible to assess these points completely, but something can be done with the transliteration and notes that Berndt provided for the original publication, and I shall attempt this a little later.[22]

In 'The Human-Hair Thread', Murray singles out features such as style, metre, tone and movement (*PT*, p. 92), and although he doesn't then provide any detailed account of these aspects of his poem, there are certainly clear stylistic and structural correspondences between the two, as in the long lines of both poems, the modelling of Murray's poem on the oral style of its Aboriginal model, and their parallel structures. Each contains thirteen sections and each moves from people in its first sections to the stars in the last (although there are different notes to the conclusion: the Moon Bone Song Cycle ends with the descent of the Evening Star into the earth, into 'the place of the white gum trees, at Milingimbi' while Murray's poem ends with the Southern Cross rising and hanging suspended over the earth).[23] As Murray says of his own poem, 'the region is *placed* in the universe' (*PT*, p. 94).

There are, however, also significant differences of emphasis in the two pieces, and one of these relates to structure. Murray himself points out that his poem is 'progressive, in a loose sort of way, while the Moon Bone Cycle is static and accretive' (*PT*, p. 94). The progression in Murray's cycle is marked, for instance, by a shadowy narrative which takes us from the arrival of the people on holiday (sections 1–3) to a foreshadowing of departure in section 13: 'people look up from the farms, before going back, they gaze at their year's worth of stars' (*NCP*, p. 145). There is no such narrative in the original, presumably (amongst other reasons) because for the 'Wɔnguri-'Mandʒikai people the poem does not concern an interlude taken out of the ordinary life from which they come and to which they return. The static and accretive nature of the poem also manifests itself in the repetition with variation common to oral poetry. Some of this comes through in Berndt's translation, but the original publication gives a sharper sense of it. The opening lines of section 13 are translated 'Up and up soars the Evening Star, hanging there in the sky. / Men watch it, at the place of the Dugong and of the Clouds, and of the Evening Star.' This is a version of an original which has a rather different effect:

'dʒu:rlpun	*'ka:ndʒiwul*	*'wurlmeii*	*'badiwadi*	*'bala'durulnaŋala*
Evening Star	Evening Star	Evening Star	Evening Star	there back saw[24]

Where Berndt uses one phrase ('Evening Star') twice in two lines, the original names the Evening Star four times in one line using four different words (and this fourfold repetition occurs again two lines later, with only two of the above words being used and two new ones introduced).

Murray's poem also puts much more emphasis on people and the traces of human habitation than does his model, in which places, animals and the totemic identities of people are more dominant. In both cases, the first three sections focus mainly on people, and in both cases the first line of the fourth section makes a transition, in very similar words, to the animal world: in Murray it is 'The birds saw us wandering along' (*NCP*, p. 139), while in the Aboriginal poem it is 'The birds saw the people walking along'.[25] There is, however, a significant difference between the two lines, which relates to the point I am addressing: this is Murray's shift from 'the people' of the original piece to 'us'. The Aboriginal poem almost stands out of the human world, in that by referring to both human beings and animals in the third person, the narrative viewpoint sees them as being of the same order of creation (and indeed the section goes on to emphasize what the birds see in relation to the totemic identifications of the people: 'the clans of the white cockatoo', the 'Shag woman'). Murray's 'us', in contrast, anchors the speaker within the human world, and identifies him with his fellow human beings, thus separating the two orders of being. Furthermore, the rest of the Aboriginal song cycle after section 3 is mainly dominated by place and animals, with human beings returning intermittently, and mostly in passing, except for section 7, which is almost entirely about people. In Murray, however, people and their activities permeate the remainder of the poem.

Another difference between the two poems concerns place-names. The Moon Bone Song Cycle is dominated by one place, the 'place of the Dugong' or elaborations of this, such as the 'place of the Dugong's tail' or its Entrails (although an inspection of the transliteration and inter-linear translation which R. M. Berndt provides in his first publication of the piece reveals that, while many of the names may refer to the same place or people, the actual words used in the original differ). The last section is pervaded by a variety of places, such as 'the place of the Eggs, of the Tree-Limbs-Rubbing-Together'.[26] In Murray's poem, however, most of the places relate either to specific people from legend and local history, such as Legge's Lake and Bingham's Ghost, or to the conse-quences of human activity, such as the Old Timber Wharf and the Dingo Trap (pp. 137, 140).[27]

In his book on Australian 'spatial history', *The Road to Botany Bay*, Paul Carter discusses, amongst other things, differences between Aboriginal and settler methods of naming places. Speaking of the names given by Captain Cook, he says:

> The very violence of their metaphorical displacements preserves the irony of the explorer's position and the contingent nature of his knowledge. The *unnaturalness* of attaching ministers to mountains, secretaries to capes, the playful tautology of calling islands 'Islands of Direction', the unlikelihood of Botany *Bay*, as if the flora in question were marine: by all these figurative means Cook preserves the differ-ence between the order of nature and the order of culture.[28]

Similarly, the place names in Murray's poem which, usually, in one form or another, impress on us the impact of human habitation, also generally differentiate between the 'order of nature and the order of culture'. In contrast, the Aboriginal names in the song cycle (which draw on the natural order) appear to blur the distinction between nature and culture, although, of course, since naming is a human practice, there can be no final abolition of the difference between the two. Martin Leer describes Murray's poem as 'an embodiment in toponymic art of the temporo-spatial differences between cultures', and this is a description which my discussion here seems to support.[29]

These points are closely linked to the question of history and the past. In section 5 of the poem, which follows the one in which Murray first turns to land and animals, he reverts to the human world and to human ancestors. The section begins as follows:

> The Fathers and the Great-grandfathers, they are out in the
>   paddocks all the time, they live out there,
> at the place of the Rail Fence, of the Furrows Under Grass,
>   at the place of the Slab Chimney.
> We tell them that clearing is complete, an outdated
>   attitude, all over;
> we preach without a sacrifice, and are ignored; flowering
>   bushes grow dull to our eyes.

> (*NCP*, p. 139)

Commenting on this section in 'The Human-Hair Thread', Murray highlights a difference between white and Aboriginal cultures:

> Section 5 broaches the subject of ancestors. This is a purely white matter; Aboriginal religion, with its reincarnationist schema and its taboo on mentioning the dead, is quite at variance with white reverence for particular, successive ancestors. In the poem, though, the particular pioneer ancestors are, as it were, given the aura of the great ancestral sires of the Central Australian sacred sites, and the timelessness of these founding ancestors is stressed as against their successivity, so there is convergence.

> (*PT*, p. 93)

As often in Murray, a consciousness of divergence is acknowledged ('a purely white matter') and then replaced by an assertion of convergence.

The white relationship to the past, with its 'reverence for particular, successive ancestors', which is connected to Western historical thinking, is brushed away and the ancestors now become timeless, thus allowing for convergence. How do we make sense of this? It seems almost as if Murray will not, or cannot, allow the double sense – one white, one aboriginal – to exist simultaneously as a mark of difference. In this case, the particularity of the relationship to the past is superseded by, or incorporated into, an Aboriginal timelessness. But when Murray says that 'The Fathers and the Great-grandfathers, they are out in the paddocks all the time, they live out there', it can be no more than a verbal assertion, rather than the lived relationship that is the Aboriginal way.

The 'fusion' which Murray was aiming at is in fact a 'translation' in my broad sense of the term. What happens, it seems to me, in the movement from the Aboriginal model to Murray's own song cycle is that, as in translation more narrowly defined, various aspects of the target culture have entered into the process and shaped the poem, and that these are embodiments of the inevitable cultural differences that exist. Whereas the impossible goal of fusion seems to want to abolish difference by melting all the elements into one, translation maintains difference, perhaps despite itself, while attempting to bridge it. The cycle is a fine achievement, but Murray's claims for it are contradicted by his own awareness of the differences between Aboriginal and white cultures.

Difficult and possibly irresolvable questions accrue round the issues I have been raising, and as an outsider to Australia, with no direct stake in the matter, I can only make tentative observations here. The wrongs of the invasion and its aftermath are by now well known, and widely, but not universally, acknowledged. Obviously nothing now can undo that past. But white Australians are in the country, and have been there for over 200 years. A numbers game as to whether 200 or 2,000 or 40,000 years are necessary before people 'belong' somewhere seems futile to me.

'The Suspension of Knock' (*NCP*, pp. 411–12), a poem in one of Murray's most strident and least appealing poetic veins, angrily expresses a feeling that the descendants of earlier generations of white settlers (outside the elite) are being rendered emotionally and spiritually homeless in Australia:

> Where will we hold Australia,
> we who have no other country?
> Not Indigenous, merely born here,
> shall we be Australian in Paraguay
> again, or on a Dublin street corner?

While one can see and feel the justice of this kind of complaint, Murray's attempts to abolish the very real differences between white and Aboriginal Australians seem to me to be overstated and unconvincing. They don't, for instance, engage with the views expressed by many Aborigines, for whom an easy reconciliation is more than a little problematic, as the writers Jack Davis and Kevin Gilbert vehemently make clear:

> I really think the majority of Australians are just buffoons. They tell us to forgive and forget what's happened in the past. Then, every Anzac day, they glorify their own history. How are we supposed to forget what's happened to us *in Australia* when White Australians keep on remembering their own violent history elsewhere? Besides, we have a lot more to remember right here.

> An onus is on Aboriginal writers to present the evidence of our true situation. In attempting to present the evidence we are furiously attacked by white Australians and white converts, whatever their colour, as 'Going back 200 years ... the past is finished ... !' Yet, cut off a man's leg, kill his mother, rape his land, psychologically attack and keep him in a powerless position each day – does it not live on in the mind of the victim? Does it not continue to scar and affect the thinking? Deny it, but it still exists.[30]

Adam Shoemaker offers a partly sympathetic and partly critical view of Murray's engagement with Aboriginal cultures. In the course of it, Shoemaker suggests that Murray's line, 'I go into the earth near the feed shed for thousands of years' goes 'too far' in making parallels between white Australian attitudes to land and those of the Aborigines: 'The sense of *belonging* of which he speaks is of a different order of magnitude to the sense of being *owned by* the land, which is the traditional Aboriginal concept, with all the sanctity of religious veneration.' Murray's 'sincere interest' in Aboriginal culture, Shoemaker concludes, is 'quasi-anthropological'.[31] While Shoemaker appears to imply that one of Murray's problems is simply that he doesn't feel conquest-guilt, unlike other Australian poets such as Bruce Dawe and Judith Wright, the different types of relationship to the land ('belonging', 'being owned by') that he mentions here are similar to the distinction I am trying to draw.[32] The belonging takes place, amongst other things, through the agency of historical narrative and historically based legendary connections (that is to say, legends based on the lives of particular, historical people). It seems to me that the most one can say is that the ways in which white Australians and the Aborigines relate or respond to the land are *different* ways, founded on long and differential histories of cultural, social and religious development, amongst other things.

To claim an Aboriginal relationship with the land is not really the mark of confidence in belonging that Murray seems to think it is. Rather it is founded on a consciousness of usurpation and belatedness. Bob Hodge and Vijay Mishra said, in a remark quoted earlier, that, because of the consciousness of usurpation, the 'new possessors must claim to know and love the land *as much as* those they dispossessed' (my italics). This focuses on the degree of feeling. Murray's claims, however, are claims of kind: he asserts that white Australians can love the land *in the same way* as the dispossessed. But, because of cultural and historical differences this simply cannot be the case, and yet Murray seems unwilling to acknowledge this. Martin Leer notes that the '"convergence" between the two cultures simultaneously brings out their divergence' and this is akin to the act of translation rather than the fusion to which Murray aspires.[33] The 'Buladelah-Taree Song Cycle' may well display a sense of belonging but the nature of that belonging has been translated from European culture. While the Aboriginal culture has clearly shaped the poem, what emerges eventually is not a fusion but something positioned in between the two cultures. The poem itself differs from and escapes the model of fusion which is put forward in the essays discussed earlier, and which was Murray's stated aim in the poem.[34]

The translational nature of the relationship with the land (this, of course, includes flora and fauna, not just the earth), the pattern of simultaneous divergence and convergence, seems to be more openly acknowledged and worked through in his sequence 'Presence: Translations from the Natural World' (*NCP*, pp. 355–78), which is 'about' various animals and plants.[35] Although the Aboriginal world is not explicit in these poems, there may be, as Robert Crawford notes, a link with Aboriginal notions of the relationship between human beings and animals.[36] For Aborigines, some of these relationships are manifested in the complex array of experiences, concepts and terms which are translated into English under the misleading and disputed terms 'Dreamtime' and 'Dreaming'. As Mudrooroo says of these 'two villains' and other concepts, 'we are not dealing with a simple word to word translation ... but with a complex metaphysical and spiritual concept for which there is simply no adequate English rendering'.[37] Some idea of the complexity of the pattern within which the human–animal relationship exists is given by Lynne Hume's description of the Dreaming as 'a cosmogony, a cosmology, a way of being, a moral system'. Hume also quotes the anthropologist W. E. H. Stanner's description of it:

> A continuing highway between Ancestral superman and living man, between the life-givers and the life, the countries, the totems and totem-places they gave to living men, between subliminal reality and immediate reality, and between the There-and-Then of the beginnings of all things and relevances and the Here-and-Now of their continuations.[38]

This is not, and cannot be, the same context as we find in Murray's sequence, which are, as his title indicates, translations. Crawford has pointed out that the poems in the sequence tend to follow two strategies – either approaching their subjects from the point of view of a human observer, or emanating from the animal or plant perspective.[39] Most, in fact, take the latter course. The mimicry of the lyrebird ('I mew catbird, I saw crosscut, I howl she-dingo') seems to be a model for what Murray is doing here (*NCP*, p. 358). A few poems, such as 'Mollusc' (p. 361), seem entirely and unambiguously spoken by a human voice. Others, such as 'Layers of Pregnancy' (p. 356), about a kangaroo, are spoken by a human voice, but translated into an in-between space by various devices (in this particular case layout, as I illustrate later on). The majority, however, seem to be spoken by plants and animals (and, in one case, a DNA molecule).

Sometimes the two strategies operate within the same poem. 'The Octave of Elephants' (p. 365), for instance, opens with a narrator setting the scene:

> Bull elephants, when not weeping need, wander soberly alone.
> Only females congregate and talk, in a seismic baritone

The rest of the poem consists of the female elephants' utterance. They speak, however, in an English which is rather like the narrator's. More radical in its contrasts between narrator and animal is 'Bats' Ultrasound', the first poem in the sequence as it appeared in the *New Collected Poems* (p. 355), but not present in the version originally published in *Translations from the Natural World*.[40] I quote the entire piece:

> Sleeping-bagged in a duplex wing
> with fleas, in rock-cleft or building

radar bats are darkness in miniature,
their whole face one tufty crinkled ear
with weak eyes, fine teeth bared to sing.

Few are vampires. None flit through the mirror.
Where they flutter at evening's a queer
tonal hunting zone above highest C.
Insect prey at the peak of our hearing
drone re to their detailing tee:

ah, eyrie-ire, aero hour, eh?
O'er our ur-area (our era aye
ere your raw row) we air our array,
err, yaw, row wry – aura our orrery,
our eerie ü our ray, our arrow.

A rare ear, our aery Yahweh.

The external human observer of the first two stanzas shifts in the
third stanza to what appears like an attempt to represent bat-language:
'words' that seem to come from the bats themselves ('words' is an
approximation here, in that the last line of the second stanza, using the
musical scale, describes the bats' sound as a 'tee' in contrast to the 're'
of the insects). Although almost every word in this third stanza, with
the exception of 'ü', is recognizable as a word in the English language
(or, like 'ur', is used reasonably regularly), and although individual
phrases make some kind of sense in isolation from other phrases, ini-
tially the particular collocation that Murray has put together eludes the
reader's sense of a syntactical and semantic direction. The sounds –
particularly the vowels and the 'r' – take over and dominate the end of
the poem. However, if one follows a hint from Bert Almon – who has
noted a similar process in 'Insect Mating Flight', a poem dropped from
the sequence as it appears in the *New Collected Poems* – some kind of
sense does emerge from the lines.[41] Thus the opening line of the bat
stanza can be seen as a kind of challenging question establishing their
rights to possession; it is their 'eyrie', their 'aero hour', their time to
occupy the air. Similarly, the next two and a half lines can be para-
phrased roughly as follows: 'over our original ('ur') area, which was ours
always or long before ('aye'; 'aye' can also be an assertion – 'yes it was')
your relatively recent arrival by sea ('ere your raw row') we display our-
selves ('air our array'), make our irregular flights ('err, yaw, row wry').

'Aura our orrery' is more difficult to make sense of. 'Aura' could be either a noun or the noun converted into a verb. An 'orrery' is, of course, a clockwork mechanism representing the movement of the planets about the sun. So perhaps the phrase refers to an order which underlies the apparent irregularity of movement depicted in the first half of the line. Finally, 'our eerie ü our ray, our arrow' might be a reference to the sound the bats make ('our eerie ü'), which, as we know, serves the function of navigation (hence the ray and arrow).

Although alternatives to these interpretations are possible ('row', for instance, has a variety of meanings – noise, argument, arrangement), some kind of sense can be made of the lines in question. Both the movement from the first two stanzas to the last lines, and the use in the third stanza of words which make a partial though not obvious sense, indicate a poem poised in between the human and animal world, an attempt to represent the unrepresentable. The last line of the poem is also interesting, since here the language recovers its humanness by making a syntactically clear (though verbless) statement. Yet this line, like the preceding five, which are clearly designated (by the preceding colon, for instance), as emanating from the bats, is also in italics. Who is this 'aery Yahweh', with his 'rare ear'? Who is represented through the first-person 'our' – bats or human beings? Although the poem doesn't make it clear, this ambiguity might be deliberate. Could the line then be seen to belong to both the human observer of the first two stanzas and the bats of the third? Both bats and human beings could in some sense claim to have an 'aery Yahweh'. For the human being this would be a God who hears them; for the bats, the referent would not be so clear to us, but perhaps Murray is inviting us to imagine a creature which can, unlike human beings, hear the bats. The bats have their own conceptions of God. Or perhaps the God of both human beings and bats is the same one, since in Christian thinking, of course, he created the entire universe. The poem flits between representation and unrepresentability; it domesticates bat language and foreignizes English, positioning the reader between two worlds, the human and the animal, and this paradox is something that Murray engages with throughout the sequence.

The kind of disorientating effect evident in the bat-language here is present, in various forms, elsewhere in the sequence as well. Some poems dislocate grammar and syntax. 'Cockspur Bush' (p. 357) begins with the line 'I am lived. I am died', 'Pigs' (p. 366) with 'Us all on sore cement was we'. Others play around with layout on the page. 'Layers of Pregnancy' (p. 356), a poem about a kangaroo spoken by a human observer, divides each line into two parts separated by a space: 'Under eagle worlds   each fixed in place / it is to kangaroo   all fragrant space'. 'Raven, sotto voce' uses the same device (p. 376). 'Migratory' (p. 377) is justified on the right-hand side of the page.[42]

These devices of layout and grammar reinforce and are reinforced by the spatial disorientations in the sequence. The eagles in 'Eagle Pair' (pp. 355–6) think entirely in terms of 'the limitless Up', which, for them, is space and freedom and the 'Down', which is 'heavy and entangled', the only good thing about it being the prey ('meats') they can find there and the thermals on which they rise again after hunting ('the rebound heat ribbing up rivers of air'). In 'Prehistory of Air' (p. 359), too, gravity seems to operate in reverse:

> Fish, in their every body
> hold a sac of dry
> freeing them from gravity
> where fish go when they die.

Here the fact that fish rise rather than fall when they die is being depicted in a syntax which suggests that they go 'to' gravity, as it were ('gravity/where fish go'). Similarly, the effect of the heron-speaker's beak striking the fish is described as their 'world turn[ing] outside-in', rather than inside-out. In 'Migratory' (p. 377), the bird in flight is instinctively conscious of 'the wrongness of here' while it is on its way to its destination, and the only thing that feels right is the vastness of movement and space:

> I am the wrongness of here, when it
> is true to fly along the feeling
> the length of its great rightness, while days
> burn from vast to a gold gill in the dark
>   to vast again

Crawford sees these poems as leading to 'an act of at-one-ment with the natural world', as being about 'escape from the corruption of the human person and cure through a bonding with all other life and a shared, exultant spirituality'.[43] Steven Matthews, while building on and developing Crawford's insights, offers a different emphasis: that the conclusion of the sequence 'becomes haunted by the possibility that language itself marks humanity's fallen state'.[44] My suggestion is that both emphases are valid and indeed central to the poems; and that this

combination of fallenness and at-one-ment, this simultaneous separa-
tion and joining are inherent in the act of translation in which Murray
is engaged throughout. The last two poems in the sequence focus on
language as the differentiating characteristic of human beings. 'From
Where We Live on Presence' (p. 378), spoken by a beetle, opens: 'A human
is a comet streamed in language far down time; no other / living is like
it. Beetlehood itself was my expression'. The final lines of the sequence,
which Matthews quotes, can be read as not just indicating that language
is a sign of fallenness, but also, in addition, that it is a way of healing
division, although complete healing can never occur. This poem, 'Possum's
Nocturnal Day' (a title which itself yokes together two opposites), is
spoken by the possum and concludes as follows:

> I curl up in my charcoal trunk of night
> And dream a welling pictureless encouragement
> That tides from afar but is in arrival me
> And my world, since nothing is apart enough for language.

> (*NCP*, p. 378)

The possum, the last line implies, since it does indeed live 'at-one-ment
with the natural world', doesn't need language; it is only those whose
world is fractured – human beings – who need the power of language in
their endless but always ultimately unsuccessful attempts to join
together the fragments.

One of the effects of the spatial and stylistic devices discussed earlier
is to convey what Crawford describes as 'a sense of otherness' by mak-
ing us aware of the 'inbuilt resistance in the language of these poems'.[45]
'Inbuilt resistance' and intractability are also, as I argued in the first
chapter, manifested in translation. To return to the distinction made
there, Murray is clearly following a 'foreignizing' translation strategy in
these poems, although as my discussion of 'Bats' Ultrasound' indicated,
in order to make sense of them we have also to follow the route of
domestication. The poems leave us poised in between, and one of the
reasons for this, as the last poem makes clear, is that what makes us dif-
ferent from animals is language. And indeed, this idea is what might
separate Murray from assimilation with Aboriginal conceptions of
animals and the land. Deborah Bird Rose says that for the Yarralin
people whom she studied, the crucial difference between human beings
and animals is not language (since 'all animals have language', even if
we cannot understand them) but shape.[46]

The sequence taken as a whole, I have been suggesting, has many affinities with the process of translation in general – whether it is translation between languages, between cultures, or, as here, between the natural world and the human. Translation – like language more generally – both is and is not a realm of fusion: it brings together, and forever separates, the two realms between which the process is occurring. It leaves us in the in-between realm which is the location of both 'The Buladelah-Taree Holiday Song Cycle' (in effect, although not in Murray's intention) and these 'translations from the natural world'.

4
Louis MacNeice, Ireland and India

Despite his Irish birth, it may seem unusual, even eccentric, to include Louis MacNeice in a book with the word 'postcolonial' in its title. He has not, to my knowledge, been discussed in such a context. One reason for this is probably the Anglicized upbringing and public school education that, in Derek Mahon's words, 'has a way of ironing out differences and turning its products into Englishmen'.[1] As a consequence of this, perhaps, he was for many years seen in one of two ways. For some, his association with the so-called Auden generation of British poets held sway: he was often thought of as secondary to Auden, and sometimes disparaged as lacking substance in comparison. Others saw MacNeice as someone stranded between England and Ireland. 'For the English reader', writes Tom Paulin, 'he appears to be Irish, while for certain Irish readers he doesn't really belong to Ireland'.[2] Francis Scarfe, for instance, sees MacNeice as 'damnably Irish', while, on the Irish side, examples often adduced are the relative neglect of MacNeice in anthologies such John Montague's *Faber Book of Irish Verse* (1974) and Thomas Kinsella's *New Oxford Book of Irish Verse* (1986).[3]

A second reason is the disputed relationship between Ireland and postcolonialism. While some have tried to link them, there have been others who question whether it is legitimate to consider the nation as having been a colony in the first place. And if this is not possible, then the idea of a postcolonial Ireland is called into question. It would not be feasible to review this debate in any detail here.[4] However, there is clear evidence in MacNeice of a divided sensibility, part colonial and part oppositional, which marks his various responses to the countries mentioned in the title of this chapter, and to England. It is his location between Ireland and England that makes him relevant here. In his unfinished autobiography, *The Strings are False*, MacNeice recounts an incident from his prep school days at Sherborne. On the twelfth of July one year, a schoolmaster asked him whether the Orange Order parades held on that day in Northern Ireland weren't all 'mumbo-jumbo', a sentiment with which MacNeice agreed. However, another master, a Mr. Cameron, was enraged by MacNeice's statement; the latter then comments:

> Oh this division of allegiance! That the Twelfth of July was mumbo-jumbo was true, and my father thought so too, but the moment Mr. Cameron appeared I felt rather guilty and cheap. Because I had been showing off to Powys and because Mr. Cameron being after all Irish I felt I had betrayed him.
>
> (*SF*, pp. 78–9)

It is such divided allegiances – the complications of his relationship with Ireland, England and then India – that I shall be concerned with here.

Over the last 30 or so years, MacNeice's reputation has undergone a considerable shift of emphasis which has seen him repositioned as an Irish writer. This shift has been to a large degree, but not exclusively, the work of Northern Irish poets and critics who came to prominence from the mid-1960s onwards, including Edna and Michael Longley, Tom Paulin, Paul Muldoon and Seamus Heaney. It is not difficult to see why this is so; for these writers he has served as a resource and a model in the polarized climate which marked northern Irish culture and politics during the Troubles. Heaney, for instance, argues that MacNeice is 'an example of how distance, either of the actual, exilic, cross-channel variety or the imaginary, self-renewing, trans-historical and trans-cultural sort, can be used as an enabling factor in the work of art in Ulster'.[5] The sharply polarized views of Ireland which these writers tried to break out of is also rejected vehemently in MacNeice's major poem of the 1930s, *Autumn Journal*:

> And one read black, where the other read white, his hope
>   The other man's damnation:
> Up the Rebels, To Hell with the Pope,
>   And God Save – as you prefer – the King or Ireland.
>
> (*CP*, p. 132)

MacNeice's cultural affiliations are in fact quite complex. More specifically, he was born into a Protestant family in Belfast. However, through his parents, who both originally came from the West of Ireland, and later through his own emotional connections, he had significant links with what in his lifetime became the Republic of Ireland. His father, moreover, although a clergyman in the (Anglican) Church of Ireland, was an Irish nationalist who supported Home Rule. While MacNeice inherited or shared some of his father's feelings about Ireland, he was educated in England and, unlike his father, chose to spend most of his life there. This is a complex heritage, as Seamus Heaney makes clear:

> MacNeice ... by his English domicile and his civil learning is an aspect of Spenser, by his ancestral and affectionate links with Connemara an aspect of Yeats and by his mythic and European consciousness an aspect of Joyce. ... He can be regarded as an Irish Protestant writer with Anglocentric attitudes who managed to be faithful to his Ulster inheritance, his Irish affections and his English predilections.[6]

Heaney's reference here to the English as well as the Irish dimensions in MacNeice is salutary; there are those who feel that the Hibernization of MacNeice in recent criticism has gone too far.[7] However, Heaney's comments may give the impression that MacNeice's situation was an easily resolved and achieved one. In fact, the faithfulness to different parts of his heritage was a much more precarious achievement than Heaney seems to imply. What I propose to do here is first to trace the way in which he reached the kind of accommodation described, and then to link it with his representations of the Indian subcontinent, which he visited on several occasions, the first time during a particularly significant period – Partition in 1947 – as part of a BBC radio team sent to India to cover the transfer of power. I shall attempt to focus on the ways in which he negotiates between the different strands of cultural experience and encounter involved, and to suggest that there are significant similarities and connections between the processes of negotiation in these cases.

There are by now many critical studies of MacNeice's relationship to Ireland, and it will not be possible here to deal with all the different aspects that have been discussed in these studies.[8] It is well documented that in his early work, there is a marked split between the North and the West of Ireland. The North, where he was born, is typically described in negative terms, as in the opening of the poem 'Belfast' (*CP*, p. 17):

> The hard cold fire of the northerner
> Frozen into his blood from the fire in his basalt

Glares from behind the mica of his eyes
And the salt carrion water brings him wealth.

Down there at the end of the melancholy lough
Against the lurid sky over the stained water
Where hammers clang murderously on the girders
Like crucifixes the gantries stand.

Masculine steeliness, stoniness and coldness are contrasted in the poem
with an oppressed and shapeless femininity:

In the porch of the chapel before the garish Virgin
A shawled factory-woman as if shipwrecked there
Lies a bunch of limbs glimpsed in the cave of gloom
By us who walk in the street so buoyantly and glib.

The poem concludes with the lines: 'the male kind murders each its
woman / To whose prayer for oblivion answers no Madonna'. In
'Valediction', Belfast is described in similar terms:

devout and profane and hard,
Built on reclaimed mud, hammers playing in the shipyard,
Time punched with holes like a steel sheet, time
Hardening the faces, veneering with a grey and speckled rime
The faces under the shawls and caps

(*CP*, p. 52)

Such images of masculine hardness feature in many of his representa-
tions of Northern Ireland. The West is presented very differently, as in
'Landscapes of Childhood and Youth', all that was written of a projected
book entitled *Countries in the Air* (reprinted by E. R. Dodds, the editor,
as an appendix to *The Strings are False*):

The very name Connemara seemed too rich for any ordinary place. It
appeared to be a country of windswept open spaces and mountains
blazing with whins and seas that were never quiet, with drowned
palaces beneath them, and seals and eagles and turf smoke and cot-
tagers who were always laughing and who gave you milk when you
asked for a glass of water. And the people's voices were different there,
soft and rich like my father's ... and not like the pious woman's or the
ferocious mill-girls' whom I always expected to pelt us with rotten eggs.

(*SF*, pp. 216–17)

It was, he says, 'the first of [my] dream worlds' (p. 216). This positive view of Ireland is mainly but not entirely confined to the West of Ireland. In the early 'Train to Dublin', for instance, he praises the movement and variety seen on a train journey from North to South:

> I give you the smell of Norman stone, the squelch
> Of bog beneath your boots, the red bog-grass,
> The vivid chequer of the Antrim hills ...
> . . . .
>   And I give you the faces, not the permanent masks,
> But the faces balanced in the toppling wave
>
> (*CP*, p. 28)

A hard and ossified Ireland is set against a fluid and living one. The ossification can take forms other than Belfast's hardness, such as a romanticized trading on familiar stereotypes of Irishness, the 'gallery of fake tapestries' he decries in 'Valediction' (*CP*, p. 52) or the feminine personification of the country as Kathleen ni Houlihan. In section XVI of *Autumn Journal*, for instance, the shawled woman at the altar from the poem 'Belfast' reappears, linked to this kind of representation of Ireland:

>   the angry voices
>   Piercing the broken fanlight in the slum,
>   The shawled woman weeping at the garish altar.
>   Kathaleen ni Houlihan! Why
>   Must a country, like a ship or a car, be always female,
>   Mother or sweetheart?
>
> (*CP*, p. 132)

Eamon Grennan has described this dualistic vision of Ireland as MacNeice's hell and heaven.[9]

It is arguable that this dualism is only a specific manifestation of another one which is central to MacNeice's aesthetic thinking: the contrast between flux and pattern – that is to say, attention to the variety and livingness of things in the world, and the desire to make sense of the variety through conceptual categories.[10] G. S. Fraser relates the dualism to more familiar philosophical concepts: 'The problem of the One and the Many, like the problem of Essence and Existence, crops up again and again in Mr. MacNeice's poetry.'[11] An important element in his poems and in his thinking about poetry is an attempt to honour both elements of these dualisms, to avoid, on the one hand, a rigid patterning which ossifies the world (as in the stereotypical figure of Kathleen ni Houlihan or in certain kinds of philosophizing, such as Plato's Idealism) and, on the other hand, sheer flux, which results in a lack of meaning. This reconciliation is not simply harmonizing, balancing or opposition. Rather the relationship is dialectical: flux makes patterning provisional and pattern makes flux, at least temporarily, meaningful, and the whole process operates constantly. We can see MacNeice returning to these ideas over and over again, explicitly in his prose, and implicitly in his poetry. In his critical book, *Modern Poetry*, he writes,

> The poet is once again to make his response as a whole. On the one side is concrete living – not just a conglomeration of animals or machines, mere flux, a dissolving hail of data, but a system of individuals determined by their circumstances, a concrete, therefore, of sensuous fact and what we may call 'universals'; on the other side is a concrete poet – not just an eye or a heart or a brain or a solar plexus, but the whole man reacting with both intelligence and emotion ... to experiences, and on this basis presenting something which is (a) communication, a record, but is also (b) a creation – having a new unity of its own, something in its shape which makes it poetry.
>
> (*MP*, pp. 29–30)[12]

An example of what can happen when the flux becomes bound into an over-rigid pattern comes in the section of *Autumn Journal* which I have quoted above. Immediately after the Kathaleen ni Houlihan passage, he writes:

> A woman passing by,
>   We did but see her passing.
> Passing like a patch of sun on the rainy hill
>   And yet we love her for ever and hate our neighbour
>
> (*CP*, p. 132)

The image of flux and movement, the 'passing' woman, is, the juxtaposition of the two passages suggests, ossified into the figure of Kathleen ni Houlihan, and this process of ossification is one source of the hostility and communal conflict which dogs Ireland.

In the early poem 'Valediction' (*CP*, pp. 52–4), his inability to recon-
cile these two Irelands in some way is 'solved' through a rejection of the
entire culture. Although he says half way through this poem 'I cannot
deny my past to which my self is wed', this is precisely what he does:

> not to have my baby clothes my shroud
> I will acquire an attitude not yours
> And become as one of your holiday visitors,
> And however often I may come
> Farewell, my country, and in perpetuum

> (*CP*, p. 53)

> I have to gesture,
> Take part in, or renounce, each imposture;
> Therefore I resign, good-bye the chequered and the quiet hills
> The gaudily-striped Atlantic, the linen-mills
> That swallow the shawled file, the black moor where half
> A turf-stack stands like a ruined cenotaph

> (p. 54)

To avoid falling into the opposing traps of what the poem calls 'indif-
ference and sentimentality' (p. 52), the only way out is to reject the
entire country; and if this means renouncing what is attractive along
with what is not, positive and negative alike, that, it seems, is the price
that must be paid. There is a current of regret in the early part of the
second quotation; the variety and fluidity MacNeice was always so
drawn to come through in 'the chequered and the quiet hills' or 'the
gaudily-striped Atlantic'. But in the end there are only the stark alter-
natives expressed in the lines: 'I have to gesture, / Take part in, or
renounce, each imposture'. This requires, as he sees it, an embrace of
Ireland's opposite: 'I will acquire an attitude not yours'. That opposite is
England: 'I must go east and stay, not looking behind' (p. 53). Here
MacNeice seems to be embroiled in those anxieties of self-definition I dis-
cussed in my introduction: he is working through mechanisms of con-
trast and exclusion. This is, however, a false choice; there is another way
which involves neither taking part in nor renouncing each 'imposture',
but accommodating these things without rejecting or participating. I shall
try to formulate this third way later through the idea of translation.

The heaven/hell dualism I have been describing is a version of some-
thing with which we have become familiar in, for instance, the language

of Orientalism or of Celticism, where the East in one case or Ireland in the other becomes either the thing to be rejected in its entirety as all that we are not, all we do not want to become, or the thing to be embraced as giving us what we lack, an image of the wholeness from which we have become estranged, the lost home to be recovered in fantasy. For the English, writes Declan Kiberd, 'Ireland was ... patented as not-England, a place whose peoples were, in many important ways, the very antitheses of their new rulers from overseas'.[13] What MacNeice is doing here is the obverse: England is not-Ireland.

In the next Irish poem I want to discuss, 'Carrick Revisited' (*CP*, pp. 224–5), which dates from 1945, the fantasy of wholeness is recognized as such under the label 'the pre-natal mountain'. In this poem, the journey back to Carrickfergus, his childhood home, is depicted as bringing about a reconnection with those days. 'The child's astonishment not yet cured', he writes,

> Who was – and am – dumbfounded to find myself
> In a topographical frame – here, not there –
> The channels of my dreams determined largely
> By random chemistry of soil and air;
> Memories I had shelved peer at me from the shelf.

The words 'topographical frame' locate him in a particular place. 'Frame' could carry a number of overlapping meanings: the ones that come most immediately to mind are the frame of a picture, or frame of reference or structural framework. The OED lists a number of associated meanings, of which I quote a few here: 'mental or emotional disposition or state (more explicitly, frame of mind, soul etc.)'; 'a structure which serves as an underlying support or skeleton, or of which the parts form an outline or skeleton not filled in'; 'a structure of timbers, joists, etc. fitted together to form the skeleton of a building'.[14] The tendency of all of them is to suggest that the frame is the structure on which his identity or identities are built, the lens (to change the metaphor) through which he peers.

The 'topographical frame' has an interesting connection with the famous radio discussion of 1939 between MacNeice and F. R. Higgins, in which Higgins urged MacNeice to realize the consequences of his Irishness: 'I am afraid, Mr MacNeice, you, as an Irishman, cannot escape from your blood, nor from our blood-music that brings the racial character to mind.' Higgins went on to praise Irish poetry for its rootedness in 'rural civilisation' and to criticize English poetry for its 'drift' to urban civilization, and modern poetry in particular for its preoccupation with the 'mechanical age' and its 'pitiful whinings'. MacNeice's response was wry and sceptical:

> I have the feeling that you have sidetracked me into an Ireland *versus* England match. I am so little used to thinking of poetry in terms of race-consciousness that no doubt this was very good for me. However, I am still unconverted. I think that one may have such a thing as one's racial blood-music, but that, like one's unconscious, it may be left to take care of itself.[15]

What MacNeice's 'topographical frame' is implying is not 'race-consciousness' or primordiality, but, still, something connected with the land where he was born, its 'random chemistry of soil and air'. As Seamus Heaney puts it, discussing an extract from the poem 'Suite for Recorders', it is 'acknowledging the relevance of concerns which are embarrassing when formulated in terms of "race-consciousness" or "racial blood-music"'.[16]

In 'Carrick Revisited' (which is central to Heaney's view of MacNeice), dualistic visions are complicated by using three terms – the North, the West and England:

> Torn before birth from where my fathers dwelt,
> Schooled from the age of ten to a foreign voice,
> Yet neither western Ireland nor southern England
> Cancels this interlude; what chance misspelt
> May never now be righted by my choice.
>
> Whatever then my inherited or acquired
> Affinities, such remains my childhood's frame
> Like a belated rock in the red Antrim clay
> That cannot at this era change its pitch or name –
> And the pre-natal mountain is far away.

There is clearly a sense of longing for the 'pre-natal mountain' – he has, after all been 'torn' away from it. And 'this interlude' suggests that Carrickfergus was a passage between two more dominant realities (although one, 'western Ireland' is a psychic rather than a physical reality, since he never lived there). The words 'what chance misspelt' go so far as to suggest that Carrickfergus was a mistake. Nevertheless, despite the fact that the pre-natal mountain is clearly the most intense psychic and emotional reality, the primordial, essential Irishness is recognized for what it is – unattainable. In these lines, England seems accepted rather than welcomed; 'Schooled from the age of ten to a foreign voice' may imply a degree of resentment. In one sense, MacNeice is nowhere, has nowhere to call home and appears to be, in the title of the Tom Paulin essay cited earlier, 'the man from no part'. But in another sense, the Carrickfergus 'interlude' is an essential term in making him the person he is, even if it was the product of chance's misspelling. Picking up once more the word he has used earlier in the poem, and which I have already discussed, he describes it as his 'childhood's frame', the structure from which he sees things. By being born into a particular culture, nation, time, any human being is, the poem recognizes, automatically and inevitably excluded from all other particularities and therefore from the fantasy of wholeness represented by the pre-natal mountain. Primordiality is a fantasy because of its amorphousness. In the stanza preceding these two he has indicated why this is so:

> Time and place – our bridgeheads into reality
> But also its concealment! Out of the sea
> We land on the Particular and lose
> All other possible bird's-eye views, the Truth
> That is of Itself for Itself – but not for me.

Our particular times and places are our bridgeheads into reality but also a concealment: bridgeheads because it is only through the particulars (of who we are) that we can get a purchase on reality, but concealment because this purchase excludes or conceals all other particularities. Or rather it is the inevitable position from which we view other positions, other cultures, other times and other realities. This is another implication of the 'topographical frame': it is the frame within which his identities are set (though not immutably), it is, as it were, where he starts from. The sea, that archetypal image of birth, rebirth and wholeness, is amorphous, at least to human eyes. When we land on a particular place at a particular time – as we must – we 'lose / All other possible bird's-eye views'. This perception is reiterated towards the end of the 1950s in the poem 'Prologue', part of an unfinished collaborative project, *The Character of Ireland*, a collection of essays which MacNeice and W. R. Rodgers were aiming to edit for Oxford University Press.[17] It is a 'chance', writes MacNeice in this poem, 'that we were born / Here, not

there', but this is 'a chance we took / And would not have it otherwise'.
He goes on to say of the Irish:

> So we, marooned between two continents
> And having missed half of their revolutions
> And more than half their perquisites can still,
> Sophisticated primitives, aspire
> In spite of all their slogans and our own
> To take this accident of time and place
> And somehow, even now, to make it happy.[18]

Here too, the 'accident of time and place' functions as what we must
work with (take'), our 'bridgeheads into reality'. Consequently, I think,
Tom Paulin's characterization of MacNeice's imagination as 'fluid, mar-
itime and elusively free', which captures an important element in his
work, needs to be balanced by the landfall described in 'Carrick
Revisited'.[19]

For reasons which will, I hope, become clearer when I come to discuss
MacNeice's Indian writings, I want to reformulate the understanding
MacNeice arrives at in 'Carrick Revisited', these negotiations between
the different parts of his inheritance, inherited or acquired, through the
metaphor of translation. I want to draw particularly on the anthropo-
logical discussions about dealing with and trying to understand differ-
ent cultures which I examined in the first chapter. In his essay 'Found
in Translation', Clifford Geertz suggests that our knowledge of other
cultures steers a path between two different positions. On the one hand,
'we can never apprehend another people's or another period's imagina-
tion neatly, as though it were our own'. But, on the other hand, this
doesn't mean that 'we can ... never apprehend it at all. We can appre-
hend it well enough, at least as well as we apprehend anything else not
properly ours, but we do so not by looking *behind* the interfering glosses
that connect us to it but *through* them'.[20] In contact with other human
cultures, we can't suddenly disburden ourselves of who we are.

MacNeice's situation in this case is not, of course, quite like that of the
European or American trying to understand Balinese cultures, which is
what Geertz is discussing. Instead he is trying to make sense of different
parts of himself and his heritage. But the process analysed in 'Found in
Translation' is, I would suggest, rather similar to MacNeice's negotia-
tions between his different realities. By landing on the particular, to
repeat MacNeice's terminology, we might lose other possible Truths, but

we can – indeed we have to – negotiate with them from the position in which we find ourselves. For MacNeice in 'Carrick Revisited', the process takes the form of negotiating with the other realities of Western Ireland and England through the necessary 'interfering glosses' of Northern Ireland, of Carrickfergus, which – to revert to his own metaphor – are his bridgeheads into reality. Or perhaps each of the three perspectives involved is an interfering gloss for the other two.

MacNeice occasionally discussed translation strategies in his book reviews, seeming to opt for 'foreignizing' rather than domestication, but also understanding that any translation will be a compromise between the two, since 'each language has its own deficiencies as well as its own capacities' (*SLC*, p. 124). Discussing a version of Virgil by R. C. Trevelyan in 1945, he rejects both the literalism of a 'school crib' and freedom. The method he advocates is 'a faithfulness that will go beyond the school crib'. He goes on to describe the method of such a translator:

> Beginning with the literal content, they then, while adding to, or subtracting from, that content as little as possible, try to salvage *via* their *presentation* of it – i.e., by phrasing, word-order, rhythm, vowel-pattern, etc. – those elements which in the original heightened the content into poetry.
>
> (*SLC*, p. 125)[21]

Ten years before this, in reviewing Gilbert Murray's translation of Aeschylus (*SLC*, pp. 7–10), MacNeice proposes the same method, but also places some emphasis on how a translation reads as English. Murray's version is criticized: 'His Greek original is so real to a scholar like Professor Murray that it is probably never out of his mind, and so he cannot see what the English looks like just as English' (*SLC*, p. 10). Translation, it seems, should involve what MacNeice elsewhere, in discussing the relationship between tradition and experiment in poetry, calls a 'concrete antinomy' (*SLC*, p. 14). Although he uses this phrase about the relationship between past and present, it applies equally to domestication and foreignization.

MacNeice sometimes equates the term 'antinomy' with 'dialectic', which he sees as a term applicable both to himself and to Ireland. Discussing the characteristics of the Irish in his book on W. B. Yeats, MacNeice finds that they can only be expressed in 'a set of antinomies', that there is an 'Irish dialectic'.[22] In his 1949 essay 'Experience with Images' (*SLC*, pp. 153–64), he describes his own cast of mind in terms of the dialectic, linking it to that veering between flux and pattern, colour and meaning, the Many and the One which I have discussed earlier:

> My basic conception of life being dialectical (in the philosophic, not in the political sense), I have tended to swing to and fro between descriptive or physical images (which are 'correct' so far as they go) and *faute de mieux* metaphysical, mythical or mystical images (which can never go far enough). 'Eternity', wrote Blake ... 'is in love with the productions of Time' and I have tried to pay homage to both.
>
> (*SLC*, p. 156)

Lionel Trilling, discussing a case of what we might call historical translation, reading Jane Austen, describes the to and fro mental movement the situation engenders as a 'dialectic, with all the dignity that inheres in that word'.[23] For MacNeice, as for Trilling, this dialectic meant a productive instability, a constant movement between, for instance, attraction and repulsion, consciousness of similarity and awareness of difference, and domestication and foreignization.

When MacNeice visited India, his bridgehead into *that* reality was of course the complex heritage that I described earlier – Ulster, Connemara, England and Europe – and the particular versions of those things that he himself embodied, such as the preconceptions and prejudices of a man with a classical education and a leaning towards Aristotelian rationalism. The understandings that are evident in a poem such as 'Carrick Revisited' were brought to bear on a new and, to him, very different scene.[24]

MacNeice's first visit to India occurred, as I have said, at the time of Partition in 1947. Before then, he already had ideas of India and the East, of course, and these are expressed in fleeting disparaging references he makes in both his poetry and his prose, references which embody the stereotypical image of India as a spiritual and world-renouncing culture. In what is perhaps the most ambitious of the projects that emerged from his visit to India, the radio drama-documentary 'India at First Sight', the main character, Edward, who appears to be a stand-in for MacNeice himself, says that amongst the preconceptions he brought to India were a dislike of 'all this yogi-cum-swami stuff', and this can serve as a summary of his attitudes before the visit.[25] This India is entirely the other and is to be rejected because of its lack of interest in the world. In section XVIII of *Autumn Journal*, for instance, he rejects 'an Indian acquiescence, / The apotheosis of the status quo' (*CP*, p. 138).

Earlier in the poem, Nirvana is equated with 'pure Not-Being' (*CP*, p. 104). In the final stanza of 'Turf-Stacks' (*CP*, pp. 18–19), he writes:

> For we are obsolete who like the lesser things
> Who play in corners with looking-glasses and beads;
> It is better we should go quickly, go into Asia
> Or any other tunnel where the world recedes,
> Or turn blind wantons like the gulls who scream
> And rip the edge off any ideal or dream.

But this retreat into Asia and what it signifies is only a desperate response to the 'mass-production of neat thoughts' in the modern world:

>   the
> Shuddering insidious shock of the theory-vendors
> The little sardine men crammed in a monster toy
> Who tilt their aggregate beast against our crumbling Troy.

The opposition in this poem between those who like colour, surface, variety and those cultures which negate the world is reiterated in 'Leaving Barra':

> O the self-abnegation of Buddha
> The belief that is disbelieving
> The denial of chiaroscuro
> Not giving a damn for existence!
>
> But I would cherish existence
> Loving the beast and the bubble
> Loving the rain and the rainbow,
> Considering philosophy alien.
>
> For all the religions are alien
> That allege that life is a fiction
>
>   (*CP*, p. 87)

The word 'chiaroscuro' here is typical of the importance of variety and flux in MacNeice's poetry and thought. It is unsurprising that a poet with his emphasis on the 'incorrigibly plural' world and the 'drunkenness of things being various' ('Snow', *CP*, p. 30), someone who once said 'the poet's first business is *mentioning* things' (*MP*, p. 5), should find unpalatable this apparent negation of phenomenal existence by Indian cultures and religions.

In his autobiography MacNeice describes a meeting in London with the Indian novelist Mulk Raj Anand who, he says, offered him an alternative view of India by telling him that he had been misinformed on the subject of a so-called spiritual India. India, Anand said, was 'earthy, matter-of-fact' (*SF*, p. 209). Whether it was for this reason or the effect of his own visit (or both), he changes his tune considerably in work produced after his 1947 trip. Indeed, if Hedli MacNeice's little parable 'The Story of the House that Louis Built' is an indication, India became of some significance for him:

> The windows on the west side looked towards Connemara, Mayo and the Sea. Those to the south scanned Dorset, the Downs and Marlborough – the windows to the north overlooked Iceland and those to the east, India.[26]

Perhaps a pentagonal house – or a variation on Seamus Heaney's figure of the quincunx as a model for the Irish literary tradition – would have been more appropriate (she leaves out the Northern Irish 'interlude');[27] however, by linking India with western Ireland and southern England, she implies that it had a powerful impact on his imagination.

Various received images of India do persist even after that first visit – India as paradox, for instance. Nevertheless, during and after the 1947 trip, there is a change. Significantly, the term 'translation' enters his vocabulary as a way of articulating his responses. In 'India at First Sight', which was broadcast on the BBC's Third Programme in March 1948, the announcer who introduces the piece tells the listener: 'The sub-continent ... is seen – or rather glimpsed – solely through Western eyes while the visitor is attended by the Western familiars of his mind. For it is only gropingly and fleetingly that any such visitor can cope with: India at First Sight' (p. 1). These familiars who accompany MacNeice's alter ego, Edward, represent different attitudes to India: Edward's nanny, who is a purveyor of old wives' tales; his uncle, the voice of the colonial administrator or businessman; a Christian missionary; and various European historical and cultural figures such as Alexander the Great. These familiars and voices encounter Indian personages, including the Mughal Emperor Akbar and the poets Kabir and Tagore. India too is personified, although always in quotation marks. Edward is also accompanied throughout by what MacNeice calls his 'still voice'.

Early in the broadcast, Edward says 'I want to start from scratch, get my own impressions', and the 'still voice' responds: 'No one can start from scratch. Here comes a whole sub-continent crowding upon you and here stand you, enmeshed in your own background, your reactions not so different from those of your Nanny or your Uncle' (p. 6). Slightly later, the voice of 'India' tells him: 'You have brought your voices with you; visitors always do. But if they stay long, sometimes those voices change – acquire a new accent or break' (p. 10). How do the voices change and new accents develop? The still voice tells Edward: 'in this country you have to proceed by translation' (p. 34). Towards the end of the broadcast Edward says 'I can't get this place at first hand. I need to have it translated'. The still voice replies: 'I will be your translator. ... We two – we one – have just had an experience. Of India at first sight. And whether one loves her or not, that is like love at first sight. For just as the love may go on but the sight must change, so India – ' (p. 43).

What is being said here in the metaphor of translation is firstly, of course, an acknowledgement that for Edward and MacNeice, India is a foreign language. Indeed, in an article also called 'India at First Sight' (*SP*, pp. 163–75), but otherwise completely different from the broadcast of the same name, MacNeice says 'India is the most *foreign* country I have ever visited. And if we use the word "foreign" for Italy or Iceland, we should really find some other word for India' (p. 163). In the drama-documentary, the responses and opinions of the 'familiars', the 'still voice', India itself and *its* voices are the languages through which Edward must chart a route, and try to translate or make sense of the sub-continent. The voices he has brought with him from Europe truly are interfering glosses.

Quite often, these glosses are those of Ireland, in that he regularly finds himself making comparisons and detecting similarities between the two countries. Thus, in the prose article 'India at First Sight', MacNeice asserts that 'educated Indians are as politics-ridden as the Irish (perhaps this is inevitable with subject or newly liberated peoples)' (*SP*, pp. 163–4). Elsewhere he describes the Pathans of the North West Frontier Province as 'v. Irish in their approach to things'.[28] On another visit to India and Pakistan in 1955, he was still drawing these kinds of parallels. Writing to his wife Hedli during this visit, he said: 'Outside this hotel the Indian Ocean is grey – just like Belfast Lough'.[29]

Responses to another culture, he argues some years after his visit to India, involve a mixture of the familiar and the foreign (as they must: if they were completely foreign, we could never make sense of them, but if they were completely familiar, they wouldn't be foreign):

> The often-met paradox of nostalgia for the unknown (how can we be homesick for homes we never had?) is confirmed by the shock of familiarity with which the unknown sometimes greets us. Such familiarity of course can be illusory and is never comprehensive. Thus in India, the most 'foreign' country that I have visited, while constantly surprised by its novelty, at the same time I often had the feeling that 'this is where I came in'. ... It is this factor of familiarity in the foreign or rather of the restoration of our own lost past or of our missing relations that must greatly influence most of us in our reactions to art.
>
> (*SP*, p. 176)

Clearly, this sense of familiarity, like his detection of Ireland in India, must, in part, constitute a domestication of the unfamiliar, in the sense outlined in the first chapter's discussion of translation strategies. But the passage tacks between two courses which echo that structure of similarity-in-difference discussed in that chapter (India is novel and utterly foreign while also being familiar), and it ends, I think, in the last sentence quoted, with something that seems to resemble Lienhardt's idea that the translation of another culture is in the end an exploration of 'the further potentialities of our own thought and language'.[30]

MacNeice's Indian poems show him enacting various processes of translation or non-translation. Three emerged after his 1947 visit ('Letter from India', 'Mahabalipuram' and 'Didymus') and some from later visits, such as 'Return to Lahore' (*CP*, pp. 453–4; Lahore was by then in Pakistan) and 'Indian Village' (*CP*, p. 498). I focus here on the first three, arising as they do from his first encounter with the reality of India. 'Letter from India' (*CP*, pp. 268–70) seems to show him floundering and overwhelmed by his experiences in the sub-continent. There are the daily experiences of dirt and mortality:

> what is Western
> Assurance here where words are snakes
> Gulping their tails, flies that endemic
> In mosque and temple, morgue and jakes,
> Eat their blind fill of man's mistakes
> And yet each carcase proves eternal?
>
> (p. 268)

And there is also the more historically specific experience of the brutal violence that accompanied Partition:

> I have seen Sheikhupura High School
> Fester with glaze-eyed refugees
> And the bad coin of fear inverted
> Under Purana Kila's trees
>
> (p. 269)

India is at once too near and too far, a 'plethoric yet phantom setting' (p. 268), a 'maelstrom / Of persons where no person counts' (p. 270), a challenge to his ways of thinking: 'what is Western / Assurance here?' (p. 268), he asks, the line-division itself unyoking the 'Assurance' from the 'Western' and destabilizing both. India interrogates European humanism at its core:

> For even should humanism always
> Have been half-impotent, debased,
> How for all that can her own children
> Break from the retina encased
> In which our vision here must waste
> Meeting but waste, the chance of Vision?
>
> (p. 269)

India functions for much of the poem in Orientalist fashion as the European's unconscious, the place where the European comes to face with things that are easy to overlook when in Europe: 'India jolts us / Awake to what engrossed our sleep'. Echoing Conrad's Kurtz, he exclaims 'This was the horror – it is deep' (p. 269). At the end of the poem, though, some redemption and resolution are found. In the concluding stanzas, his wife Hedli, to whom the 'Letter' is addressed, and who has seemed, in the overwhelming environment of India, a far-off figure in Europe, returns more strongly as a resource and a refuge:

> Yet standing here and notwithstanding
> Our severance, need I think it loss
> If from this past you are my future
> As in all spite of gulf and gloss
> However much their letters cross
> East and West are wed and welcome;

> And both of us are both, in either
> An India sleeps below our West,
> So you for me are proud and finite
> As Europe is, yet on your breast
> I could find too that undistressed
> East which is east and west and neither?

(p. 270)

In the context of the floundering and disorientation evident through-out the poem, these concluding stanzas seem to offer a somewhat unconvincing resolution, willed into existence rather than prepared for and achieved; the nightmare which India had seemed to be is put to bed in a vision which simultaneously and contradictorily asserts (or reasserts) the bounded identity of Europe and speaks of merger, of boundaries being crossed. Europe, like Hedli MacNeice, is 'proud and finite' and at the same time part of an undifferentiated or merged whole: 'East and West are wed and welcome'; the 'undistressed / East which is east and west and neither'. That 'breast' on which he hopes to rest reveals, I think, the wish-fulfilling element here, the merger with the maternal, that constant symbol of wholeness (to spell it out in a way that MacNeice avoids). And the fact that this comes as part of a question (which began several lines earlier in 'need I think it loss') signals more clearly its wish-fulfilling nature.

In 'Didymus' (*CP*, pp. 295–9), this kind of forced resolution is missing. Didymus is the Apostle Thomas, who is said to have travelled to India (according to tradition and apocryphal literature; there is no confirmed historical evidence). There are, even now, particularly in the southern state of Kerala, Christian families who claim to be descended from peo-ple baptized by St Thomas; many of these St Thomas Christians, as they are known, are in communion with the Syrian Orthodox Church, some with the Anglican and some with the Catholic. Didymus is a figure who had appeared before in another poem, also called 'Didymus', which was part of a short sequence with the overall title 'Entered in the Minutes'. This earlier Didymus is depicted in what seems a rather ambivalent way:

> Refusing to fall in love with God, he gave
> Himself to the love of created things,
> Accepting only what he could see, a river
> Full of the shadows of swallows' wings

(*CP*, p. 187)

This 'love of created things' is something that MacNeice approves of in other writings, as I indicated earlier. However, it is possible to detect a note of what one might call Platonic criticism as well in this poem: the idea that the created things are, by themselves, only 'shadows' of a truer reality, that 'the love of created things' by itself – sheer flux – is not enough. Didymus 'would not / Ask where the water ran or why' and 'When he died a swallow seemed to plunge / Into the reflected, the wrong, sky'. Thomas's doubt, his empiricism, his scepticism towards absolute belief, are things that MacNeice is drawn to, but here it seems incomplete: the 'reflected' sky is also 'wrong'.

Didymus in India is somewhat different from the earlier poem, his doubt possibly an emblem of MacNeice's wary but attracted response to the country; the dualism which is contained in his name (it means 'twin'), and which MacNeice emphasizes throughout the poem, is perhaps a figure for the bemused Westerner confronted with India. All Thomas has, the opening part of the poem tells India (although it is couched in form of a question), are 'two plain crossed sticks / To flout your banyan riot of dialectic'. This banyan riot is depicted in the first part through a dazzling and dazzled list of details from the Indian scene, reminiscent of his similar detailing of Ireland in a poem such as 'Valediction':

> Red spittle on the flagstones of the temple,
> Green flash of parrots, phosphorescent waves,
> Caparisoned elephants and sacred bulls,
> Crystal-gazers, navel-gazers, pedants
>
> ('Didymus', *CP*, p. 295)

> the horses' feet like bells of hair
> Shambling beneath the orange cart, the beer-brown spring
> Guzzling between the heather, the green gush of Irish spring.
>
> ('Valediction', *CP*, p. 52)

The listing does not always work, in the Irish or the Indian case – Terence Brown, for one, considers the technique 'overdone', 'enervating' and 'an irritating indulgence' in 'Didymus' – but it can be seen as a way of stressing the overwhelming nature of the country which confronts Thomas (and MacNeice), the bewildering variety of sense impressions which force themselves on the observer.[31] The dualism already hinted at in the two crossed sticks here is emphasized further in the next section, which tries to imagine Thomas in India and keeps returning to the word 'two', emphasizing his two hands. The dualism is reiterated in a different manner in the third section, which is spoken by Thomas. As Kit Fryatt notes, homophones run through this section: 'soar' and 'sore', 'right' and 'write', for instance.[32] Throughout the poem, Thomas seems dissociated, both from himself (by his doubt) and from India (by its difference):

> I doubt and I doubt; in a crumbling exposed redoubt,
>   Enfiladed by heathendom, here to the end
> I watch in the endless rain to herald the reign
>   Of the Friend of Man – but can he be Thomas's friend?
>
> (p. 298)

Yet by the end, the 'Doubting Thomas' of the first section has become a 'Believing Thomas':

> Believing Thomas,
> Apostle to the Indies! If never there,
> The Indies yet can show in a bare church
> On a bare plaque the bare but adequate tribute
> To one who had thrust his fingers into the wounds of God.
>
> (p. 299)

The replacement of doubt by belief marks in part MacNeice's sympathy for, and identification with, Thomas, besieged, isolated, overwhelmed in India, unsure of his own capacities: 'His two hands only, only two – / What could they prove against Shiva and Krishna?' (p. 296). But I think it also signals what is more clearly indicated in the following lines. 'If never there' shows MacNeice's awareness of the fact that there is no strict historical evidence for Thomas's presence in India; on the other hand, the plaque in the Little Mount Church (which he has referred to previously in section II) most definitely *is* there. Doubt about Thomas's actual presence in India is counterbalanced by belief in the reality of the plaque, which the poet has seen. This is an unusual kind of belief, and I will return to it shortly.

'Didymus' is an uneven poem; the wordplay in the third section, for instance, one of MacNeice's favourite linguistic devices, becomes an overdone verbal tic. Nevertheless, the poem marks clearly the dilemma of the Western visitor to India without trying to impose the kind of solution (in reality, an escape) that is given at the end of 'Letter from India'. What happens in the two poems I have been discussing so far can be described as a failure of translation in the sense suggested by 'India at First Sight'. In 'Letter from India', the merger proposed at the end seems forced, and, indeed, is undermined by the image of a 'finite' Europe which figures in the same stanza. In 'Didymus', the failure is not evaded in the same way. The saint himself cannot translate India, cannot make sense of it, his two hands – perhaps an image for dualistic ways of thinking – being seen as ineffective when faced with the plethoric reality of India and its gods. The narrator of the poem, largely effaced behind the figure of Thomas, appears in the end to suggest the possibility of a representation or translation (if I may so – a little tendentiously – describe the plaque) without a corresponding reality or an original (since we do not know for sure that the saint was ever actually in India). The neat certainty of the plaque contrasts with the bewildering reality of India, Thomas's confusion as depicted in the poem and the possibility that what it represents did not in fact occur. Rather than enforcing a resolution, as in 'Letter from India', 'Didymus' focuses for the reader the disjunction between a possibly illusory sense of certainty and Thomas's bewilderment.

In the first section of 'Didymus', MacNeice draws a contrast between the seething variety of India and its gods, and the single resistant emblem of one god, Śiva: the 'restful purposeful indifferent phallus', or lingam, which figures also in the final poem I discuss, 'Mahabalipuram' (*CP*, pp. 273–5). Here the variety and singleness are brought together in a way that, I think, shows translation in operation as a creative activity. Mahabalipuram, near Madras (now officially Chennai), is the location of a famous complex of temples and sculptures on the seashore. In stanza four of this poem, MacNeice sees the monuments at Mahabalipuram as representative of the Hindu world:

> And now we look, we to whom mantra and mudra mean little,
> And who find in this Hindu world a zone that is ultra-violet
>> Balanced by an infra-red,
> Austerity and orgy alike being phrased, it seems, in a strange
>> dead language

(p. 274)

The Hindu world, then, being like a 'strange dead language', seems at this point untranslatable and incomprehensible. In the second half of this stanza, however, he is able to overcome the exclusion:

> But now that we look without trying to learn and only look in
>   the act of leaping
> After the sculptor into the rockface, now we can see, if not hear,
>   those phrases
>   To be neither strange nor dead.
>
> (p. 274)

The image of leaping into the rockface 'without trying to learn' is an act of sympathy or identification with the Hindu world as represented in this sculpture – precisely what Godfrey Lienhardt terms a 'temporary assent' to the other's way of thinking – instead of simply rejecting it as alien. In the last two stanzas of the poem, after describing the details of the largest of the rock reliefs at Mahabalipuram, the one known as Arjuna's Penance, he proceeds to an interpretation of his experience:

> A monochrome world that has all the indulgence of colour,
> A still world whose every harmonic is audible,
>   Largesse of spirit and stone;
> Created things for once and for all featured in full while for once
>   and never,
> The creator who is destroyer stands at the last point of land
> Featureless; in a dark cell, a phallus of granite, as abstract
>   As the North Pole; as alone.
>
> (p. 274)

His interpretation is guided by a series of oppositions: monochrome and colour, stillness and sound, stone and spirit, and abstraction and concreteness. The two different sides of these oppositions are represented in the poem by two features of the monuments at Mahabalipuram. One of these is the abstract and solitary 'phallus of granite' (the lingam), which is located in a 'dark cell' of the famous shore temple at Mahabalipuram. The other feature is the variety of creatures and things he finds represented in the carvings and sculptures: the 'cowherds and gods continue to dance in the rock (p. 273). Both are part of the same reality.

What MacNeice sees in the scene is in fact a version of something that is familiar to readers from elsewhere in his poetry and prose, that contrast between flux and pattern which I have discussed earlier, that is to say, attention to the variety and livingness of things in the world, and the desire to make sense of the variety through conceptual categories. It may seem odd to describe the lingam as, in some sense, a 'conceptual category'. I mean only that, like any conceptual category, it unites in itself a variety of phenomena; and although it thereby obliterates or effaces difference and individuality, it also serves the function of 'tidying' or ordering the world. There is, perhaps, also something else he is seeing here: Ireland, which as I suggested above, he regularly saw in India. A number of his descriptions of the Irish landscape and climate echo or are echoed by this mixture of some kind of variety and colour with some kind of monochrome. In discussing the Irish background of Yeats's poetry, for instance, MacNeice writes:

An Irish landscape is capable of pantomimic transformation scenes; one moment it will be desolate, dead, unrelieved monotone, the next it will be an indescribably shifting pattern of prismatic light. The light effects of Ireland make other landscapes seem stodgy; on the other hand, few countries can produce anything more depressing than Ireland in her grey moments.[33]

A similar description can be found in a typescript of *circa* 1941–4, 'Northern Ireland and Her People':

Owing to the moisture in the air sunlight in Ireland has the effect of a prism; nowhere else in the British Isles can you find this liquid rainbow quality which at once diffuses and clarifies. When the sun is not shining, however, (and this is often the case) the landscape relapses to a sodden grey monotony.

(*SP*, p. 151)

Here too, there is the combination of shifting variety and singleness (although it takes the form of 'grey monotony') that MacNeice later finds in India. In seeing what he sees in the monuments at Mahabalipuram, MacNeice is, to return to Geertz's terminology, possibly seeing the Hindu world through the 'interfering glosses' of his cultural and intellectual make-up.

It could be argued, however, that he is simply imposing a familiar pattern on an alien experience, domesticating the scene into categories which he has brought with him, and not really seeing anything apart from himself. Reviewing Edward Lear's *Indian Journal* in 1953,

MacNeice wrote that because India was 'too large and too complex to be "comprehended", [it] invites us to select from her vastness only our own pet properties, rediscovering in fancy dress things which we have always fancied'.[34] Is this what it is happening here?

In part, it is: MacNeice is selecting his own 'pet properties' of flux and pattern. But if there were no points of contact between one conceptual scheme and another, then any scheme apart from our own would make no sense, and there would be no understanding, contact or communication across conceptual schemes or languages. What MacNeice said in his essay 'Poetry To-day' (*SLC*, pp. 10–44) is also true of translation: 'A poem, to be recognizable, must be traditional; but to be worth recognizing, it must be something new' (p. 12). So, to comprehend another language or culture, we must bring our own traditions or languages to bear on it; but then, if we engage with its otherness, it will bring something new to us. This is one of the implications of Geertz's discussions of cultural translation.

However, in addition to this use of his own glosses, the end of 'Mahabalipuram' seems to recognize that his conceptual categories have been altered. The poem concludes:

> But the visitor must move on and the waves assault the temple,
> Living granite against dead water, and time with its weathering
> action
>   Make phrase and feature blurred;
> Still from to-day we know what an avatar is, we have seen
> God take shape and dwell among shapes, we have felt
> Our ageing limbs respond to those ageless limbs in the rock
>   Reliefs. Relief is the word.
>
> (*CP*, p. 275)

There is something of a reversal of MacNeice's usual scale of values: the moving sea is now 'dead', while the static 'granite' is 'living'. The speaker's conceptual world and language have had to change to accommodate this experience of the foreign – 'from today we know what an avatar is'. This knowledge is also accommodated in the paradoxical 'living granite'. Strictly speaking, 'granite' here seems to refer at this point to the temple as a whole, rather than simply to the lingam as it did in the previous stanza. Yet, because the granite has had such a recent appearance in the previous stanza as a description of the phallus, the use of 'living' in this final stanza must infiltrate also our sense of the granite lingam. The previously 'abstract' granite phallus acquires a degree of life. It is clear that his categories have changed; the granite is alive because it contains the god and the gods, the creatures carved in the rock relief. The lineation of these words, splitting 'rock' from 'reliefs', may be a way of highlighting the two elements: the rock being static, like the granite phallus and temple, and the reliefs emphasizing movement, variety and contrast, since a relief projects outwards from the surface in which it is carved. (I think that MacNeice weakens the effect by going on to make a too-easy pun – a habit to which he was prone – on the word 'relief', but that is a different issue.)

MacNeice had used the idea of a dead language in a much earlier poem, 'A Contact' (1933), where a train passing by at night is described in the following terms:

> The familiar rhythm but the unknown implications
> Delight like a dead language
> Which never shocks us by banal revelations.

> (*CP*, p. 21)

This combination of the familiar and unfamiliar with the possibility of new rather than banal revelations is, I think, what the observer in 'Mahabalipuram' finds in the temple complex: the rhythm (the mixture of flux and pattern) is familiar, but the 'unknown implications' (the idea of the avatar) are unfamiliar. He may have known in theory what an avatar was, but now, after this visit, he has a realization of it. He does not, however, pretend that he has some inward knowledge; he is, finally, despite his momentary act of identification, seeing it from the outside ('the visitor must move on', after all), with the weight of his own cultural baggage and interfering glosses which he can't simply disregard, as if they never existed. Time may blur whatever grasp he has achieved of this new language.

In the ways that Geertz describes, MacNeice's India in this poem is mediated by the 'interfering glosses' he brings to bear on the act of interpreting it – an act which is a translation. He is able to translate it because he finds something similar, something he recognizes: flux and pattern, multiplicity coexisting with provisional unity. At the same time, though, it is not the same, because he has to alter the categories of his thought to accommodate the category of the avatar as a way of mediating between flux and pattern. As Godfrey Lienhardt suggests, the contact allows him – even forces him – to explore and extend the 'further potentialities of [his] own thought and language'.[35] Interestingly, in the broadcast 'India at First Sight' MacNeice anticipates the terminology Lienhardt is using here: the 'still voice' tells MacNeice's surrogate, Edward:

> The point is not what people know in words, the point is not what opinions they think they have, the point out here is what they *potentially* know; their potential sympathy with things that, as words go, are alien; their potential identity with their opposite numbers. (emphasis in original)
>
> (pp. 27–8)

In the radio debate referred to earlier, F. R. Higgins attacks the 1930s poets for what he sees as their flouting of tradition. Defending his generation against this charge, MacNeice also goes on to make a wider and more general point:

> In some of them I see the continuance of the specifically English feeling of past English poets – the feeling for the typical English virtues and the English landscape. Over and above that, I would suggest that there is such a thing as a European tradition, which is inherited by some of these poets, and in fact I think it possible that sooner or later national traditions will be taken up into some wider traditions of this kind, corresponding to the superseding of narrower national feelings by creeds or philosophies which cut across national frontiers.[36]

Although he is speaking here of European traditions, the supersession of 'narrower national feelings', as I have tried to show in this chapter, applies also outside Europe. It is precisely this process of cutting across national frontiers to try and work towards these 'wider traditions', but without losing his own bridgeheads into reality, that can be seen in MacNeice's evolving relationships with Ireland, England and India. Where he had initially worked through exclusionary contrasts between Asia and Europe, his Indian poems show him moving towards creative processes of translation which lie somewhere between Judith Wright's sense of incommensurability and Les Murray's fusion.

5
Seamus Heaney's Acoustics

The Ireland of Seamus Heaney's imaginings, it has been argued by a number of critics, is something organic, autochthonous, mythical, beyond and outside history. It glosses over difference of various kinds, and both feeds from and feeds back into stereotypical notions, particularly a feminized version of the land. (My compressed summary, of course, necessarily brushes over the different nuances and perspectives of different commentators.) Criticisms along these lines include well-known ones by David Lloyd, Elizabeth Butler Cullingford, Clair Wills and Patricia Coughlan.[1] A more recent example is an essay by David Kennedy, who, writing about the poem 'Broagh', concludes that 'Heaney's real interest ... is in what lies beneath. Under the present-day speech community lies a Celtic point of origin: pre-modern and mystical'. Kennedy does, it is true, identify another strain within the poem, 'the poem's focus on linguistic difference as the valuable embodiment of a wider difference'; but he sees this as being 'at odds with Heaney's organicism', arguing that 'the possibility of accessing an originary, essential identity through language ... is contradicted by the fact that "the strangers" cannot "manage" the shibboleth of "the last *gh*". The identification of difference through linguistic performance actually makes difference relational'.[2] For Kennedy, the organicism seems to invalidate or override the differential identity.

In defence of Heaney against this type of criticism, one might offer the preliminary argument that he has always stressed the in-betweenness of his historical and cultural situation. In an early prose piece, he describes the location of the family farm, Mossbawn, between the villages of Castledawson and Toome as positioning him 'symbolically ... between the marks of English influence and the lure of the native experience, between "the demesne" and "the bog"' (*P*, p. 35). A further

101

consideration is that he has often warned against reversions to the past as a consolatory fantasy or as a spur to revenge. In his lecture on Brian Merriman's eighteenth-century dream-vision poem *Cúirt an Mheán Oíche*, which he has partially translated under the title *The Midnight Verdict* (it is usually rendered as *The Midnight Court*), he describes the woman who wakes up the sleeping poet as 'a burlesque version of the visionary beauty who is a constant feature of an Irish poetic genre called the *aisling*'. The *aisling*, as Heaney goes on to point out, evolved in the seventeenth and eighteenth centuries as 'a political fantasy about the future liberation of Ireland by the Stuarts' (*RP*, p. 48). Merriman's anti-*aisling* figure, described in Heaney's translation (*MV*, p. 24), as 'Bony and huge, a terrible hallion', is a way of ridiculing this fantasy: 'She directs attention to the demeaned realities of the here and now rather than deflecting the imagination into consoling reverie' (*RP*, pp. 48–9). In *The Cure at Troy*, Heaney's version of Sophocles' *Philoctetes*, Neoptolemus tells Philoctetes to stop brooding on the past: 'Stop just licking your wounds. Start seeing things.' Only by letting go of these resentments can we, in the words of the Chorus shortly afterwards, 'hope for a great sea change / On the far side of revenge' (*CT*, pp. 74, 77).

It is of course true, as Kennedy implies at the beginning of his essay, that we should not necessarily take Heaney's poetry on the terms he has set out for himself in his poems or his prolific sideline as a critic. It is equally true that in a number of places (although, I think, mainly in his earlier work), he does depict autochthonous, organic models of identity and rely on easy gender stereotypes of Ireland. His essay, 'The Sense of Place', for instance, concludes that 'it is to … the stable element, the land itself, that we must look for continuity' (*P*, p. 149). In 'Toome', the speaker becomes almost one with soil and water:

> I am sleeved in
>
> alluvial mud that shelves
> suddenly under
> bogwater and tributaries,
> and elvers tail my hair.

> (*WO*, p. 26)

And in the essay 'Belfast', he states: 'I suppose the feminine element for me involves the matter of Ireland, and the masculine strain is drawn from the involvement with English literature'(*P*, p. 34). This organicism can be understood, at least in part, as the kind of grounding movement followed by many writers in the earlier stages of their development – particularly those from split and colonized cultures, often haunted by the fecundity and power of what seems to be an authoritative canon from England (or other 'metropolitan' cultures) and needing to sink roots in their native soil. Nevertheless (if one is interested in drawing up this kind of charge-sheet), there is evidence to put Heaney in the dock.

In this chapter I want to explore whether the idea of translation – which exists between languages and cultures – helps to provide another perspective on this debate, since it is intimately connected to the in-betweenness that I have referred to above. Translation in the strict sense has become an increasingly significant part of Heaney's output since the late 1970s, as his versions of *Buile Suibhne* (*Sweeney Astray*), Sophocles, *Beowulf*, Dante, Merriman and Ovid testify. But if we extend the idea of translation, we might also include the place-name poems in *Wintering Out*, which are modelled on a genre from Irish poetry, *dinnseanchas*, or the sequence 'Sweeney Redivivus' (*SI*, pp. 97–121) which takes as its starting point the figure of Sweeney from *Buile Suibhne*. Pushing the term still further, one might even point to the bog poems in *North*, which 'translate' (the etymology of the word, 'carry across', is relevant here) the Irish situation to ancient Scandinavia, and vice versa. One could also invoke in this context the parable poems in *The Haw Lantern* (1987), such as 'From the Frontier of Writing', which draw on the modes of certain kinds of Eastern European writing. He also regularly uses the words 'translate' and 'translation' as metaphors; in the first of his 'Sonnets from Hellas', he describes a goatherd in the forecourt of a filling station as 'Subsisting beyond eclogue and translation' (*EL*, p. 38), and in 'Keeping Going', he wonders whether the childhood experiences he shared with his brother Hugh 'might not translate beyond / Those wind-heaved midnights' (*SL*, p. 11).

Heaney has written extensively about translation – in relation to *Beowulf*, for instance, and in essays such as 'The Impact of Translation' (*GT*, pp. 36–44), which explores the influence of Eastern European poetry on English-language poets in the West, concluding that this has led to a displacement of the latter 'from an old at-homeness in their mother tongue and its hitherto world-defining poetic heritage' (p. 40). However, such displacement is not necessarily a negative phenomenon, he adds. The effect of translation on English poets has been an awareness of 'the insular and eccentric nature of English experience in all the literal and extended meanings of those adjectives' (p. 41).

By allowing a clearer perception of the limitations of English culture and poetic tradition from a position 'on the very edge' (a quotation from Edwin Muir's poem 'The Interrogation', with which Heaney closes his essay), translation extends the possibilities open to the poet. But, as a reference to Stephen Dedalus earlier in the essay implies (p. 40), this extension of possibility is not confined to translation in the strict linguistic sense of the word; it can extend to the use of the English language by a writer from a colonized or formerly colonized culture who might, because of his in-between position, see not only his own culture more clearly, but also the culture of England. This enables such a writer to create a space in which he can lay claim to the English language in a different way.

Some of the issues involved in this situation are clarified in the essay 'Earning a Rhyme' (*FK*, pp. 59–66), where Heaney discusses his translation of *Buile Suibhne*. He begins by suggesting that 'considerations other than the strictly literary', ones that are 'historical, cultural and political', are relevant to translations from Irish into English by Irish writers: 'a canonical literature in English creates the acoustic within which the translation is going to be heard; an overarching old colonial roof inscribed "The land was ours before we were the land's" is made to echo with some such retort as "You don't say!"'. There is an 'element of answering back' (*FK*, p. 59).

He situates his Sweeney translation in the context of the cultural politics of Northern Ireland during the late 1960s and early 1970s:

> The whole unfinished business of the England/Ireland entanglement presented itself at a local level as a conflict of loyalties and impulses, and consequently the search was on for images and analogies that could ease the strain of the present. The poets were needy for ways in which they could honestly express the realities of the local quarrel without turning that expression into yet another repetition of the aggressions and resentments which had been responsible for the quarrel in the first place.
>
> (*FK*, p. 60)

Here some of the impulses behind the translation he is discussing in the essay are linked to that need to avoid entrenchment in the past which I referred to earlier. One past is seen as an alternative to the repetition of other pasts which are suffused with revenge and rancour, allowing us to see that there have been alternatives to the way we think and feel now. In the space of translation new possibilities can be held in mind and change can begin to take place. Heaney hoped that 'the book might render a Unionist audience more pervious to the notion that Ulster was

Irish, without coercing them out of their cherished conviction that it was British' and also that, because it dealt with a pre-colonial Ireland, it 'might complicate that sense of entitlement to the land of Ulster which had developed so overbearingly in the Protestant majority' (*FK*, p. 61).

The first quotation from the essay uses the word 'acoustic' ('a canonical literature in English creates the acoustic within which the translation is going to be heard'). This is a word with some significance for Heaney. Discussing *Krapp's Last Tape* in his Richard Ellmann lectures on modern literature, he argues that the 'final speech belongs again to the voice of cornucopia, but it is being listened to within the acoustic of the empty shell'. The cornucopia referred to here is something he has described earlier as 'young trust in the possibilities of love and transcendence' (*PW*, p. 66). In the 'Translator's Note' to *The Midnight Verdict*, he writes that the three segments of Ovid and Merriman translated in the book all came from a 'single impulse', and that 'the end of *The Midnight Court* took on a new resonance when read within the acoustic of the classical myth [of the death of Orpheus], and this gave me the idea of juxtaposing the Irish poem (however drastically abridged) with the relevant passages from Ovid's *Metamorphoses*' (*MV*, p. 11).[3]

The term 'acoustic' and the notion of a 'new resonance' are elucidated in his long discussion of Merriman in *The Redress of Poetry*, where he argues that the poem's anti-climactic ending evades a potentially 'archaic beast' [which] has ... stirred beneath the poem's surface' (*RP*, p. 60), the violence which the women are about to inflict on the narrator when he suddenly wakes from his dream. The 'archaic beast' is not hidden in Ovid, where Orpheus is dismembered by the Maenads. Through his juxtaposition of Merriman and Ovid, Heaney adds, the power of *The Midnight Verdict* is 'augmented by being located within the force-field of an archetype' (*RP*, p. 61). The 'acoustic' provided by Ovid adds to the significance and meanings of *The Midnight Verdict*, helping us to see more clearly what, according to Heaney, Merriman's 'tidy outcome' evaded, namely, 'male anxiety about suppressed female power, both sexual and political' (p. 61).

The way Heaney uses the term 'acoustic' suggests, amongst other things, that the translations are heard (in their English versions) within another music, other reverberations, sometimes formed by 'a canonical literature in English'. These translations become a kind of counterpoint or secondary phenomenon, an 'echo', to use his own term, which answers or qualifies another sound without negating it. However, Heaney's use of the word 'acoustic' does not simply imply inferiority; it does not seem to be like Stephen Dedalus's crisis over the word 'tundish', when he feels that the Dean of Studies has a greater claim to the English language than he himself does. An acoustic could be more like Stephen's subsequent realization that the word 'tundish' is as much his as it is the Dean's (in fact, more so, because, although the word originally came from England, the Dean had not heard it before). This is what Heaney argues in his St Jerome lecture on translation:

> By finding that his Dublin vernacular is related to the old English base, Stephen discovers that his own linguistic rights to English are, as it were, pre-natal. He may not be the true-born English man, but he is the new-born English speaker. And at this moment, he is also born as a writer, liberated from subject-people status, freed of the language question to become part of the language issue. ... Or to put it another way, the flicker of illumination in the word 'tundish' is an intimation of those ghostlier demarcations and keener sounds of the ideal poetic order.[4]

Stephen's possession of 'tundish', which is surer than the Dean's, gives him an intimation of an 'ideal poetic order', which I take to be something like a world without the kinds of borders and dualities within which he had been imprisoned when he thought the Dean's claim on English was superior to his own. So, beside the claim that the 'canonical literature in English creates the acoustic within which the translation is going to be heard', we can also place the reverse proposition. The ripples spread back from the colony into what is thought of as the canonical language. Stephen's liberation from the imprisonment that links language to national boundaries, that is, might provide an acoustic for the Dean. For Heaney, Stephen's realization is, however, only an 'intimation', an imagined state rather than an achieved reality.

I have been moving between discussion of translation into English and discussion of those in the position of Stephen Dedalus (Joyce and Heaney amongst others); and the implication is that the situations of writer and translator are not different. And indeed Heaney explicitly argues in the St Jerome lecture that they have similar problems; each is 'poised between his own idiolect and the vast sound-wave and sewage-wash of the language's total availability'.[5] This ambivalent significance of the term 'acoustic', formulated here in the terms 'idiolect' and 'the language's total availability', points, I believe, to a dual aspect of Heaney's relationship with the English language. On the one hand, there may be a resentment that another culture or language is providing an acoustic for him; and this can issue in a desire to withdraw within borders, to ground himself in Ireland, in continuity and in the past; on the other hand, though, there is a sense of expansion and transgression, a crossing of boundaries between languages, cultures and nations.

In the essay 'Something to Write Home About' (*FK*, pp. 48–58), Heaney discusses some lines from his poem 'Terminus' which depict an event that took place in 1599, a parley between Hugh O'Neill and the Earl of Essex, with the former seated on a horse standing in the middle of the River Glyde. At that particular historical juncture, he says, the two men were trapped:

> There was no room for two truths. The brutality of power would have to decide the issue, not the play of mind. And yet ... we want each of them to be released from the entrapment of history. We want the sky to open above them and grant them release from their earth-bound fates. And even if we know that such a release is impossible, we still desire conditions where the longed-for and the actual might be allowed to coincide. A condition where borders are there to be crossed rather than to be contested.
>
> (*FK*, p. 56)

Heaney then goes on to link his poem, particularly the 'stasis' at the end, with the 'locked and blocked' political situation in Northern Ireland during the mid-1980s:

> The poem is saying that the inheritance of a divided world is a dis-abling one, that it traps its inhabitants and corners them in deter-mined positions, saps their will to act freely and creatively. But before that moment and since that moment, things nevertheless were and have been different.
>
> (p. 56)

The borderland, the space of translation, is a place where freedom is imagined, an intimation of the ideal poetic order. Whether or not this is an Edenic fantasy, an evasion of actual history and politics, is something I shall return to later.

The dual impulses I have been discussing – the need for 'grounding' (which is necessarily divisive, since each nation has, in Philip Larkin's phrase, a different 'proper ground') and the desire to cross boundaries – can be felt in two poems which are in a way foundational for Heaney's poetry: the opening and concluding poems of his first book,

Death of a Naturalist. Heaney felt that in 'Digging' (*DN*, pp. 13–14), he 'had let down a shaft into real life' (*P*, p. 41). This is connected to a grounding in the land through the hole being dug by his father in the poem. There is also an assertion of continuity on Heaney's part: He has a pen rather than a spade, but the poem is keen to assert a filial piety and a similarity between the generations, since although the speaker has 'no spade to follow men like them' (his father and grandfather), he will, as the concluding line tells us, dig with his pen. Yet this pen is sinister as well: it is 'snug as a gun'. What does this implement of destruction represent here? One interpretation sees the spade and gun as representing the choices facing the young Irish Catholic male: 'agricultural tradition' and 'Republican militarism'.[6] But there could be at least another meaning of the gun. It could represent the destruction of the very continuity Heaney is asserting in the poem, since he has broken away from the farming background of his family. Although he has repeatedly expressed his affection and gratitude towards his parents and family, a consciousness of betrayal surfaces from time to time in poems such as the fourth sonnet in the 'Clearances' sequence (*HL*, p. 28), where his mother tells him 'You / Know all them things.', but does so 'With more challenge than pride', leading him to a difficult and divided position:

> So I governed my tongue
> In front of her, a genuinely well-
> adjusted adequate betrayal
> Of what I knew better. I'd *naw* and *aye*
> And decently relapse into the wrong
> Grammar which kept us allied and at bay.

The simile of the gun, then, points to an element in 'Digging' that signals a movement away from origin, roots and family.

This movement may also be signalled through the other 'foundational' poem in that first book, 'Personal Helicon' (*DN*, p. 57), which recounts Heaney's childhood fascination with wells. Although this fascination is now, from the point of view of adulthood, dismissed as childish, the poem nevertheless sees it as having links with his adult poetry, which is a mutated form of those childhood impulses:

> Now, to pry into roots, to finger slime,
> To stare big-eyed Narcissus, into some spring
> Is beneath all adult dignity. I rhyme
> To see myself, to set the darkness echoing.

'I rhyme / To see myself' at first suggests a secure process, a self which is stable and rooted, there to be seen; yet this is rapidly counterpointed or undermined, even, by the appositional infinitive phrase which follows: 'to set the darkness echoing'. This phrase indicates something which cannot be seen in the darkness, and which does not have a stable centre, since the echo is bouncing back and forth round the sides of the well so that no point of origin can be located. Significantly, 'echoing' is the last word of the poem.

'Personal Helicon' is one of the first of those poems of empty space and/or darkness which recur in Heaney's work. A later poem of this kind, the last in the 'Clearances' sequence (*HL*, p. 32), takes as its main image a chestnut tree which has been cut down. At the beginning of the poem, the space once occupied by the tree is described as 'Utterly empty, utterly a source', a line which simultaneously affirms and denies origin. Then, after imagining the cutting down of the tree, the poem concludes:

> Deep planted and long gone, my coeval
> Chestnut from a jam jar in a hole,
> Its heft and hush become a bright nowhere,
> A soul ramifying and forever
> Silent, beyond silence listened for.

'Clearances' is a sequence commemorating Heaney's mother, who had died three years before *The Haw Lantern* was published, and in these closing lines the 'long gone' tree seems to merge with the soul of the mother who is now forever silent. But there is something apart from absence in these lines, something enduring – 'a bright nowhere', 'a soul ramifying'. And yet this enduring thing proves elusive, without proper location or limits: it is 'nowhere' and it is 'ramifying' (a poem about a tree must take seriously the etymology of this word, which comes from the Latin *ramus*, 'branch'). It is silent, but always 'listened for' beyond that silence (with the implication that this is an infinitely enduring process which always falls short of success; what is always being listened for 'beyond silence' is never finally heard). What that enduring and elusive thing might be is illuminated by an essay on Patrick Kavanagh (*GT*, pp. 3–14). An aunt planted the chestnut tree, Heaney explains, outside the family home in 1939, the year of his birth, and because he and it were 'coeval', he came to identify it with his own life. It was later cut down by new owners after the Heaneys sold the house, and gradually faded from his mind, only to resurface imaginatively as a 'luminous emptiness' (p. 3) years later. There was, however, a difference from his earlier identification:

> This time it was not so much a matter of attaching oneself to a living symbol of being rooted in the native ground; it was more a matter of preparing to be unrooted, to be spirited away into some transparent, yet indigenous afterlife. The new place was all idea, ... it was generated out of my experience of the old place but it was not a topographical location. It was and remains an imagined realm, even if it can be located at an earthly spot, a placeless heaven rather than a heavenly place.
>
> (*GT*, p. 4)

Here we seem to be moving towards the idea of place – of Ireland – as an 'imagined community'. It is true, of course, that any imagined realm can remain a nostalgic reversion, an autochthonous place of the mind. There are occasions when Heaney seems to flirt with such ideas. In his lecture 'Correspondences', he speaks of 'Irishness' as constituting 'a big unconscious voltage and all it needs is some transformer to make it current in a new and significant and renovative way'.[7] Such mental states can easily merge with nostalgia for vanished (or non-existent) material states. So, for instance, the disappearance of the hearth from kitchens and its replacement by central heating radiators is a mark of a new world in which something has been lost, in which the modern Irish citizen is 'vaguely in exile from somewhere inside or outside yourself' but retains a 'vestigial capacity to focus around an old field of force that is neither marked on the map nor written into the schedule'. Yet on the following page he argues that what he has been saying 'are not sighs for a lost Ireland', but 'chancy manifestations of affection and connection' upon which 'we must build a work of meaning'.[8] Early on in the lecture, he describes a detour he once took in his car to Boolavogue in Co. Wexford, a site of resistance during the 1798 uprising:

> I was driving not towards any civic or ecclesiastical entity called Boolavogue. I was rather driving towards the ever-receding centre of yearning in a musical cadence. I was following a signpost which brought me not so much into the geography of a parish as into the acoustic of a song.[9]

The song he refers to is one about Father Murphy, who played a role in the 1798 rising. Here, too, geographical rootedness is replaced by something else. In linking the word 'acoustic' to 'the ever-receding centre of yearning in a musical cadence', he seems to articulate the idea that an acoustic is something like a persistent reverberation, perhaps like the echoing darkness of 'Personal Helicon'. But the word 'yearning' also acknowledges the constant pull that lies behind the yearning, a pull towards a centre, even if this centre is never locatable. The two sides exist concurrently, in entanglement with each other.

There is a tug or dialectic between two ideas of Ireland, a primordial Ireland, somehow rooted deep down in the psyche or the soil, and an ever-receding spot on the horizon, always there, and always out of reach. The fact that he refers to the 'acoustic of a *song*' (my italics) is also important. For it suggests that this identity which is always receding is one that exists in representation and signification, and not in the soil or the primordial Irish psyche or some such entity. And representation is always extendable with more representation. In another essay, Heaney quotes the Australian poet Vincent Buckley's remark: 'Language is an entry to further language' (an idea repeated in the introduction to *Beowulf*).[10] This, I think, is one of the possible significances of translation (in all the narrow and wide senses of the term which I have been using in this book) for Heaney. Translation, too, is an unending process, in the sense that there can be no final and ultimate translation, not only because of historical and linguistic changes, but because, even within the same historical period and the same states of the language, there are different and valid versions possible, even of relatively simple sentences, let alone more complex structures such as poems.

It is notions such as these that I want to pick up now in proceeding to an analysis of some more of Heaney's poems and translations: Ireland as a place that is both potential and memory, a pull towards a centre and a rippling outward from a centre into 'further language'. I want to begin with perhaps the most celebrated of the poems in which Heaney brings together land and language: the place-name poems, which, as I have mentioned earlier, draw on an old Irish genre, *dinnseanchas*.[11] There are three of these in *Wintering Out*: 'Anahorish', 'Toome' and 'Broagh' (*WO*, pp. 16, 26, 27). These poems have been widely discussed, and, in one sense, there is little new to say about their details. I shall draw on these prior discussions, but what I hope to add is a reshaping of the details into a different pattern. Each of the titles is both place and word – Anahorish (a townland and the name of Heaney's primary school) means, as the poem itself says in the first line, 'place of clear water', the villages of Toome and Broagh get their names from the Irish *tuaim*, tumulus, and *bruach*, riverbank, respectively.[12] Each poem links

the place name with aspects of its sound. Anahorish is a 'soft gradient /
of consonant, vowel-meadow', the repeated sounds *'Toome, Toome'* are
'soft blastings', and 'Broagh' refers to both the 'black *O*' of the name –
the vowel sound in the word – and 'that last / *gh* the strangers found /
difficult to manage'. These connections between sound and place might
be read in the way David Kennedy reads the 'black *O*' (which is also a
heelmark made in mud), as asserting organicism, delving beneath the
surface to 'a Celtic point of origin'.[13] One might also argue that they
attempt to make some kind of 'natural' connection between language
and place. Each poem, however, also has currents which oppose its
undeniable flirtation with organicism. Thus Anahorish, 'the first hill in
the world', apparently linked indissolubly with the sounds of the word,
gives way to something else:

> after-image of lamps
> swung through the yards
> on winter evenings.
> With pails and barrows
>
> those mound-dwellers
> go waist-deep in mist
> to break the light ice
> at wells and dunghills.

The Edenic Anahorish has slid now into an 'after-image' of people
moving through farmyards on winter evenings. Although the linking
of Anahorish to these people (presumably farmworkers of Heaney's
childhood) may appear to make them, too, into inhabitants of Eden,
the poem also says that this Eden is an *image*, something represented in
memory and, by implication, prone to the distortions and falsifications
of memory and representation. By associating them with the 'mound-
dwellers' (probably ancient inhabitants of Ireland), it is implying further
that they are almost as much products of conjecture, reconstruction, and
mythologizing as those inhabitants. One could even see a patronizing
element in this description of them. The poem embodies, as Helen
Vendler and Neil Corcoran have pointed out, a distanced view both in
time and in cultural vantage point. 'Anahorish', in Corcoran's words,
'accommodates, even as it places, nostalgia'.[14]

   'Toome' is also marked by a double movement. As I suggested at the
beginning of this chapter, the poem, which ends with a description of
Heaney 'sleeved in / alluvial mud', seems to embody an organic conception

of identity in which he is literally one with the soil. To arrive at this state, he has moved from the sound of the place-name into a 'souterrain', pushing beyond the archaeological remains of history and conflict:

> prospecting what new
> in a hundred centuries'
>
> loam, flints, musket-balls,
> fragmented ware,
> torcs and fish-bones

Yet this push beyond history into contact with the soil is not a comfortable state. Instead of being rooted and stable, there is a sense of uncertainty, even perhaps danger. For, as Corcoran notes, the alluvial mud 'shelves / suddenly', undermining the sense of stability, and the elvers which tail the speaker's hair give him a resemblance to Medusa, who, of course, turned anyone looking at her into stone – an apposite image for the kind of hanging on to the past which Heaney has often attacked.[15]

'Broagh', too, oscillates between different movements, in this case inclusion and exclusion. Heaney has explained that the early lines of the poem incorporate words deriving from the different sources which have gone into the making of the language spoken in Ireland – Irish, English and the Scots which came in with plantation.[16] In doing this, they embody, one might say, a community which spreads across the sectarian divides of Northern Ireland, and they do so through an activity which can be described as translation in the sense of carrying across – 'bruach' into 'Broagh', for instance, or the carrying over the water of 'rig', 'pad' and 'docken' from England and Scotland to Ireland. But the poem also contains at the end, as many people have noted, a movement of exclusion – the difficulty of pronouncing the sound 'gh', which is experienced by those who are described as 'the strangers', and which functions here as a shibboleth. This sound, however, is not 'difficult to manage' for the Irish themselves, whether Catholic or Protestant. Language, as George Steiner has pointed out, is both a movement of inclusion (it is 'outwardly communicative') and one of exclusion (it is tribalistic, 'inward and domestic').[17] This is why, perhaps, translation is equated with betrayal – the betrayal of the secrets of the tribe to the outsider, who then becomes privy to knowledge which only the members of the tribe should have. Translation, like all liminal activities, is hedged round with danger, because it is a movement away from the comfort of the familiar into the unfamiliar or unknown.[18] Inclusiveness, while it may be in principle a desirable goal, is also infused with ambivalence.

In each of these poems, it seems, a double movement is occurring. The nostalgic longing which suffuses the evocation of an Eden at the beginning of 'Anahorish' gives way to a recognition that the past *has* passed. In 'Toome', the descent into the soil is marked by intimations of danger, and in 'Broagh', exclusion and inclusion go hand in hand. What marks the negative critical readings of these poems by Clair Wills and David Kennedy, amongst others, is the assumption that one of these movements is finally chosen and the other rejected, or that there is a 'contradiction' in the poem. It should scarcely be necessary to point out here that few poems aim at constructing a logical argument; in these poems, both movements must be held. Discussing Heaney's early poems about family, farming and the Irish countryside, Helen Vendler describes him, in a suggestive phrase, as 'an anthropologist of his own culture'.[19] And an anthropologist, as Clifford Geertz and others have argued, is a kind of translator, located between identification with a culture and analytic distance, just as Heaney is in these poems.

The second group of poems I want to consider here consists of the so-called bog poems in *Wintering Out* and *North*. As is well known, these poems draw on material Heaney first came across in P. V. Glob's *The Bog People* about the Iron Age bodies found in the peat bogs of Jutland. Some of these bodies, Glob argued, were of people who had been ritually sacrificed. As is also well known, and as Heaney has made clear (*P*, pp. 57–60), he found this material provided him with poetic points of entry into the Northern Ireland Troubles. There is, in a loose sense, an act of translation occurring in this movement from Iron Age Jutland to 1970s Ireland. These poems have been the subject of a huge volume of debate, both positive and negative. Many of the arguments ranged against Heaney here parallel those sketched at the beginning of this essay and again in relation to the place-name poems. A well-known example is the early review by Ciaran Carson, 'Escaped from the Massacre?':

> The real difference between our society and that of Jutland in some vague past are [*sic*] glossed over for the sake of the parallels of ritual. ... In 'Punishment' he seems to be offering his 'understanding' of the situation almost as a consolation. ... It is as if he is saying, suffering like this is natural; these things have always happened; they happened

then, they happen now, and that is sufficient ground for under-
standing and absolution. It is as if there never were and never will be
any political consequences of such acts; they have been removed to
the realm of sex, death and inevitability.[20]

Others, such as Elizabeth Butler Cullingford, add to this criticism by
suggesting that Heaney's parallels between the bodies of Iron Age
Jutland (some of whom were victims of ritual sacrifice) and victims of
the IRA in contemporary Belfast are symptoms of an identification with
repressive myths of gender:

> He vacillates between the positions of detached anthropological
> observer and dismayed devotee of the Goddess. Although he
> describes the psychological economy underlying the conflict between
> 'feminine' Catholic and 'masculine' Protestant as 'bankrupt', he
> seems unable to understand how the habit of thinking in immutable
> gender polarities helps to sustain the political problem he deplores:
> to call the Republican ethos a 'feminine' religion is to imply that
> femininity and barbarism are inseparable. ... Heaney is possessed by
> and even reproduces the atavistic myth which he deplores.[21]

As I noted earlier in this chapter, it is undeniable that Heaney has been
known to endorse gender polarities. The question, however, in relation
to the bog poems, and notwithstanding what Heaney says in his prose
about his conceptions of gender, politics and the nation, is whether
these particular poems might embody less clear-cut notions than
Carson and Cullingford allow for. Here again (in the use of the evalua-
tive verb 'vacillates'), there is that inability to see that there might be (at
least) two sides to the question, and that they can coexist.

Cullingford draws on David Lloyd's well-known essay, ' "Pap for the
Dispossessed" ', in which he has pointed out Heaney's syntactical deft-
ness in the following lines of 'The Tollund Man':

> In the flat country nearby
> Where they dug him out,
> His last gruel of winter seeds
> Caked in his stomach,
>
> Naked except for
> The cap, noose and girdle,

> I will stand a long time.
> Bridegroom to the goddess,
>
> She tightened her torc on him
> And opened her fen,
> Those dark juices working
> Him to a saint's kept body

(WO, p. 47)

The death of the Tollund Man is depicted as a sexual encounter with the goddess (Nerthus, the fertility goddess to whom some of the bog bodies were sacrifices, according to Glob). Syntactically, Lloyd observes, 'Naked, except for / The cap, noose and girdle', and 'Bridegroom to the Goddess' could apply to both the Tollund Man and the speaker. The effect of this is to contract the 'distance of the historical observer ... into an imaginary immediate relation to the corpse', and this identification 'facilitates the elimination of human agency, which is distilled to thematically equivalent operations of sacrifice (by which the corpse is worked 'to a saint's kept body') and poetic rememoration which reverses, by analogy with exhumation, the direction of sacrifice without invalidating it'.[22]

The force of this criticism about 'elimination of human agency' – which one regularly comes across in recent criticism – is not, in my view, as compelling as Lloyd assumes it ought to be. It seems to take for granted an agreement about a scale of literary and other values which may not be shared by everyone, and it seems to want to preclude as illegitimate situations where a lack of agency might indeed be experienced by the subjects involved. It also overlooks the argument that a *representation* of lack of agency might in fact be an act *of* agency. In any case, I am not entirely convinced that 'The Tollund Man' does collapse the distance between the historical observer and the corpse, and so pave the way for the 'elimination of human agency'. On the contrary, one could argue that the poem arrives at an in-between space, a distance from both Ireland and Jutland, which serves as a location where critique (and through that, change) become possible. It is notable that the poem insists on its hypotheticality and futurity.[23] Each of the three sections of the poem emphasizes this in its first stanza by the use of the future, the conditional or the subjunctive (the italics in the quotations below are mine):

> Some day *I will go* to Aarhus (section I)
>
> *I could risk* blasphemy (section II)
>
> Something of his sad freedom

> As he rode the tumbril
> *Should come* to me, driving (section III)

And it concludes on a similar note:

> Out there in Jutland
> In the old man-killing parishes
> I *will feel* lost,
> Unhappy and at home.
>
> (*WO*, p. 48)

The speaker of the poem, located in the present, writes about a future event (the anticipated trip to Denmark) in which he will or might see things and have experiences partly engendered by a past event (the ritual sacrifice of the Tollund Man). Indeed, there are two pasts here; the middle section of the poem, in which he imagines himself praying 'Him to make germinate' the bodies of twentieth-century victims of the Irish conflict, includes a reference to an incident from the 1920s:

> Tell-tale skin and teeth
> Flecking the sleepers
> Of four young brothers, trailed
> For miles along the lines.
>
> (*WO*, p. 48)

This, says Heaney, derives from a killing by Protestant paramilitaries, in which the bodies of the victims 'had been trailed along the railway lines, over the sleepers as a kind of mutilation'.[24] Here, too, there is a kind of macabre and perverted ritualistic element in the disposal of the bodies. This fourfold temporal layering already complicates any simple contraction of the distance between the present observer and the Iron Age corpse. In addition to being located between different times, the poem is also located between different places (Ireland, Denmark) and different languages (English, Danish). He will be unhappy, one presumes from the poem, for a number of reasons. One is that the marks of violence on the Tollund Man's body (although, at this point, he has only seen it in photographs) remind him of Ireland (and this is, of course, the motive propelling the poem onwards). But he will be unhappy also because he is lost or disoriented geographically and linguistically, as he imagines himself driving and asking the local people for directions to the places where the bodies were found, and receiving the responses in a language he does not understand:

> driving,
> Saying the names
>
> Tollund, Grabaulle, Nebelgard,
> Watching the pointing hands
> Of country people,
> Not knowing their tongue.

(WO, p. 48)[25]

And yet, of course, the place is not just foreign. While he will be disorientated and 'unhappy' in an unfamiliar language, landscape and culture, he will also be 'at home' (because it will remind him of Ireland, which also makes him unhappy). The syntactical ambiguities discussed by Lloyd can be related to this. If the speaker of the poem identifies with the Tollund Man, it is for a number of reasons – sympathy with him, and revulsion at the violence done to him, certainly, but also because he *understands* (which is not the same thing as excusing) the sacrificial motives leading to his death: as Heaney points out in his essay 'Feeling Into Words', Ireland has similar patterns in the form of 'political martyrdom for that cause whose icon is Kathleen Ni Houlihan' (*P*, p. 57). This understanding, he must feel, makes him complicit. At the beginning of section III, in lines that I have already quoted, Heaney imagines his future trip to Denmark as having similarities with the Tollund Man's journey towards his execution:

> Something of his sad freedom
> As he rode the tumbril
> Should come to me, driving

The phrase 'sad freedom' here is puzzling. One can understand the sadness of the Tollund Man, confronted with his imminent death (although 'sad' seems something of an understatement). But why should he also have a sense of freedom? Is there a suggestion that his freedom might come from the fact that, as a product of the culture which institutes these sacrifices to the fertility goddess, he is invested in (even supports) the beliefs which are leading him to his death? And a similar set of feelings and beliefs is in action for Heaney, too: the killings in Ireland horrify him, but, as a product of Irish Catholic culture, he understands the patterns which lead to them. If this is so, he might feel 'lost' or dislocated not only geographically and linguistically but also morally. In which case, the 'pointing hands / Of country people' might have a sense of accusation about them, and not just be indicating directions. Is there not perhaps something macabre about the activity which he envisages himself in here: driving around in search of a dead body?

The sense of complicity I have been discussing is something that we are familiar with in these bog poems (and again, this has been widely noted). In 'The Grauballe Man' (*N*, pp. 35–6), there is discomfort about the very aestheticization which Lloyd criticizes; both the series of metaphors round which most of the poem is constructed and the 'beauty' of that aestheticization are counterpointed with and judged by the word 'atrocity':

> but now he lies
> perfected in my memory,
> down to the red horn
> of his nails,
>
> hung in the scales
> with beauty and atrocity:
> with the Dying Gaul
> too strictly compassed
>
> on his shield,
> with the actual weight
> of each hooded victim,
> slashed and dumped.

The beauty of the sculpture of the Dying Gaul and the series of metaphors earlier in the poem are answered with the final stanza – particularly the terse monosyllables of the last line – which depict the violence perpetrated on the 'actual' contemporary victims of sectarianism in Northern Ireland. Even better known than this is 'Punishment' (*N*, pp. 37–8), in which the speaker exposes himself as an 'artful voyeur' of one of the bog bodies, this time a woman's, and castigates himself for his failure to condemn the tarring and feathering of women in contemporary Ireland.

> I who have stood dumb
> when your betraying sisters,

> cauled in tar,
> wept by the railings,
>
> who would connive
> in civilized outrage
> yet understand the exact
> and tribal, intimate revenge.

However, his self-castigation and condemnation of the act, as the words 'connive / in civilized outrage' tell us, are immediately undercut by something else. His 'civilized outrage' is hobbled by something deeply rooted, since he is, in the words of 'The Tollund Man', also 'at home' with the tribal motivation of revenge which powers the tarring and feathering. There is an understanding of – also experienced as moral complicity with – the motivations which have led to the acts committed against both modern and Iron Age victims. At the same time, there is a distance: 'civilized outrage' in one case, historical and geographical distance in the other.

It is these various dislocations and in-between positions which connect the bog poems with the notion of translation. A point that I have returned to a number of times during this book is the idea that translation and understanding, whether linguistic or cultural or temporal, involve a closeness to another language or culture or time, and at the same time a distance and difference from it. The translator in each of these cases is both there and here (in the other language, culture, period; and in his or her own language, culture, period) and neither here nor there. In doing this, one is capable of understanding better – to the degree that one can – not only the other culture or language or period, but one's own, clarifying things about it which may be more clearly graspable from that in-between position. In the freeing up of space which cultural or linguistic translation can achieve (although, of course, this need not necessarily happen), distance and reflection are possible. The location that Heaney arrives at in these bog poems allows him to articulate the limits of certain aspects of Irish republican culture. And this is a step towards critique and reform. The vacillation 'between the positions of detached anthropological observer and dismayed devotee of the Goddess' that Elizabeth Cullingford depicts as a problem might be, instead, a *platform* for something else.

I move on here to look at 'From the Frontier of Writing' (*HL*, p. 6), one of the parable poems in *The Haw Lantern*. The mode and method of these poems register the influence of the Eastern European poetry Heaney discusses in various essays and reviews reproduced in *The*

Government of the Tongue, such as 'The Impact of Translation', which I referred to earlier. In his introduction to this book, he explains that the reason for his repeated invocation of Mandelstam and other Eastern European poets is their affinity with the situation in Northern Ireland:

> One of the challenges they face is to survive amphibiously, in the realm of 'the times' and the realm of their moral and artistic self-respect, a challenge immediately recognizable to anyone who has lived with the awful and demeaning facts of Northern Ireland's history over the last couple of decades.
>
> (*GT*, p. xx)

The amphibious state described here is another form of that in-betweenness I discussed earlier. 'From the Frontier of Writing' and the other parable poems must be read, then, as coming out of this amphibiousness.

Like some of the bog poems, 'From the Frontier of Writing' is a poem both about the act of representation and about Ireland. In an essay which includes a discussion of this poem, Heaney has compared the 'the crossing of the lyric barrier' to 'the experience ... of getting through a road-block or a border checkpoint manned by the British army'. The constrictions of the latter experience, he says, 'can represent the repressions and self-censorings which hamper a writer and keep him or her stalled at the barrier of composition'; yet the movement as one is cleared and waved on represents 'the beginning of the slide into fluency which initiates poetic composition'. The poem depicts in its parabolic manner two road blocks – the first, Heaney says, is 'an incident on a journey', the second 'an occasion recollected and transformed by the writing'.[26] Both of these experiences are described in terms of in-betweenness and stasis:

> The tightness and the nilness round that space
> when the car stops in the road, the troops inspect
> its make and number

These lines indicate the limbo-like nature of the situation ('nilness'), and the nervousness of the feeling engendered (the 'tightness' here is partly a tautening of the nerves). Yet there is perhaps a different note in the third stanza:

> and everything is pure interrogation
> until a rifle motions and you move
> with guarded unconcerned acceleration

'And everything is pure interrogation' seems to recount an unwelcome experience; interrogation is what security services do. Yet is it not conceivable that a sense of possibility is at work here too? 'Pure interrogation' may also be openness to different outcomes: everything is possible and nothing has been fixed. This double note continues in the apparent contradictions of the last line quoted: 'with guarded unconcerned acceleration'. There are both negative and positive feelings here. The speaker and his vehicle move cautiously and under the guards' eyes (both meanings are contained in the word 'guarded', as perhaps more distantly and questionably is the feeling of *being* protected) but also undergo an experience of liberation ('unconcerned acceleration'). The multiplicity of meaning is also present in the next road block, this time the 'recollected and transformed' one. Having undergone another nervous interrogation, the speaker is allowed to move on, both accused of a crime and liberated: 'And suddenly you're through, arraigned yet freed'. In part these multiplicities touch on the feeling of somehow being guilty (even if one is not) which one might feel in contact with the forces of law and order. But if, as the title indicates, the poem is in some sense also about writing, then what do they represent? They may indicate that feeling within the act of writing itself – the sense of simultaneous opening and closing of possibility, freedom and constriction – that comes from turning an embryonic poem (which is 'pure interrogation') into definite words. The closure of possibility occurs because in fixing on certain words, ones which the poet and poem must stand by, other possibilities are necessarily excluded. And yet, in the completion of a poem, something is freed up, some space is created; hence one is 'arraigned and freed'. One is freed also because of the reverberations that persist at the edges of the actual, the 'acoustic' or 'further language' which is heard around the poem. In this arraignment and freedom, poet and poem participate in the simultaneous making and unmaking that is inherent in translation.

The final example of Heaney's work I wish to discuss here is a translation in a stricter sense of the word, his version of *Beowulf*. The original poem is itself positioned between cultures. It was composed in England and addressed to an English audience, but is set entirely in Scandinavia; it is also located between pagan and Christian world views. The era of the events described is a pagan era, and there is, throughout, evidence of an imaginative identification with the values of the heroic code, such as its emphasis on earning *lof* or fame through warrior-like deeds, and its sense of the inevitability of *wyrd* (fate). Yet it is also infused with Christian attitudes, as when the narrator describes the

Scyldings' resort to pagan gods for protection against Grendel as a 'heathenish hope' (*B*, p. 8). It has also been suggested that archaeological traces of the Roman Empire in England can be observed in some of the details of the Old English poem. For instance, shortly after Beowulf's arrival at Heorot, Grendel tears down the door of the hall:

> Then his rage boiled over, he ripped open
> the mouth of the building, maddening for blood,
> pacing the length of the patterned floor
> with his loathsome tread

(p. 24)

The phrase Heaney translates here as 'patterned floor' (*fāgne flōr* in the original) has been thought to refer to a mosaic floor of the Roman type, leading to the suggestion that Heorot might be modelled on 'something like a Saxon hall built on the tessellated floor of an abandoned mansion'.[27]

As the poem infuses an earlier era with the details and concerns of its own era, so too does Heaney's version, as is inevitable in any act of translation. While Beowulf's funeral pyre goes up in flames at the end of the poem, a woman mourns:

> A Geat woman too sang out in grief;
> with hair bound up, she unburdened herself
> of her worst fears, a wild litany
> of nightmare and lament: her nation invaded,
> enemies on the rampage, bodies in piles,
> slavery and abasement. Heaven swallowed the smoke.

(p. 98)

This woman, Heaney suggests in his introduction, 'could come from a late-twentieth-century news report, from Rwanda or Kosovo' (p. xxi). Indeed, as Seth Lerer has said, it is possible that 'what we have here is no "translation" at all, but an evocative reflection on an editorial invention'.[28] The editorial invention occurs because the Old English manuscript is badly damaged at this point, and some of the readings are conjectural, differing between different editions of the text. Heaney has also imparted a particular edge to his translation, as Lerer notes of the phrase 'slavery and abasement'. The original reads *hynðo ond haeft-nyd* (which can be translated as 'humiliation and captivity').[29] Heaney's rendering increases its emotional weight, and one effect of this, Lerer suggests, is to evoke the Northern Ireland situation.[30] Other aspects of the world of *Beowulf* have a similar effect: in his introduction (p. xiii), Heaney mentions the 'laws of the blood-feud' in *Beowulf*, and this might well remind him of the cycles of violence and revenge in Ireland's own history.

But in addition to these reminders of modern violence and political conflict, the language of Heaney's translation also comes out of his own cultural locations. The introduction and his 1999 St Jerome Lecture have much to say about how he incorporates words and phrases from his Northern Irish vocabulary into the translation. In the introduction, Heaney explains that he heard the 'enabling note' which provides a translator's 'right of way into and through a text' as 'a familiar local voice, one that had belonged to relatives of my father, people whom I had once described (punning on their surname) as "big-voiced scullions"'. The relatives referred to here were the Scullions, who 'came across with a weighty distinctness' (p. xxvi). Another point of entry was the Old English word *Þolian* ('to suffer', 'endure'), since it had survived into the speech he had heard in his childhood from his aunt, amongst other people. '*Þolian*', he says in his introduction, 'had opened my right of way' (p. xxvi).

The opening lines of the translation come out of this enabling note:

> So. The Spear-Danes in days gone by
> and the kings who ruled them had courage and greatness.
> We have heard of those princes' heroic campaigns.
>
> (p. 3)

The word 'So' here renders the Old English *Hwæt* (other translators have used 'Attend!', 'Listen!', the now archaic 'Lo', and even, disastrously, the Bertie Woosterish 'What ho!').[31] Heaney's choice of 'So', he explains in his introduction, was governed by the fact that he wanted these opening lines to be framed in 'cadences that would have suited [the Scullions'] voices' (as he wanted the whole poem to be 'speakable' by them). In what Heaney calls 'Hiberno-English Scullion-speak', the word '"so" operates as an expression that obliterates all previous discourse and narrative, and at the same time functions as an exclamation calling for immediate attention' (p. xxvii).

Other words derived from the Hiberno-English idiom include 'graith', 'hoked', 'hirpling', 'bothies', 'bawn', 'wean' and 'brehon', which are all explained by glosses (in the Norton edition, though not in the Faber one).

Heaney's use of these Ulsterisms has been criticized by some Old English scholars, who have dubbed his translation 'Heaneywulf'.[32] And there may well be justice to this criticism, given that the translation was from the start destined for a canonical publication (canonical in US academic circles anyway), *The Norton Anthology of English Literature*. Howell Chickering's review argues that, as a strategy of translation, this 'does not accurately represent the language of *Beowulf*. ... it does a disservice to students to make it look like there is an amalgam of Irish and English in the original poem'. He points also to a more fundamental difficulty: Heaney's aim is for 'his posited connections between Old English and the Ulster dialect to work so that when successful "the flash of the right word choice should create a tremor that makes readers feel they exist as 'full strength' members of the language group"'. Yet, Chickering asks, 'the problem for the majority of his audience is, which language-group is it, Irish or English? It can't be both, given the history of Northern Ireland'.[33]

In discussing the issues raised by these remarks, I will focus particularly on the word 'bawn', since this has a complex political edge to it. Heaney had used and commented on the word before. Mossbawn was the name of the family farm (*P*, pp. 35–6), and there are also the two dedicatory poems in *North* (pp. 8–10) given the collective title 'Mossbawn'. 'Bawn', Heaney explains (*P*, p. 35), was the 'name the English colonists gave to their fortified farmhouses'. This definition is slightly at odds with other sources. The *Concise Ulster Dictionary*, it is worth noting, glosses the word as 'a walled enclosure, usually with towers at the angles, used as a cattle-court normally, and for defence in an emergency'.[34] The OED also defines it as the enclosure rather than the house itself. The word also means a cattlefold (without the suggestion of a military use). Although 'bawn' derives from the Irish *bábhún*, there is a clear association with the colonial era as well. But Heaney also infuses it with a different Irish flavour; in the poem 'Belderg', he says

> I could derive
> A forked root from that ground
> And make *bawn* an English fort,
> A planter's walled-in mound,
>
> Or else find sanctuary
> And think of it as Irish,
> Persistent if outworn.

> (*N*, p. 14)

The nature of this Irish sanctuary is clarified in his prose; the name of the farm, he tells us, was pronounced 'Moss bann, and *bán* is the Gaelic word for white. So might not the thing mean the white moss, the moss of bog-cotton?' *(P,* p. 35). As far as I can tell, this is a piece of revisionist etymology which is intended to reclaim the word from its colonial associations.

Heaney singles out the word for specific discussion in his introduction:

> In Elizabethan English 'bawn' ... referred specifically to the fortified dwellings that the English planters built in Ireland to keep the dispossessed natives at bay, so it seemed the proper term to apply to the embattled keep where Hrothgar waits and watches. Indeed, every time I read the lovely interlude that tells of the minstrel singing in Heorot just before the first attacks of Grendel, I cannot help thinking of Edmund Spenser in Kilcolman Castle, reading the early cantos of *The Faerie Queene* to Sir Walter Raleigh, just before the Irish would burn the castle and drive Spenser out of Munster back to the Elizabethan court. Putting a bawn into *Beowulf* seems one way for an Irish poet to come to terms with that complex history of conquest and colony, absorption and resistance, integrity and antagonism, a history that has to be clearly acknowledged by all concerned in order to render it ever more 'willable forward / again and again and again'.
>
> (p. xxx)

Chickering finds this explanation 'deeply confused'. To equate Spenser in his bawn with Hrothgar in Heorot 'makes the historical equation read: the oppressed Irish = Grendel, and the colonizing English = Hrothgar'. He doubts that Heaney intended to take his 'Elizabethan Irish forebears to have been monsters from the race of Cain, nor the exploitative English planters to have been wise rulers like Hrothgar' (as the above analogy implies).[35] Chickering might also have referred to another locution. After Grendel's mother has attacked Heorot as a reprisal for her son's death, Hrothgar describes them as follows:

> One of these things,
> as far as anyone can ever discern,
> looks like a woman; the other, warped
> in the shape of a man, moves beyond the pale
>
> (p. 45)

'Beyond the pale' here translates the Old English *wraeclāstas* (line 1352 of the original), which means, according to the glossary in the Wrenn/Bolton edition, 'paths of exile'.[36] The resonances of the phrase Heaney uses are somewhat different from this. 'Pale' has, of course, a particular significance within Ireland, since it was the part of the island where English jurisdiction had been established. Beyond the pale were the uncertain and threatening Irish realms. Indeed, the phrase 'warped / in the shape of a man' could easily be the kind of phrase that an English colonist might have used to describe what some saw as the wild sub-human Irish. Here is Charles Kingsley writing of the Irish as late as 1861: 'I am haunted by the human chimpanzees I saw along that 100 miles of horrible country. ... to see white chimpanzees is dreadful'.[37] The use of 'beyond the pale' to refer to Grendel equates him once more with the Irish 'other'. Here again the Old English poem cannot have meant to make Hrothgar the oppressor and Grendel the oppressed, since, as Chickering points out, Grendel is depicted as one of the race of Cain, and Hrothgar is clearly meant to be a model ruler. It is quite likely that Heaney, in wanting to tune his translation to the pitch of his own version of English, has overlooked the confusion that Chickering describes.

Nevertheless, there is a possible significance here for us as readers of the translation rather than the Old English text. Seth Lerer has pointed out that there is a sense in which Hrothgar and his warriors can be seen as 'colonizers of some strange landscape', and that in at least one passage of the translation, 'we are meant to see Heorot through Grendel's eyes: a castle thrown up by invaders, a mansion that has no business being in the moor-land'.[38] Whether we are *meant* to see it this way or not (and I am not sure that we are) there is, I think, a symptomatic significance in the kinds of ambiguities or, less charitably, confusions, that Chickering discusses. They point to an important element in Heaney's work, whether or not Heaney had spotted the difficulties with locutions such as 'bawn' and 'beyond the pale'. This view is consonant with Chickering's suggestion that Heaney wants his *Beowulf* to be seen as one of his own poems rather than as a translation.[39]

This significance can be approached via Spenser's Kilcolman Castle, which has figured in Heaney's writings before his introduction to *Beowulf*. In 'Frontiers of Writing' (*RP*, pp. 186–203), Heaney refers to a lecture delivered earlier in his tenure as Oxford Professor of Poetry in which he depicted an 'integrated literary tradition' for Ireland in terms of a quincunx of five towers. At the centre is the 'tower of prior Irelandness'; to the south is Kilcolman Castle, representing 'English conquest and the Anglicization of Ireland'; on the left is Yeats's Thoor

Ballylee, which symbolizes the 'effort ... to restore the spiritual values and magical world-view that Spenser's armies and language had destroyed'; the Eastern one is Joyce's Martello tower, indicating the 'attempt to marginalize the imperium which had marginalized him' (p. 199); and to the North is Carrickfergus Castle, associated with Louis MacNeice. As the only one of these symbolic towers to be located in Ulster, this last has a particular significance for Heaney. MacNeice, in Heaney's reading, discussed in chapter four, combines attributes from Spenser, Joyce and Yeats and can, consequently, be regarded as 'an Irish Protestant writer with Anglocentric attitudes who managed to be faithful to his Ulster inheritance, his Irish affections and his English predilections' (p. 200). With the exception of 'Protestant', all these affiliations can be related to Heaney as well, although certain modifications may be necessary. Whether Heaney can be described as Anglocentric may be open to debate, but in reviews and essays he has certainly declared the significance of the English literary tradition for his own work (the formative influence of that very English writer, Ted Hughes, for instance). For Heaney, MacNeice 'offers a way in and a way out not only for the northern Unionist imagination in relation to some sort of integral Ireland but also for the southern Irish imagination in relation to the partitioned north' (*RP*, p. 200).

The issues I have been raising here can be related back to Heaney's *Beowulf* and, in particular to his use of Ulsterisms. As mentioned earlier, the word *Þolian* was one of his points of entry into the translations. In addition to being linked to a word he had heard in childhood, it also gave him a sense, he says, of the transnationality of language:

> My aunt's language was not just a self-enclosed family possession but an historical heritage, one that involved the journey *Þolian* had made north into Scotland and then across into Ulster with the planters, and then across from the planters to the locals who had originally spoken Irish, and then farther across again when the Scots Irish emigrated to the American South in the eighteenth century.
>
> (p. xxv)

Earlier experiences of the kind he had with *Þolian* had helped him to question his idea that English and Irish were 'adversarial tongues', and to arrive at 'a more confident and creative way of dealing with ... the question ... of the relationship between nationality, language, history and literary tradition in Ireland', a way which included the idea of a 'pristine Celto-British Land of Cockaigne, a riverrun of Finnegans

Wakespeak pouring out of the cleft rock of some prepolitical, prelapsarian, ur-philological Big Rock Candy Mountain'. As a result of this the 'Irish/ English duality, the Celtic/Saxon antithesis were momentarily collapsed', and he saw the possibility of 'an escape route from what John Montague has called "the partitioned intellect", away into some unpartitioned linguistic country, a region where one's language would not be simply a badge of ethnicity or a matter of cultural preference or an official imposition, but an entry into further language' (pp. xxiv, xxv).

It could be argued – as indeed has been argued against Montague's idea of the unpartitioned intellect – that Heaney's Utopian vision here (and elsewhere) evades difficult differences of politics and history, and aspires to what John Wilson Foster describes as 'a politico-spiritual impossibility – a mythic landscape of beauty and plenitude that is pre-Partition, pre-Civil War, pre-famine, pre-Plantation and pre-Tudor'.[40] It is even possible that Montague's and Heaney's notions can become a guise under which familiar hegemonies are asserted under the apparent Edenic harmony. Is a 'Celto-British Land of Cockaigne' simply a dangerous fantasy, though? I do not think that Heaney is suggesting that this is a place outside the difficult realms of reality, difference and conflict which can actually be reached. The entry into 'further language' is only a glimpse of a possibility, a constantly receding horizon.

Heaney's St Jerome Lecture, which I quoted earlier, may shed some light on this. Here the state of the writer and that of the translator are compared, since both are positioned somewhere between their own idiolects and what Heaney describes as the 'language's total availability'.[41] In exploring this state further, he draws on Ted Hughes's essay 'Myths, Metres, Rhythms'. Any group's language communicates and conserves what Hughes calls the 'voltage of the whole group's awareness and energy'. Yet, for different reasons, the group and the wider society each find the other's language unsatisfactory. 'From the point of view of the lingua franca', says Hughes, 'the solidarity system and mythology of any sub-group tends to appear parochial, old-fashioned, limited and limiting – to be indulged, if at all, only as local colour.' To the sub-group, however, 'the lingua franca appears shallow, arbitrary, empty, degraded and degrading, even destructive, if not altogether meaningless'. Hughes adds:

each modern literary work has to take its place on a continuum between some sub-group's (author's) system of shared understandings ... and the most inclusive, ideally global wave-length of a multicultural lingua franca.[42]

It is with this dilemma that Heaney's *Beowulf* engages. On the one hand, something destined for the *Norton Anthology of English Literature* clearly needs to be tuned to the 'most inclusive, ideally global wavelength of a multi-cultural lingua franca'. And, on the other hand, as Heaney states in his introduction and in the St Jerome lecture, for him it needed to meet the demands of what Hughes describes as his 'sub-group's ... system of shared understandings'.[43] There is, I think, a further implication, one with which Heaney does not explicitly engage: that the demand to tune into the wave-length of the sub-group may create ripples, extensions and shifts within the lingua franca, which will, in consequence, be challenged and altered. There is another implication as well. Heaney also suggests that a parable Hughes narrates in his essay 'could equally well be a parable for the indissolubility of individual consciousness, shared language and cosmic at-homeness that we suppose existed in the world before Babel'.[44] Here again we meet Walter Benjamin's 'pure language'.

Several issues have emerged in this discussion of *Beowulf* which can be related to the discussion of the earlier groups of poems as well, and to more general issues of translation. Heaney's translation of, and commentary on, the Old English poem ties in with two sets of demands that he has engaged with throughout his career: those of the sub-group's 'shared understandings', particularly as sedimented in its language, and those of the lingua franca, a language that can be understood throughout the British Isles, or throughout the English-speaking world. Adherence to the sub-group might mean that crossing over to the linguistic or ideological or ethical lingua franca is seen as a betrayal. Each language, Steiner suggests, 'hoards the resources of consciousness, the world-pictures of the clan, ... is secret towards the outsider and inventive of its own world'. Consequently, 'there is in every act of translation ... a touch of treason. Hoarded dreams, patents of life are being taken across the frontier'.[45] This is a feature of Northern Irish culture, as Heaney has made clear in a poem such as 'Whatever You Say, Say Nothing', where he refers to Northern Ireland's 'tight gag of place' and describes it as a 'land of password, handgrip, wink and nod', where your name betrays your religion (*N*, p. 59). Manifestations of this tendency in the poems I have been discussing include the burrowing down into the Irish word-hoard in the place-name poems, the exclusion through language of the 'strangers' in 'Broagh', the understanding of the 'exact / And tribal, intimate revenge' in 'Punishment', and the use of the Ulsterisms in *Beowulf*.

On the other hand, as we have been seeing throughout, and as Walter Benjamin, Godfrey Lienhardt and Clifford Geertz have made clear in essays I have used at various points as touchstones, translation, as in 'Heaneywulf', is also an extension of possibilities, an evanescent glimpse, perhaps, into that never-to-be-achieved universality which Heaney describes as an 'unpartitioned linguistic country … an entry into further language'. Since the 'further language' is unending, Heaney's poetry seesaws productively between an exclusionary localism and an inclusive but unreachable universalism. It is this dilemma that he has been negotiating throughout his poetic career, beginning with those emblematically positioned first and last poems in *Death of a Naturalist*.

6
Indian Palimpsests: The Poetry of A. K. Ramanujan

Of the poets discussed in this book, Ramanujan is perhaps the most distinguished and influential as a translator. It is true that Seamus Heaney's translations have been widely acclaimed, and since Heaney is better known amongst readers of poetry in the English-speaking world (and beyond), my claim on Ramanujan's behalf may seem excessive. Heaney's translations, however, have generally been of works and authors that have been translated on numerous occasions – often with great distinction – and are already in reasonably wide circulation in the West: Sophocles, Dante, *Beowulf* and Ovid, amongst others. Ramanujan, on the other hand, has worked largely with material that was little known in the West outside scholarly circles, particularly ancient and 'medieval' poetry in South Indian languages.[1] He has not only brought this to the attention of a wider public, but has done so by producing translations of a regularly high quality that work as English poems in their own right. Despite this achievement as a translator, however, the focus of this chapter will be less on his translations than on his own poetry, although I will touch on the former where necessary. There are many points of contact between the two bodies of work, as there are between them and his scholarly essays, which I shall draw on as well.

My initial – somewhat circuitous – approach to his poetry is through a consideration of some debates about Indian nationhood which have taken on a particular edge and importance in the last 30 years or so. These debates are about the inter-relationship of India's different cultures, religions and ethnicities and about how (or if) they can coexist within a single nation-state. 'India will go on', the novelist R. K. Narayan told V. S. Naipaul in the 1960s.[2] His assurance on this point is precisely what has been in question. In what form will it go on?

At independence in 1947, secularism and multi-ethnicity were among the founding principles of the new nation-state. In recent years, though, this vision has been under threat from a number of sources. On the one hand, Hindu nationalism, which is strongly anti-secularist, and which had been bubbling under for decades, has become increasingly assertive, even finding its way into political power, both nationally and locally. On the other hand, separatist and dissident movements – sometimes intertwined with religion – have been active in various parts of the country. The most widely reported ones have been those in Kashmir, and, during the 1980s, in Punjab, but the north-eastern states of India have been simmering as well. The multi-lingualism of India has also been a source of discontent, with the 'Hindi nationalism' of the more powerful north being resented and opposed by speakers of the very different languages of South India.[3]

These political and cultural forces have been paralleled by vigorous debates about the nature of Indian nationhood, debates encapsulated in the title of Partha Chatterjee's book *The Nation and Its Fragments*.[4] The two nouns of this title set unitary conceptions of India against the 'fragments', or groups subordinated by the unitary views and marked by characteristics such as language, caste, class, region and (minority) religious affiliations. Two unitary ideas of India, in circulation since the nineteenth century, have been powerful in the post-Independence years: secular modernizing nationalism, particularly in the Nehruvian era, and, more recently, Hindu nationalism. One of the issues animating these debates has been the question of how the fragments can constitute part of the nation without simply existing in a state of subordination.

Chatterjee is associated with *Subaltern Studies*, and although there are differences of perspective between the various contributors to this project, a number of them certainly share the view that the vision of secular modernity supported by the national elite is one that steamrollers over the interests and needs of the various fragments, trying to impose a view of India which is not shared by large numbers of people – the peasantry, dalits and minority religions, amongst others. This kind of debate goes back at least to the different visions of what an independent India should look like, which were advocated by Mahatma Gandhi and Jawaharlal Nehru. *Subaltern Studies* has been engaged in trying to reorient Indian historiography by questioning what it sees as this imposition of one view of the nation – secular modernity – on the people.

Hindu nationalism (at least in its present form) has few difficulties with modernity, even though, paradoxically, it projects itself back to ancient India as a source. It fought the elections of 2004, for instance, under the slogan 'India Shining', which was intended to indicate its vision of a modern India. On the other hand, as I have already mentioned, Hindu nationalists are strongly opposed to the idea of secularism. For them, India is essentially, primordially and organically a Hindu nation. Hinduism is defined broadly, as one of the main ideologues of *Hindutva*, V. D. Savarkar, indicates: 'he is a Hindu to whom Sindhustan is not only a Pitribhu [Fatherland] but also a Punyabhu [Holyland]'.[5] This definition is capacious enough to include other religions originating in India (Buddhism, Jainism and Sikhism), for whom therefore India is the holy land, but it clearly excludes Islam and Christianity.

Although both these would-be unifying versions of the nation are disputed, a political entity such as India, with its many religions, languages, and ethnicities clearly needs *some* 'idea of India', as the title of an excellent book by Sunil Khilnani puts it. Khilnani's own idea, based on the thinking of Jawaharlal Nehru, is of a 'layered' and 'palimpsestic' India (I shall qualify Khilnani's use of the layer model later on in this chapter); for Khilnani, as for Nehru, India is a place of cultural interaction and of 'interconnected differences'.[6] The Indian palimpsest includes modernity, and while this implies the necessity of a central state, Khilnani notes that Nehru also had a 'de-centred' conception of India, so that 'no part of the country could be called the heart of that culture'.[7]

Such debates may seem remote from Ramanujan's cultural and literary concerns, which, in his prose and translations particularly, centre on religious and love poetry, folklore and anthropologically informed discussions of the cultures of India. While there may not be immediately obvious political implications in his work, there are many intersections between his preoccupations and the themes discussed so far: the contention between modernity and countervailing movements, for instance, or the relationship between centralizing and decentring forces. His own poetry can be seen in one of its dimensions as a kind of palimpsest, a rewriting of the Indian texts he translated; his poems write over those ancient poems, and are in turn written over by them, as they write over and are written over by Western modernist influences. His scholarly work also traverses different layers of Indian culture, such as 'high' and 'low' cultural forms (although in many Indian cases, this distinction is not as clear-cut as it might seem). Ramanujan does not openly engage with the kinds of political debates I have been sketching; yet there is in his work a model of an India which can accommodate the various 'fragments'.

The multi-lingualism and multi-ethnicity of India have, I suggested above, led to structures of domination and subordination, such as the aspirations to hegemony which are reflected in Hindu nationalism or in attempts to impose the Hindi language. On the other hand there have been attempts to resist the imposition of such structures. Amongst Indologists, these structures of domination and subordination, and the idea of the nation and its fragments, used to be paralleled by a pair of terms which have now fallen into disfavour: the so-called Great and Little traditions. The distinction here is between a pan-Indian cultural system on the one hand, and a multiplicity of local and fragmentary systems on the other. The reason it has been discredited, Stuart Blackburn and Alan Dundes argue, is because the Great Tradition came to be associated with 'division, hierarchy, and a bias in favor of written, brahmanical, Sanskrit traditions' (*CE*, p. 348).

The distinction, however, is one that Ramanujan reconceptualized and undermined, as Blackburn and Dundes note (*CE*, p. 348). Ramanujan points out that 'the Great Tradition is not singular but plural'; he describes it as 'a set of interactive pan-Indian systems, Brahmanism, Buddhism, Jainism, with *tantra* and *bhakti* interacting variously with these'. To these systems he also adds 'Islam, Christianity, et cetera, and modernity itself as the other active systems that participate in this give-and-take' (*CE*, p. 536). This list of systems requires two comments. One is that, in practice, Ramanujan does not deal with non-Hindu cultures, and the second is that, unlike the *Subaltern Studies* historians or neo-Gandhians such as Ashis Nandy, Ramanujan has a more welcoming attitude to modernity.

While dispersing the unitariness of the so-called Great Tradition, Ramanujan also finds unifying elements in the supposedly fragmentary Little Traditions, pointing out their all-India and even international currency:

Not only do folklore items – arising and current in apparently narrow incommunicable corners and very localised dialects – travel within the country or culture area, they are also part of an international network. ... Here we begin to glimpse a paradox: where the so-called pan-Indian Hindu mythologies of Viṣṇu or Śiva, or the great classics like the *Mahābhārata* and the *Rāmāyaṇa* are unique to India, folklore items such as proverbs and tales participate in an international network of motifs, genres, types, and structures – using them all, of course, to say something particular, local, and unique.

(*CE*, p. 537)

He is wary of 'terms such as "classical" and "folk" as terms in simple opposition' (these terms being versions of the Great/Little distinction), arguing that 'they should be seen as parts of a cline, a continuum of forms, the endpoints of which may look like two terms in opposition' (*CE*, p. 429). Out of such critiques of the Great/Little distinction, he develops an idea that becomes vital to his work, the idea of 'reflexivity' or 'mirroring' as a way of thinking about the relationships between Indian cultures. This view is most fully set out in his essay 'Where Mirrors Are Windows: Toward an Anthology of Reflections':

> Cultural traditions in India are indissolubly plural and often conflict-ing but are organised through at least two principles, (a) context-sensitivity and (b) reflexivity of various sorts, both of which constantly generate new forms out of the old ones. ... They are responses to previ-ous and surrounding traditions, they invert, subvert, and convert their neighbours. Furthermore, each of these terms, like what we call India itself, is 'a verbal tent with three-ring circuses' going on inside them. Further dialogic divisions are continuously in progress.
>
> (*CE*, p. 8)

The forms that reflexivity can take include 'awareness of self and other, mirroring, distorted mirroring, parody, family resemblances and rebels, dialectic, antistructure, utopias and dystopias, the many ironies con-nected with these responses, and so on' (*CE*, p. 8). One of the central features of reflexivity is, of course, that pattern of simultaneous resem-blance and difference which is characteristic of translation.

Given the importance of reflexivity in Ramanujan's thinking, it is no surprise to find him having repeated recourse to images of mirroring in his poems. The early 'Self-Portrait' (*CP*, p. 23), for instance, describes his reflec-tion in a shop window as 'the portrait of a stranger', yet one which is 'often signed in a corner / by my father'. This simultaneous difference from and affinity with his parents is marked also on the cover of his second book of poems in English, *Relations* (1971), which shows, in what can be described as both a form of mirroring and a palimpsest, Ramanujan's face with a por-trait of his parents superimposed on his forehead. (Although this was, apparently, not chosen by him, and, indeed, he showed a degree of ambivalence towards it, he finally allowed it to stand.[8]) The posthumously published poems 'Not Knowing'(*CP*, p. 216) and 'Lines' (*CP*, p. 267) use the mirror to represent a self which is also multiple and other:

> I roam the city walk into movies
> hurtle down a roller coaster

till mirrors in a mirror shop
break me up into how many I was
show me in profile and fragment

whose head I have whose nose ('Not Knowing')

Who's this out there
with your face and not your hair?
Images detached from mirrors
float through the room ('Lines')

The lines quoted from 'Not Knowing' embody a theme present elsewhere in his poems (in 'Drafts', which I discuss later, for instance), the use of genetic inheritance as an image of 'mirroring, distorted mirroring, parody, family resemblances and rebels'. Ramanujan suggests that Yeats's line (from the poem 'The Statues') 'mirror on mirror mirrored is all the show' is an apt description of Indian cultures (*CE*, p. 9).

In this reflexivity, there can be no original India or Indian culture, no core, centre or heartland. Such views clearly produce an India contrary to the ideology of Hindu nationalism, with its emphasis on an Aryan Hindu essence and past as lying at the origin of India's identity. At the same time, Ramanujan also qualifies the hegemony of modernizing elite nationalism; although, as we have seen, Ramanujan sees modernity as *one* of the systems within Indian culture, he also makes room for, and attaches considerable value to, forms which are usually thought of as non-modern and subaltern, such as folklore, *bhakti*, women's tales and others.[9] In diversifying 'our notions of Indian civilization. ... away from the purely Brahmanical view of Indian civilization' (the classical and hierarchical view), based on Sanskrit, and focusing instead on the mother tongues, he offers a more democratized view of India, since, for him, the 'mother tongues represent a democratic, anti-hierarchic, from-the-ground-up view of India' (the folk).[10]

Reflexivity has significant connections with notions of Indian identities, since it emphasizes permeability across cultural boundaries and the ability to inhabit multiple dimensions and worlds simultaneously, a feature which is manifested in the bi- or even multi-lingualism of many Indians, and in the ability to navigate between 'modernity' and tradition.[11] Reflexivity also qualifies the idea of 'layered' identities. The layer model, Arvind Krishna Mehrotra argues, 'treats the Indian poet as someone who chiefly transports linguistic and cultural materials from the bottom to the surface, from Indian mother tongue to English' – that is, from a supposedly deeper or more fundamental level to a more superficial, more recently acquired one, which suggests a unidirectional movement.

Reflexivity, however, can be seen as more of a bouncing back and forth, like the echoes in Seamus Heaney's poem 'Personal Helicon'. In a 'multilingual sensibility', Mehrotra argues, the different languages are 'tissued' rather than layered. Mehrotra describes Ramanujan's multilingualism in precisely these terms of permeability across borders: 'Instead of assigning languages fixed positions in a hierarchical system, he sees them as territories with soft borders across which movement is unrestricted' (although 'unrestricted' may be stretching the point a little, since it takes no account of possible resistances).[12]

The idea of reflexivity also resonates with important currents in Indian theories of translation. There is, as has often been noted, no single exact equivalent in Indian languages of the English word 'translation'.[13] Harish Trivedi has pointed out that *anuvād*, one of the words for 'translation' in Hindi and some other Indian languages, is derived from Sanskrit, where it means, primarily, according to the Sanskrit-English dictionary of Monier Monier-Williams, 'saying after or again, repeating by way of explanation, explanatory repetition or reiteration with corroboration or illustration, explanatory reference to anything already said'. As Trivedi notes, the metaphor here is temporal ('after') rather than spatial, as in the English word 'translation' ('carry across').[14] The etymology of *anuvād* is symptomatic of the dimension of flexibility in Indian attitudes to translation. Traditionally, Ayyappa Paniker writes, 'the concept of the transference of a literary text from one Indian language into another was not confined to a literal paraphrase ... a literal word-for-word rendering of the original'. Such transferences were more like retellings, and 'deviations were not only tolerated but welcomed and encouraged too'.[15] Ramanujan describes each different *Rāmāyaṇa* as 'a unique crystallization, a new text with a unique texture and a fresh context' (*CE*, p. 158). K. Satchidanandan goes further, arguing that the *Rāmāyaṇas* in the various Indian languages were thought of as 'neither translations nor adaptations, but original works as they were the most brilliant manifestations of the genius of the respective languages'.[16]

Such ideas form a striking contrast with much Western thinking about translation, which has been shaped by a sense of fallenness from an original perfection or unity (as in the story of the tower of Babel), and has been haunted by the idea of recovering that unity and perfection.[17] In India, the notion of 'fidelity' has not had the same force as in Western theories of translation, and the boundaries between translation and 'original' composition have been more fluid. The sense of creativity in translation this indicates is marked in the word 'transcreation' which has been used in the Indian context for a considerable time now by the indefatigable and prolific P. Lal (apparently independently of the Brazilian cannibalists' use of the same word).[18] These kinds of approaches to translation in Indian traditions can be seen as a form of reflexivity, fitting indeed what Ramanujan wrote in his definition of the term, quoted earlier: that cultural systems in India are 'responses to previous and surrounding traditions, they invert, subvert, and convert their neighbours'.

Some of these themes and principles also mark Ramanujan's discussions of his own attitudes to, and procedures of, translation. In the essay 'On Translating a Tamil Poem' (*CE*, pp. 219–31), Ramanujan remarks that while Tamil syntax is 'left-branching', that of English is 'right-branching', making the two languages 'mirror images of each other' (p. 223). In such a situation of language difference, 'what is a translator to do?', he asks, before going on to answer his own question: 'Many of my devices (e.g., indentation, spacing) and compromises are made in order to mimic closely the syntactic suspense of the original, without, I hope, estranging the English' (*CE*, p. 223). This strategy is extended and clarified in his concept of 'structural mimicry':

> One attempts a structural mimicry, to translate relations, not items – not single words but phrases, sequences, sentences; not metrical units but rhythms; not morphology but syntactic patterns. ... Translations are transpositions, re-enactments, interpretations. Some elements of the original cannot be transposed at all. One can often convey a sense of the original rhythm, but not the language-bound metre; one can mimic levels of diction, but not the actual sound of the original words. Textures are harder (maybe impossible) to translate than structures, linear order more difficult than syntax, lines more difficult than larger patterns. Poetry is made at all these levels – and so is translation. That is why nothing less than a poem can translate another.
>
> (*CE*, pp. 230–1)

As in other Indian theories of translation, there seems to be a flexible attitude here: a translator of Ramanujan's type transposes, re-enacts and interprets, represents structures, patterns and relations. The devices and 'compromises' he discusses include elements of form such as indentation and spacing which were not in the text being translated. He is, he says of one set of translations, concerned 'not to match the Kannada with the

English, but to *map* the medieval Kannada onto the soundlook of modern English; in rhythm and punctuation, in phrase-breaks, paragraphs and lineation to suggest the inner form of the originals as I see them'.[19] The distinction here between matching and mapping is the difference between what, in his preface to Ovid's *Epistles*, Dryden called metaphrase ('turning an author word by word, and line by line, from one language into another') and what Ramanujan here terms structural mimicry.[20] On a formal level, such variations seem to be a version of reflexivity, allowing a degree of subversion, conversion and inversion of the source text.

I am not concerned here to offer an evaluation of Ramanujan's theory or practice from the point of view of translation studies more generally.[21] My aim is to see if and how the themes I have been discussing will illuminate his poetry. I want to focus here particularly on two dimensions of Ramanujan's poems, their provisionality and their incompleteness, both of which are inherent in what he says about reflexivity and translation. Translation emerges out of an interaction between a previously existing text and a current reader, and, if, as Ramanujan argues, 'a translation has to be true to the translator no less than to the originals', the vantage point differs for each observer so that any specific translation can only be a provisional one.[22] Similarly, reflexivity implies that no one culture or translation can be understood as a self-contained unit; it will always reach out in dialogue or quarrels across its boundaries. This is one sense in which cultures and languages are incomplete. Another is indicated in Ramanujan's 'Translator's Note' to *Poems of Love and War*, where he draws on Paul Valéry's famous dictum to assert: 'Translations too, being poems, are "never finished, only abandoned"'.[23]

These characteristics appear in a variety of shapes in his poems, but I will focus on two of them: his sense of the past (which manifests itself both thematically and formally) and some common devices of style and language. Amongst these devices are structural features of his poems, his use of older models and his construction of a web of images between poem and poem. In conclusion, I shall try to suggest ways in which these might link up with the debates on the nation outlined at the beginning of this chapter.

Reading the past, I have argued elsewhere in this book, can be seen as a translational relationship, a view that Ramanujan supports in his poem 'Waterfalls in a Bank':

> As I transact with the past as with another
> country with its own customs, currency,

> stock exchange, always
> at a loss when I count my change
>
> (*CP*, p. 189)

Here the loss involved is stressed, but this is not always the case. 'The past', Ramanujan asserts, 'like other cultural constructions, changes as we attend to it. ... One is changed by it and the past itself is changed by one's study of it' (*CE*, pp. 184–5). The shape of the past, of the present and of the observer are malleable, all emerging in part through such acts of translation between past and present. Like translations, historical interpretations are moulded by our personal, cultural and temporal reading positions and locations. It follows that there is no single definitive past. 'India', Ramanujan states, 'does not have one past, but many pasts' (*CE*, p. 187). A good example of these characteristics is the poem 'History,' (*CP*, pp. 107–8; the comma is part of the title). This poem begins:

> History,
>
> which usually
> changes slowly,
> changes sometimes
> during a single conversation:
>
> the petite little aunt
> in her garden of sweet limes
> now carries a different
> face, not merely older or colder
> or made holy
> by deaths and children's failures.

The comma in the title is a signal which leads us to anticipate syntactical continuation, and the modulation of the title into the first sentence imparts a sense of process, countering any implications of reification which might cling to the abstraction 'History'. The remainder of the poem illustrates precisely how this sense of historical process operated. On the day his great-aunt died, the speaker (then a child) tells us, he observed his aunt looking for something under the cot on which her mother's body was lying. The description of the aunt as a sculpture suggests that her image became fixed and static in the observer's memory: 'nose eyes and knee-bend cut / fresh from stone for a Parvati statue'. The rest of the poem brings us into the present, recounting a conversation in which the speaker's mother tells him what actually happened on that day: the great-aunt's two daughters

> unknown each to the other
> alternately picked their mother's body clean
> before it was cold
> or the eyes were shut,
> > of diamond ear-rings,
> > bangles, anklets, the pin
> > in her hair

These lines are marked by that indentation and spacing which Ramanujan uses in his translations as, he tells us, a way of mimicking the 'syntactic suspense of the original, without ... estranging the English'. Such typographical devices occur frequently in his poetry, suggesting a family resemblance – a kind of reflexivity – between his own poems and his translations. 'History,' goes on to list other things that they took from their mother's body, concluding:

> and the dark
> stone face of my little aunt
> acquired some expression
> at last.

The apparently rigid 'stone face' (the image picks up the reference to the 'Parvati statue' earlier) has become mobile, as the past is. This mobility, though, is not because of a physical change in the aunt's face, but because of a mental shift in the speaker's perceptions.

The link between family history and wider cultural forces and contexts apparent in 'History,' is characteristic of Ramanujan, as we can see in another poem, the well known 'Small-Scale Reflections on a Great House' (*CP*, pp. 96–9), where Ramanujan moves between the individual, the extended family, and, beyond that, the nation, to present a different aspect of history as process.[24] The capacious and unstable house, the contents of which are constantly being added to and lost, is both a physical building and a lineage:

> Sometimes I think that nothing
> that ever comes into this house
> goes out. Things come in every day

> to lose themselves among other things
> lost long ago among
> other things lost long ago

> > (p. 96)

And later in the poem, he says:

> anything that goes out
> will come back, processed and often
> with long bills attached

> > (p. 97)

Disobedient runaway sons return in the shape of their dutiful children who, unlike their fathers, respect their elders and do their duty: they 'recite Sanskrit / to approving old men / or bring betelnuts for visiting uncles'. The poem could almost be an illustration of a remark Ramanujan makes in a somewhat different context: 'Nothing is lost, only transformed' (*CE*, p. 438). The affectionateness of the portrait in the poem goes hand in hand with a sense of the chaotic nature of the house and of India: the clutter, the stray cows appropriated by the family, the skeletons in the cupboard, such as the daughters who 'get married to short-lived idiots' and then return. Tragedy hovers on the fringes of the comedy, as in the conclusion of the poem, which depicts the deaths in warfare of two members of the family. The origins of things disappear like the lost objects of the two opening stanzas quoted above, or the cows which have wandered in 'from nowhere'. The absence of origins is also a feature of the poem 'Drafts' (*CP*, pp. 157–8), in which everything is seen as a copy, even the original, which is 'Itself a copy of lost events'.[25]

Although the past is originless and fluid, Ramanujan is aware of the temptation to ossify it by trying to pin down origins, as in the case of the Hindu nationalism discussed earlier. 'Prayers to Lord Murugan' (*CP*, pp. 113–17) is a poem that deals with this danger. Murugan, a deity worshipped particularly in the state of Tamil Nadu, is described in a note to the poem as the 'ancient Dravidian god of fertility, joy, youth, beauty, war, and love'. He later came to be identified with the god of war Kārttikeya, who is, according to one significant tradition, a son of Śiva.[26] Ramanujan explains in his essay 'Classics Lost and Found' (*CE*, pp. 184–96) that his starting point here was a sixth-century Tamil devotional poem, part of which he also translated and which 'tells where to go and how to find

Murugan' (*CE*, p. 190).[27] The earlier poem was itself modelled on an even older genre, the 'Guide Poems ... where one poet guides a poorer colleague toward a patron who would recognise his talent and reward him handsomely' (*CE*, p. 190); but this secular and worldly precursor was redirected towards devotion. Ramanujan re-secularizes his model, using the sixth-century religious poem and various iconographic details from it (the fact that the god is red in colour, and has six faces and twelve hands, for instance) to develop new meanings about India's past, present and future. At the time of writing his poem, Ramanujan tells us, he was 'somewhat despondently preoccupied' with the Indian past: 'I had felt that Sanskrit itself and all that it represented had become an absence, at best a crippling and not an enabling presence, that the future needed a new past' (*CE*, p. 192). This feeling comes through in the poem:

> Deliver us O presence
> from proxies
> and absences
>
> from sanskrit and the mythologies
> of night and the several
> roundtable mornings
>
> of London and return
> the future to what
> it was.

> (*CP*, p. 117)

The mythology is associated not only with Sanskrit, but also with the freedom struggle against the British, which seems in the poem to have become a fetish rather than a lived and living presence (the 'round-table mornings' mentioned here being a reference to the Roundtable Conferences between Indian leaders and the British government which took place in London during the early 1930s).

Section 5 of this poem (p. 115), in particular, details a mythologized, stereotyped and ossified India, complete with rajahs who 'stand in photographs / over ninefoot silken tigresses / that sycophants have shot'. In the second half of this section, his despondency comes to the fore:

> We eat legends and leavings,
> remember the ivory, the apes,
> the peacocks we sent in the Bible

to Solomon, the medicines for smallpox,
the similes

for muslin: wavering snakeskins,
a cloud of steam.
Ever-rehearsing astronauts,
we purify and return
our urine

to the circling body
and burn our faeces
for fuel to reach the moon
through the sky behind
the navel.

The 'legends and leavings' here are fixations to and with the past. The import of all the details here is not clear, although some are obvious. The recycling of urine is presumably a reference to the late Prime Minister Morarji Desai's practice of drinking his own urine for health reasons. The contrast between modernity (astronauts and moon travel) and entrenchment in the past ('legends and leavings') is also clear enough. There may, it seems to me, also be a reference to myths (which were certainly current when I was at school in India) to the effect that many modern discoveries and inventions could be found in the *Vedas* and other scriptures, that ancient India had known and discovered virtually everything. The detail of the 'wavering snakeskins', which constitutes one of the 'similes / for muslin' is also noteworthy, since it appears elsewhere, in a poem already mentioned, 'Waterfalls in a Bank':

And then one sometimes sees waterfalls
as the ancient Tamils saw them,
wavering snakeskins,

cascades of muslin.

(*CP*, p. 189)

Here, unlike the Murugan poem, the use of the simile is, as Jahan Ramazani points out, a creative one; Ramanujan's split vision 'decommodifies and Indianizes the confined waterfall in an American bank'.[28] Although 'Prayers to Lord Murugan' invokes the god and repeatedly prays to him for deliverance from being entrenched in the past, its last stanza unravels its own status as a prayer ('Lord of answers, / cure us at once / of prayers'), thus inserting a note of scepticism, and treating prayer (including his own) as an aspect of the clinging to the past which the poem has been trying to counteract. 'Prayers to Lord Murugan' can be seen in a loose sense as a kind of translation; Ramanujan suggests that he uses 'an old poem in a well-known genre to make a new poem to say new things. The past works through the present as the present reworks the past' (*CE*, p. 192). Ramanujan's model, as I said, was a religious adaptation of an earlier, secular kind of poem. So, in a reverse movement, Ramanujan redirects his poem in ironic and sceptical directions, rooted in his own experiences of modernity and India. 'Indian creativity', Ramanujan argues, is characterized by 'a presence of reflexive worlds', in which traditions, cultures and languages can coexist 'in one space, parodying, inverting, facing and defacing each other, sharing and taking over characters, themes, motifs and other signifiers, but making them signify new and even opposite things' (*CE*, p. 447). This seems to me an apt description of what is happening in 'Prayers to Lord Murugan'. Ramanujan's poem is both a prayer and an anti-prayer. He reorients a poem of faith and devotion in order to ask for a disturbance of the misconceived faith which is founded on 'legends and leavings'. He takes over from the older poem and the traditions associated with it various characters, themes, iconographic details, motifs and other signifiers, and makes them signify something new, something which is recognizably modern while also linking itself to the past and looking towards a possible new future. The very conception and form of the poem are examples of creative fluidity, of mobile and malleable mythologizing in action, unlike the frozen mythology of those 'legends and leavings'.

Although the poem is a translation only in a loose sense, it nevertheless resembles translation in one of its Indian incarnations by reading and writing the past text from the vantage point of the present. The word *anuvād*, I noted earlier, has the etymological sense 'saying after or again', and that is what Ramanujan is doing in this poem. Myths of the past play, as we know, crucial roles in constituting the idea of any nation; consequently, to put the past into question, to see it ironically, sceptically and as subject to change in the way that Ramanujan does is to see both past and nation existing as transactions between past and present, as, in short, acts of translation. It is also to see them as incomplete and incompletable in the way that a poem or a translation is. Hindu nationalists locate the core of India in an ancient (and mythical) Hindu past. In this poem and more generally, Ramanujan rejects that kind of revivalism. Although the past is always with us, 'disconnection is as much an understanding of the past as making the connection. And people living in the present have to see both, because to assert continuity where there is none, where we cannot see any, is to be a revivalist'.[29] The dialectic here between connection to and disconnection from the past is precisely parallel to the position of the linguistic or cultural translator poised between cultures and languages (and the past *is* another language and culture, as L. P. Hartley's celebrated aphoristic opening to *The Go-Between* implies: 'The past is a foreign country: they do things differently there.').[30]

Incompleteness and provisionality are also characteristic of many of the devices and techniques used in Ramanujan's poetry. The epigraph to his 'Is There an Indian Way of Thinking? An Informal Essay' (*CE*, pp. 34–51) reads: 'Walter Benjamin once dreamed of hiding behind a phalanx of quotations which, like highwaymen, would ambush the passing reader and rob him of his convictions.' By putting forward different points of view through the quotations, without nailing his colours to any single mast, the compiler of the 'phalanx' disturbs the reader's certainties. This is a procedure Ramanujan tries to follow in his own essays, many of which do in fact circulate round a network of quotations and examples, a procedure he draws attention to by using the word 'anthology' in a number of the titles or subtitles he attaches to his essays: 'Toward an Anthology of Reflections', 'Towards an Anthology of City Images', 'Towards an Anthology of Hindu Food-Images' (*CE*, pp. 6, 52 and 73). In his preface to the *Collected Essays*, Vinay Dharwadker comments on some aspects of Ramanujan's method in his scholarly work, linking it to the devices of his poetry:

> While each piece was structured simply, so that it never strayed far from its stated theme, it was also surrounded by a field of multiple resonances, leading the reader outward in several directions at once. This 'ripple effect' was a function of Ramanujan's poetic style as a writer of critical prose, in which wit, irony, humour and polyphony enabled him to condense several perspectives or insights into a few aphoristic phrases. ... Ramanujan, in fact, constructed an essay much like a poem, which shows more than it tells, suggests more than it reveals, and echoes more than it acknowledges.
>
> (*CE*, p. x)

His anthological style is also part of this. Beyond their suggestiveness, these techniques have other consequences which are relevant to the context of translation and reflexivity. What they do in his poetry is to decentre individual poems or parts of poems by setting up dialogues between one poem or part and another, and allowing the poem to evade definiteness (which is not to say that they evade precision). The ripple effect that Dharwadker draws attention to here is evident in a number of ways, of which I shall single out two. One is a characteristic way of structuring many of his poems by circulating round their themes through a series of different contexts or images, considering them from different perspectives. The other is the creation of a network of reference and allusion between one poem and others.

'Prayers to Lord Murugan' is one illustration of the former method, its 11 parts nosing through the relationship between past, present and future from a variety of perspectives and in different contexts. Another poem about the ossification of the past is 'Some Indian Uses of History on a Rainy Day' (*CP*, pp. 74–5), which approaches its themes through three brief narratives. The first, set in 1965, depicts the struggle of bank clerks in Madras trying to go home after work, but finding themselves unable to board the crammed buses. After a number of such experiences, they begin to speak of the reign of the seventh-century ruler King Harsha, who once gave gifts of 'a hundred pieces of gold, / a pearl, and a length of cloth' to 'ten / thousand monks', and a 'single visiting Chinaman'. This comforts and sustains them: having missed the eighth bus, they 'begin to walk, for King Harsha's / monks had nothing but their own two feet'.

The second part of the poem depicts a number of Indian Fulbright scholars travelling by sea to take up their scholarships in the United States; when the ship stops in Egypt en route, they visit a museum and are 'amazed at pyramidfuls / of mummies swathed in millennia / of Calicut muslin'. Here, as in 'Prayers to Lord Murugan', the image of muslin represents a past which has been ossified. In part three, an Indian Professor of Sanskrit on an exchange programme in Nazi Germany is confused and thrown off balance by the unfamiliarity of the country, culture and language; in attempting to orient himself, he locates with relief something familiar, the ancient Hindu symbol of the swastika. The Professor

> suddenly comes home
> in English, gesture, and Sanskrit,
> assimilating
>   the swastika
> on the neighbour's arm
> in that roaring bus from a grey
> nowhere to a green.

There is little overt statement in the poem; instead, we are provided with three laconic vignettes in each of which the past seems a diversion from the realities of the present. The recollection of King Harsha's reign in the first section can be seen as an evasion of the realities of modern India: instead of being motivated to protest about the decrepit transport system, the clerks accept it. The amazement of the 'Fulbright Indians' at the connection they discover between ancient Egypt and India mesmerizes them in a way that seems static rather than creative; in the words of 'Prayers to Lord Murugan', they seem to be eating 'legends and leavings'. The Professor of Sanskrit's view of the swastika is more dangerous; in his desire for orientation, he ignores, or is unaware of, the Nazi misappropriation of it. His homecoming and assimilation of the symbol domesticate it back into its Hindu contexts and so miss the threatening meanings it has acquired in the 1930s. He misreads its contemporary significance – translates it wrongly, domesticates it, in effect – because he is stuck in the past. Without openly pointing out a moral, the poem does in part what Ramanujan said of 'Prayers to Lord Murugan': it embodies his feeling that 'Sanskrit ... and all that it represented had become an absence, at best a crippling and not an enabling presence'. I use the qualification 'in part', because there is a way in which the first section, at least, can be read as enabling: the recollection of the incident from the past clearly enables the clerks to take positive and independent action, as they start to walk home. This use of the past, unlike the other two, might be creative as well as nostalgic. The triple-pronged approach to India's relationships with its past probes the subject from different perspectives, dispersing itself into an unresolved dialogue between its parts, without explicitly pointing out a conclusion.

A similar structure can be seen in 'Drafts' (*CP*, pp. 157–8), a four-part poem which circles round the motif of the original and its copy or representation, a theme which manifests itself in an anthology of images: a police artist's attempt to reconstruct the features of a suspect from an eyewitness account; the Indus valley seals; adopted children searching for their parents; the unpredictability of genetic inheritance and so on. What seems to link these different images is the notion of the elusiveness or non-existence of the original, the idea that all we have or can ever have are copies or representations. The suspect in the first example is absent, for instance, and we have only the artist's reconstructions of his appearance. And with the Indus valley seals the point is made explicitly: 'Itself a copy of lost events / the original is nowhere'.

What we have are, in effect, translations, as the last part of the poem makes clear:

> mother's migraines translate, I guess,
>   into allergies, a fear of black cats,
> and a daughter's passion
>
> for bitter gourd and Dostoevsky

The original (migraines) is not reproduced exactly but translated in its passage between generations: to draw on Ramanujan's distinction, the migraines are *mapped* onto the allergies, fear and passion, rather than *matched* with them. And the migraines themselves must be translations of a previous generation's characteristics. The process therefore extends indefinitely both backwards into the past and forwards into the future. Earlier in the poem, writing itself is seen as a kind of translation: the act of representation, like that of translation, displaces the original:

> dinosaur smells, that leave no copies;
>   and copies with displaced originals
> like these words

Each part of the poem can be thought of as a provisional shot at embodying aspects of the poem's themes, so that the finality and authority of any one viewpoint are disturbed. The structure thus reinforces the meanings of the poem. This kind of structuring produces an effect similar to that which Ramanujan attributes to the use of insets or implicit comparisons in classical Tamil poetry:

> An inset is an implicit comparison. ... Unlike metaphor and simile, it often leaves out all the points of comparison and all explicit markers of comparison (e.g., 'like,' 'as'); such an omission increases manyfold the power of the figure. ... image intensifies image, associations flow into each other. These 'montage' and 'dissolve' effects are aided by the flowing syntax of the language.[31]

'Flow', 'montage' and 'dissolve' are precisely the kinds of terms one might use to describe the effect of the structure of poems such as 'Prayers to Lord Murugan', 'Drafts' or 'Some Indian Use of History on a Rainy Day': in these poems, scene dissolves into scene, context into context and image into image. In poems such as these Ramanujan follows the strategy of many of his scholarly essays and provides the reader with an anthology of examples which set up 'multiple resonances', ripples and echoes 'leading the reader outward in several directions at once'.

One effect of this type of structure is, if not exactly to rob the reader of his convictions, at least to disturb, through the provision of multiple viewpoints, the perceptions and attitudes which he or she might have brought to the act of reading the poem. There is here a structural similarity to the act of translation, which, by positioning translators and readers in between the two or more terms of the cultures and languages concerned, may cause them to reflect on the fact that the assumptions they carry with them are not inevitable or natural, may, indeed, lead them to think otherwise.

The second aspect of technique I referred to earlier was Ramanujan's use of a network of echoes between poem and poem. Montage and dissolve effects work not only through the large structure of poems but also at the local level, in phrases, images and details, so that 'every poem resonates with the absent presence of others that sound with it. ... one text becomes the context of others' (*CE*, p. 15). In 'Looking for the Centre' (*CP*, pp. 184–5; the title itself highlights the kinds of themes discussed in this chapter), Ramanujan uses the image of a zilla spider for the self. This species is one that, apparently, waits for its prey at the centre of the web rather than constructing a retreat from which it can then advance on its trapped prey. This centredness and sense of control are depicted in the poem as delusions: the speaker is 'a zilla spider / on LSD', spinning 'enormous webs', yet 'unaware / in my ecstasy I'm not at the centre'. This delusion unravels in a vertiginous image of disorientation and dislocation during the next, concluding section of the poem:

> Suddenly, connections severed
> > as in a lobotomy, unburdened
> of history, I lose
>
> my bearings, a circus zilla spun
> > at the end of her rope, dizzy,
> terrified,
>
> and happy. And my watchers
> > watch, cool as fires
> in a mirror.

> > > > > (p. 185)

The 'watchers' here are figures that appear in other poems. In 'Questions' (*CP*, pp. 130–1), the speaker asks 'were the watchers there / with me, being born over and over ...?'; in 'Connect!' (*CP*, p. 178), 'my watchers are silent as if / they knew my truth is in fragments'; and they form the title and entire subject of one poem (*CP*, p. 137). They seem to represent parts of the self: 'parts of me watch, parts of me burn' runs a line from 'Questions', which also indicates their provenance in its epigraph:

> Two birds on the selfsame tree:
> one of them eats the fruit of the tree,
> the other watches without eating.

This is from the *Muṇḍaka Upaniṣad*, 3. 1.1 (it appears also in the *R̥g Veda* and the *Śvetāśvatara Upaniṣad*). The birds, according to Sanskrit scholars, represent *puruṣa* (or the 'inner part of a human being') and *deva* (god), while the tree represents *prakr̥ti* ('Nature', although nature is understood in a different sense from the modern English meaning, and includes 'matter, body, mind and senses – everything ... that is not *Puruṣa*').[32] The watching birds of Ramanujan's source are thus connected with the ideas of selfhood found in the *Upaniṣads*, yet in Ramanujan's poems they do not retain the exact meanings of the source. His watchers effect a decentring or dissolving of the unified self and do so, as it were, by 'translating' traditional and ancient Hindu concepts into something also allied to modern psychological notions of the self as composed of multiple elements, so that they exist between the modern and the traditional. And indeed the image of the spider which is central to this poem may be doing the same thing. The spider is possibly also drawn from the *Muṇḍaka Upaniṣad*, where, however, it fulfils a very different function:

> As a spider emits its thread and seizes on to it,
> As plants grow on the earth,
> As head- and body-hair from a living person,
> All here arises from the imperishable.[33]

Here the spider indeed represents the centre of creation, the very notion that Ramanujan undermines.

This circulation of images, phrases and themes through his poetry can be seen as a version of that reflexivity I discussed earlier, that 'awareness of self and other, mirroring, distorted mirroring, parody, family resemblances and rebels, dialectic, antistructure, utopias and dystopias, the many ironies connected with these responses'. The different uses of an image or phrase in Ramanujan's poems are forms of mirroring, distorted mirroring and so on. Indeed, circulation itself is one of the important motifs of Hindu culture, including religion, as Ramanujan notes in an essay on Hindu food-images:

> Food is brahman, because food is what circulates in the universe, through bodies which in turn are food made flesh and bone. According to this view, in the organic world, there is no other stuff: food is the primal substance, all animate beings are its forms. One may stretch it further and see this cycle as including inorganic matter as well. All forms arise out of food and return to it – which is, after all, one of the descriptions of brahman, the ground of being. In the transformations of food, inorganic becomes organic, one form is metamorphosed into another; the eater is eaten, big fish eat little fish, and if you wait long enough, little fish eat big fish.
>
> (*CE*, p. 75)

Preceding this passage is Ramanujan's translation of a verse from the *Taittrīya Upaniṣad* (2. 2) which concludes:

> From food all beings
> come to be,
> by food
>
> they grow,
> into food
> they pass.
>
> And what eats is eaten:
> and what's eaten, eats
> in turn.[34]

This image of the eater being eaten is one that Ramanujan himself recycles, as in 'Elements of Composition' and 'Questions' (*CP*, pp. 123, 130), and the idea of circulation and recirculation is, as we have seen, a feature of 'Small-Scale Reflections on a Great House'. Both the individual self, then (in the first two of these poems), and India itself (in 'Small-Scale Reflections') are conceived of as process and circulation.

What the circulation of images does is to create a kind of web of internal allusions and echoes between poems, as one reaches out to another in a way that provides a formal analogue to the permeable boundaries that I described earlier as constituting Indian identities. The individual poem, like India itself, is dispersed and decentred. Through devices such as those I have discussed, Ramanujan creates, in effect, a body of work rather than single poems. The techniques I have been discussing also seem to resemble certain features of the poems he translates. In the 'Afterword' to his *Poems of Love and War*, he notes the way images and themes appear and reappear through the body of Tamil poetry:

> No good bard is only a reciter, nor does his art simply reproduce a past poem. He uses the whole tradition as his instrument, a key-board, a language of possibilities. The signifiers may remain the same, but what is signified continually changes. ... Every instance resonates in counterpoint with all the other uses of the whole tradition of themes, pictures, formulas.[35]

Ramanujan's various uses of the watchers, for example, set up precisely this kind of resonant counterpoint both within the body of his own poetry and with the wider Hindu tradition represented by his source in the *Upaniṣads*. The same can be said of the muslin image discussed earlier. In the case of 'Waterfalls in a Bank', it is used to establish a living and creative connection with the past, a way of negotiating with the present, whereas in 'Prayers to Lord Murugan', it is a symptom of the ossification of the past and the present (as it is, again, in 'Some Indian Uses of History'). A number of the poems I have discussed, such as 'The Watchers', 'Connect!' 'Elements of Composition' and 'Questions' were, according to Vinay Dharwadker's introduction to the *Complete Poems*, originally parts of a long poem, itself called 'Elements of Composition', which Ramanujan then dismembered, dispersing them through his second collection, *Second Sight* (*CP*, p. xxxvii), so that the circulation of images and phrases can partly be explained by that. But the same circulation also occurs in poems which were not originally parts of a whole in this way (the muslin in 'Prayers to Lord Murugan' and 'Some Indian Uses of History', for instance).

In a statement quoted earlier, Ramanujan said that the appropriate relationship to the past was to see both the connections and the disconnections between present and past. This oscillation between connection and disconnection, between unifying and fragmenting motions is characteristic of many of his poems and is enacted through the kinds of structural and verbal devices I have been discussing. While there are unificatory family resemblances and connections between many of his poems, and between his poems and translations, such as the indentations and spaces touched on earlier, at the same time, some of the devices I have discussed also fragment any individual poem, pulling it apart, unravelling it, making it reach out beyond its boundaries. As Vinay Dharwadker says in his introduction to the *Collected Poems*, Ramanujan's work is characterized by a 'double movement ... "stitching and unstitching", building and dismantling, or constructing wholes and producing fragments' (*CP*, p. xxxvii). Ramanujan himself makes the point in his poem 'Connect!' (*CP*, p. 178): 'my truth is in fragments'.

This double movement and the aesthetic of fragmentation are derived not only from Indian sources but also have connections with European modernism. Many of the terms that have been used here to describe Ramanujan's work – fragmentation, flow, montage and dissolve – have also been regularly used to characterize modernism.[36] Furthermore, the decentring of the self which I have discussed as a significant feature of his work has many equivalents in European philosophy and psychology. What Ramanujan does with these multiple sources from both East and West is to produce a body of work that exists within the in-between space that marks all translation. Culturally, his poems are positioned between India and the West; formally, as I have been suggesting, they enact a modernist aesthetic of the fragment, while acknowledging an aspiration to the unity of a whole body of work and drawing on Indian sources for both theme and language. As a consequence of their fragmentation and dispersal, they resist meaning in the very act of conveying it; in Bruce King's apt description, Ramanujan's poetry is in fact a 'house of mirrors'.[37]

Early on in this chapter, I suggested that the links between Ramanujan's poems and the versions of India outlined earlier would be oblique rather than immediate. I want to conclude here by briefly spelling out some of these links. Ramanujan's model of Indian cultures highlights the processes of dialogue, mirroring and reflexivity which take place amongst them. They are simultaneously in communion and separate, related to, but also refracting, each other. His own poetry, I have suggested, enacts movements of reflexivity and fragmentation. Ramanujan's aesthetic theory and practice, as well as his explicitly articulated views on India's cultures, are opposed to any monolithic conceptions of India, such as those of Hindu nationalism. India's cultures are palimpsestic, reflexive and translational, and if R. K. Narayan's confidence in the country's going on is to be proved right, it can only be in some such form.

7
Fragmentation and Restoration in Derek Walcott's *Omeros*

Creolization is usually taken to be an important and distinctive feature of the Caribbean. Edward Brathwaite defines the process in the case of Jamaica as involving the 'formation of a society which developed, or was developing, its own distinctive character or culture which, in so far as it was neither purely British nor West African, is called "creole"'. In the course of this process, during which two cultures had to 'adapt themselves to a new environment and to each other' within a context dominated by slavery, a 'friction' was generated which was both 'cruel' and 'creative'.[1] One aspect of this process is the development of creole languages and of what linguists call the creole continuum, which refers to the existence of a number of language varieties, ranging from the 'acrolect', a local version of the standard language (English or French, for example), to the 'basilect' or variety furthest removed from the standard. The existence of this continuum allows speakers to move between different language varieties – a characteristic known as code-switching. Although creolization is not synonymous with translation, it is nevertheless one manifestation of a translational structure within Caribbean cultures. By a 'translational structure' I mean here the structure of similarity-in-difference or difference-in-similarity that Clifford Geertz identifies as a feature of cultural translation.

Creolization takes on a variety of inflections in the Caribbean context. Like A. K. Ramanujan in the case of India, a number of Caribbean writers are drawn to images involving reflection and refraction. The poet, novelist and critic Edouard Glissant describes creolization as diffraction – a dispersal rather than a centring.[2] Antonio Benítez-Rojo sees it in similar terms; for him, cultural interaction in the Caribbean is like 'a ray of light within a prism', involving 'phenomena of reflection, refraction, and decomposition'. The Caribbean is marked by the existence of the 'syncretic artifact', which is 'not a synthesis, but rather a signifier made of difference', and hence cannot constitute 'a stable point'. In the Caribbean, he writes,

> the binary oppositions Europe/Indoamerica, Europe/Africa, and Europe/Asia do not resolve themselves into the synthesis of *mestizaje*, but rather they resolve into insoluble differential equations, which repeat their unknowns through the ages of the meta-archipelago.[3]

The similarity-in-difference (or vice versa) which I have described as a translational structure is a version of the paradoxes hinted at in Benítez-Rojo's pairings of 'resolve ' and 'insoluble', 'equations' and 'differential', and 'repeat' and 'unknowns'. Although Europe always constitutes one of the binary oppositions he specifies, there is no reason to doubt that a similar process operates between the other sides. We could thus have oppositions such as Africa/Asia, Indoamerica/Africa and Indoamerica/Asia. There is also no need to confine oneself to binaries; we could have triple or quadruple (or more) oppositions. And, as Benítez-Rojo points out in discussing the Cuban cult of the Virgen de la Caridad del Cobre, each side of each of these oppositions is itself a 'syncretic object'.[4] Caribbean literature, as a product of this kind of society, displays similar qualities:

> The literature of the Caribbean can be read as a *mestizo* text, but also as a stream of texts in flight, in intense differentiation among themselves and within whose complex coexistence there are vague regularities, usually paradoxical. The Caribbean poem and novel are not only projects for ironizing a set of values taken as universal; they are, also, projects that communicate their own turbulence, their own clash, and their own void.[5]

Both cultural and linguistic dimensions of creolization (understood in something like the sense described by Benítez-Rojo) are directly relevant to Walcott's writing. Much of his work in poetry, drama and prose has been concerned with the interaction of Europe and the Americas, and he has also consistently explored the resources of the various language varieties available to him in the Caribbean, a device he makes use of in poems such as 'The Schooner *Flight*' (*CP*, pp. 345–61), 'The Spoiler's Return' (*CP*, pp. 432–8) and *Omeros*, although I shall not be dealing here with his uses of these possibilities.[6] Nor shall I be concerned here with another feature of his work which has an etymological kinship with translation, the stylistic device of proliferating metaphor, whereby one seems to sprout out of another.[7]

My emphasis in this chapter will instead be on the way translational structures operate in *Omeros*, and, in particular, on the 'turbulence' and 'self-undoing' of the poem.[8] This long narrative work is, in a number of ways, a culmination of preoccupations present from relatively early on in Walcott's career: amongst them are his sense of the parallels between the Greek and Caribbean archipelagos, and the interconnected issues of history, myth and the Adamic vision.[9] My initial approach to *Omeros* is through the idea of the Caribbean as an empty space. Although we can trace this back at least to the nineteenth-century writer J. A. Froude's notorious claim that 'there are no people there in the true sense of the word, with a character and purpose of their own', in our own time it is associated more with V. S. Naipaul's equally notorious statement: 'The history of the islands can never be satisfactorily told. ... History is built around achievement and creation; and nothing was created in the West Indies'.[10]

Naturally this view has not gone unquestioned. Edward Kamau Brathwaite, for instance, challenges it early on in *The Arrivants*:

> for we who have achieved nothing
> work
> who have not built
> dream
> who have forgotten all
> dance
> and dare to remember[11]

'Achieved' evidently links back to 'achievements' in the quotation from *The Middle Passage*, and 'built' to Naipaul's use of the same word. The paradox of simultaneous forgetting and remembering is one that parallels Walcott's account of Caribbean amnesia, which I discuss shortly.

Walcott himself engages with the idea of nothingness on a number of occasions in his earlier poetry. In 'Crusoe's Journal' he writes

> So from this house
> that faces nothing but the sea, his journals
> assume a household use;
> we learn to shape from them, where nothing was,
> the language of a race

> (*CP*, p. 94)

The long autobiographical poem *Another Life* reiterates the sentiment: 'they will absolve us, perhaps, if we begin again, / from what we have always known, nothing' (*CP*, p. 286). In his essay 'The Caribbean: Culture or Mimicry?', Walcott responds more explicitly to Naipaul. After (mis)quoting *The Middle Passage* ('nothing was created in the West Indies, and nothing will ever be created'), he comments: 'Nothing will always be created in the West Indies, for quite [a] long time, because what will come out of there is like nothing one has ever seen before' (*CM*, p. 9). Naipaul speaks only of the past; Walcott's extension of Naipaul's statement into the future emerges out of his own concern with the creative possibilities of West Indian culture. Walcott's nothingness and Naipaul's are very different; whereas the latter seems to be paralysed by it, for Walcott, as for Brathwaite, the nothingness is the source of a kind of creation *ex nihilo* (although, as it turns out, for Walcott 'nothing' is not literally privation or absence; it is permeated by presence). In Walcott's writings, nothingness and creativity in Caribbean culture are closely linked to the related figures of Robinson Crusoe (as in 'Crusoe's Journal', amongst other places) and Adam, both of them translated and creolized. 'My Crusoe', he says, 'is Adam because he is the first inhabitant of a second paradise'.[12]

The idea of the Americas as a new Eden and of the writer as Adam is scarcely unique to Walcott.[13] For Walcott, as for many of his predecessors, the Adamic vision is the particular province of poets of the Americas, such as Whitman and Neruda:

> It is this awe of the numinous, this elemental privilege of naming the New World which annihilates history in our great poets, an elation common to all of them, whether they are aligned by heritage to Crusoe and Prospero or to Friday and Caliban. They reject ethnic ancestry for faith in elemental man. The vision, the 'democratic vista,' is not metaphorical, it is a social necessity. A political philosophy rooted in elation would have to accept belief in a second Adam, the re-creation of the entire order, from religion to the simplest domestic rituals.
>
> (*MH*, p. 40)

Yet because of the history of the Americas, this Adamic vision cannot be purely innocent, in the way that the first Adam might be thought to have been: 'its savour is a mixture of the acid and the sweet, the apples of its second Eden have the tartness of experience' (p. 41).

An important aspect of the second Adamic vision is its relationship to the past. Walcott distinguishes between two attitudes which he finds prevalent in Caribbean writers. There is, on the one hand, a 'servitude to the muse of history', out of which comes 'a literature of revenge written by the descendants of slaves or a literature of remorse written by the descendants of masters' (p. 37). A sense of linearity seems to lie at the core of these attitudes: 'That is the bitter secret of the apple. The vision of progress is the rational madness of history seen as sequential time, of a dominated future' (p. 41). This attitude embodies an allegiance to what he describes in the quotation above as 'ethnic ancestry'. The Adamic writers with their 'faith in elemental man' have a different conception of history:

> These writers reject the idea of history as time for its original concept as myth, the partial recall of the race. For them history is fiction, subject to a fitful muse, memory. ... Their vision of man is elemental, a being inhabited by presences, not a creature chained to his past.
>
> (p. 37)

History as time is associated with fixity; Walcott describes it as the 'Medusa of the New World' (p. 36). Myth, on the other hand, is flux: 'No history, but flux, and the only sustenance, myth' (p. 48).

Myth as 'partial recall' relates also to Walcott's idea of amnesia: 'In time the slave surrendered to amnesia. That amnesia is the true history of the New World' (p. 39). This amnesia, however, is not total, since some memories ('partial recall') remain. In 'The Caribbean: Culture or Mimicry?', further light is shed on both the amnesia and the partial recall:

> A return is also impossible, for we cannot return to what we have never been. The truth in all this is, of course, the amnesia of the American, particularly of the African. Most of our definitions of American culture are fragmentary, based on the gleam of racial memory which pierces this amnesia.
>
> (p. 7)

Because amnesia is fragmentary, Walcott makes clear in a later essay, it helps the Caribbean amnesiac to avoid the linearity of history as time: 'what America offers ... is an obliteration of the old linear idea of progress'.[14] Amnesia clears a space where imagination can operate:

> In the Caribbean history is irrelevant, not because it is not being created, or because it was sordid; but because it has never mattered,

what has mattered is the loss of history, the amnesia of the races, what has become necessary is imagination, imagination as necessity, as invention.

(*CM*, p. 6)

For Walcott, as Paul Breslin notes, amnesia is both 'psychic scar of historical violence and ... release from historical burden'.[15] How the move from the former to the latter can be made, how the imagination operates on the fragments of cultures will be developed and illustrated at greater length in my discussion of Walcott's Nobel lecture 'The Antilles: Fragments of Epic Memory'.

In European thinking, the Adamic idea is of course closely connected with language, since it was Adam who named the creatures. But, through the Tower of Babel, seen as a second Fall, there is also a link with translation, since it was only then that translation became necessary. In *After Babel*, George Steiner examines the mythology of this subject. The most common mythological explanation for the multiplicity of languages sees it as a punishment for the hubristic act of building the tower. Originally, there was a single Adamic language:

> The occult tradition holds that a single primal language, an *Ur-Sprache* lies behind our present discord, behind the abrupt tumult of warring tongues which followed on the collapse of Nimrod's ziggurat. This Adamic vernacular not only enabled all men to understand one another. ... It bodied forth, to a greater or lesser degree, the original Logos, the act of immediate calling into being whereby God had literally 'spoken the world'. ... The tongue of Eden was like a flawless glass; a light of total understanding streamed through it. Thus Babel was a second Fall, in some regards as desolate as the first. Adam had been driven from the garden; now men were harried, like yelping dogs, out of the single family of man. And they were exiled from the assurance of being able to grasp and communicate reality.[16]

The metaphysical and theological tradition on this subject contains much speculation on the possibility of undoing this second Fall through the recovery of the *Ur-Sprache*:

> If man could break down the prison walls of scattered and polluted speech (the rubble of the smashed tower), he would again have access to the inner penetralia of reality. He would know the truth as he spoke it. Moreover, his alienation from other peoples, his ostracism into gibberish and ambiguity, would be over.[17]

The Caribbean equivalent of the tower's rubble would be the fragments of cultures present through the archipelago (African, European, Indian, Chinese, Arawak, Carib and so on). In 'The Antilles', Walcott offers some suggestions as to how the fragments might be brought together. He begins by describing the presentation in a Trinidad village of the *Ramleela*, a dramatization of the deeds of the Hindu god-hero Rama. Walcott's first inclination, he says, was to search for 'some sense of elegy, of loss, even of degenerative mimicry'. 'Purists', he thinks, see the occasion as a manifestation of 'memory that yearns to join the centre, a limb remembering the body from which it has been severed. ... In other words, the way that the Caribbean is still looked at, illegitimate, rootless, mongrelized'. For these purists, as for Froude, there are no people, only 'fragments and echoes of real people, unoriginal and broken' (*A*, pp. 67–8).

He concludes that these ways of looking at the scene misread its meaning:

> The performance was like a dialect, a branch of its original language, an abridgement of it, but not a distortion or even a reduction of its epic scale. Here in Trinidad I had discovered that one of the greatest epics of the world was seasonally performed, not with that desperate resignation of preserving a culture, but with an openness of belief that was as steady as the wind bending the cane lances of the Caroni plain.
> (p. 68)

What he now sees is gratitude and celebration, not the 'sigh of History'; too much emphasis, he feels, is placed on 'that long groan which underlines the past' (p. 68). The backward-looking perspective – obsessed with the 'sigh of History' – is one that he comes to question. Instead of seeing the scenes as 'evocations of a lost India', he asks himself, 'Why not "celebrations of a real presence"? Why should India be "lost" when none of these villagers ever really knew it, and why not "continuing," why not the perpetuation of joy'? (pp. 68–9).

The possibilities he sees in the scene before him are available not only to the Indo-Caribbeans he is observing, but to any Caribbean person. In fact, he concludes, *all* the cultures of the region are resources potentially available to him, and to which he is entitled:

> Break a vase, and the love that reassembles the fragments is stronger than that love which took its symmetry for granted when it was whole. ... It is such a love that reassembles our African and

Asiatic fragments, the cracked heirlooms whose restoration shows its white scars. This gathering of broken pieces is the care and pain of the Antilles, and if the pieces are disparate, ill-fitting, they contain more pain than their original sculpture, those icons and sacred vessels taken for granted in their ancestral places. Antillean art is this restoration of our shattered histories, our shards of vocabulary, our archipelago becoming a synonym for pieces broken off from the original continent.

(p. 69)

Walcott's 'nothing', then, turns out to be more than nothing: the 'shards' and 'fragments', are 'celebrations of a real presence' from which a start can be made. 'There is too much nothing here', he says paradoxically in 'Air' (*CP*, p. 114).

The restored vase with its 'white scars' is both whole and not whole: it displays cracks, it carries the sign of the fragments which constitute it. What Walcott is engaged in can fairly be described as an act – or multiple acts – of translation ('carrying across') between the cultures of the Caribbean. These tensions between coming together and falling apart are inherent in the nature of translation as such. Linguistic and cultural translation, too, are involved in a constant negotiation between contrary forces, a bringing together and a differentiating; an accommodation between the forces goes along with what Steiner calls the 'resistant particularity of the "other"'.[18]

Walcott's (metaphoric) equivalent of this bipolarity or antinomy, this simultaneous accommodation and resistance is, I suggest, the reassembled vase whose 'restoration shows its white scars'. It is in the combination of the restoration with the white scars of the joins that the unison and plurality make themselves felt, it is through the scars that the 'resistant particularity of the "other"' is manifested. The fragments can be said to represent one of the roles of language: that of preserving the (exclusionary) identity of the group, even in as vestigial a form as Walcott sees in the West Indies; but in the movement across the borders or scars from one fragment to another that Walcott (a Dutch-English-African fragment) as observer of the *Ramleela* (an Indian fragment) makes as he reads and re-reads the meaning of the scene before him, we can see another of the functions of language and of translation, their ability to generate '"counter-worlds". ... to gainsay or "un-say" the world, to image and speak it otherwise'.[19]

In trying to apply these ideas to *Omeros*, I want to pursue Walcott's metaphor and consider the poem as the reassembled vase. From this perspective, it is clear that it is constituted of a number of different types of fragments. Most obviously there are the different cultural traditions which go into its making, primarily Caribbean, African and European (despite his main example in 'The Antilles', Indo-Caribbean culture generally plays a fleeting role in Walcott's poetry).[20] These cultures enter the poem partly through its various locations. The most dominant setting for the action of the poem is the Caribbean, but significant portions of the plot take place in Africa, Europe and North America. The poem also draws on resources from both European epic traditions (in its plot, imagery and use of certain epic conventions) and the Caribbean (through code-switching, for instance).

The relationship of the poem to the epic tradition is a matter of debate. For some readers, such as Mary Lefkowitz, *Omeros* is unquestionably an epic.[21] Walcott himself has a more ambivalent attitude on the subject. In his talk 'Reflections on *Omeros*', he both asserts and denies that it is an epic, comparing it at one point to *The Odyssey* on the grounds that 'the story of wandering is the classical epic', but later repudiating this label, and calling it a 'very intimate work'.[22] Although the epic is not an exclusively European form, some of the conventions and material he draws on are clearly modifications of materials and devices from Homer and Dante, amongst others. The manifestations of such traditions in the poem have been widely discussed and I do not propose to go over this ground in any detail here. Nevertheless, I think it is worth quickly mentioning a few examples in order to highlight the mutations they undergo. The journey to the underworld (Book 11 of *The Odyssey*), for instance, mutates into Achille's journey to Africa (chapters 25–8 of *Omeros*), although instead of meeting his dead mother as Odysseus does, he meets his ancestral father Afolabe. The statement of theme which comes at the beginning of epics such as *The Odyssey* and *Paradise Lost* is positioned retrospectively towards the end (chapter 64). The link with Homer's epics is, of course, obvious from the title and the names of some of the characters: Achille, Hector, Helen, Philoctete and so on. Connections such as these, however, are usually not neat ones: the men competing for Helen are not Paris and Menelaus, but Achille and Hector. The Cyclops make recurrent appearances as an image for, variously, a telescope (p. 102), a lighthouse (p. 204), a cyclone (p. 51) and a camera (p. 299). Like Penelope in *The Odyssey* weaving her shroud, Maud Plunkett is recurrently depicted as being at work on a piece of handicraft (in her case embroidering a quilt). These links between the Caribbean and Homer are not new for Walcott; in the title poem of *Sea Grapes* (1976), for instance, 'a schooner beating up the Caribbean / for home, could be Odysseus', and towards the end of the poem, the tide is described in terms of Homeric verse: 'the great hexameters come / to the conclusions of exhausted surf' (*CP*, p. 297). Another European epic, Dante's *Divine Comedy*, is referred to in *Omeros* through the use of the tercet form, slipping in and out of *terza rima*, and through the references to the circles of Hell (for instance, chapter 58, in which a Homer-Virgil figure leads the narrator up the slopes of the Soufrière volcano where he sees the 'Pool of Speculation' containing those politicians who have sold out the land for profit).[23]

The fragmentary nature of the poem also manifests itself in the multiplicity of narratives. The Caribbean triangle of Achille, Hector and Helen is the centrepiece of the poem, of course, and Dennis and Maud Plunkett's lives weave in and out of the three main characters' stories, especially that of Helen, who used to work for them. But they have independent stories of their own – particularly the accounts of how they came to the Caribbean, how they lived there, and Plunkett's labour on writing the history of the island. There is also the African story of Achille's dream-return to Africa and of the slave trade. Less successfully interwoven, I think, is the story of the American woman Catherine Weldon, who worked on behalf of Sitting Bull against the US government's attempts to persuade him to sign away his people's land (see, for instance, pp. 176, 178–82, 208–9, and particularly 212–18); this seems much more of an intrusive anomaly than any of the other narratives. Although one can see thematic connections with the rest of *Omeros*, it is, as Robert Hamner remarks, one of the 'least defensible aspects of the poem'.[24] Then there is also the intermittent autobiographical account of the narrator, which resembles Walcott's own. The narrator's father, like Walcott's, is called Warwick (p. 68); like Walcott, whose late twin brother was named Roderick, the narrator has a brother called 'Roddy' (p. 166); and, like Walcott, the narrator spends time in Boston (e.g. chapter 36).

With such a variety of people, narratives and places, there is clearly a potential structural problem. Not all of the different levels seem to me to fit in, as I have already indicated. Nevertheless, there is a fair degree of success in integrating these different elements. One of the ways in which this is done is by making certain patterns and motifs weave in and out of the poem. I use the image of weaving deliberately here, since stitching forms one of these motifs and patterns. There is, first of all, the quilt which Maud is embroidering with birds (e.g. pp. 55, 88–9). It is also used metaphorically, as when martins 'sew the silk sky' (p. 66). The narrator is himself an embroiderer: 'This wound I have stitched into Punkett's character' (p. 28). The wound referred to here is itself one of the most important of these recurrent motifs, and I will deal with it towards the end of the chapter. Helen's yellow dress weaves through the text both as itself (e.g. pp. 29, 38, 40, 62, 64, 103 and 275) and in such linked guises as a yellow immortelle flower (p. 93) and yellow butterflies (p. 272). Another recurrent pattern in the poem is the vase – an interesting link with the image that Walcott uses in 'The Antilles'. It first appears as a metaphor in the context of the girl who, early on in the poem, tells the narrator the Greek name for Homer (p. 13) and then reappears on a number of occasions, usually with some reference back to that first appearance (e.g. pp. 33, 219, 230, 279–80, 284 and 323).

More significant is the pervasive sea-swift. Its most momentous role in the poem is as the guide for Achille's symbolic healing journey back to Africa (pp. 133–52). God is depicted as telling Achille: 'Is I send the sea-swift as a pilot, / the swift whose wings is the sign of my crucifixion' (p. 134). The swift recurs in another context of healing as the bird which, centuries before, carried a seed in its stomach to the Caribbean (pp. 238–9), a seed from which grew the plant used by Ma Kilman to cure Philoctete of his wound. The sea-swift is also one of the birds which Maud is embroidering on her quilt (e.g. p. 88). And it is used as an image for the stitching together of the poem: 'I followed a sea-swift to both sides of this text; / her hyphen stitched its seam' (p. 319). Elsewhere, too, the swift is associated with writing, as when Plunkett's annotations on the books he is reading for his history of St Lucia are described as a 'flock of V's, winged comments' (p. 95).[25]

Another integrating technique Walcott uses is to have his character experience various kinds of connections: coincidences, meetings and shape-shifting. There are several father–son meetings during the poem (a connection with James Joyce, who is also referred to in the text [pp. 200–1]). During the course of his research into the Battle of the Saints (1782), for instance, Major Plunkett comes across the name of a Midshipman Plunkett who died during the engagement, and adopts him as 'a namesake and a son' (p. 94), a substitute for the son he has never had. Two other examples have already been mentioned: the narrator's encounter with the shade of his father (pp. 68–76), and Achille's dream-journey back to Africa in the course of which he has a significant meeting with *his* ancestral father Afolabe (pp. 136–9). Shape-shifting is most evident in the figure of Omeros, who turns up variously as a marble bust (p. 14), as a tramp in London (p. 194), as an Indian shaman (pp. 216–17) and towards the end of the poem as the Virgil-like guide to the narrator's Dante (pp. 289–94). Omeros is also linked with the blind prophet figure Seven Seas who mutates into and out of Virgil/Omeros towards the end of the poem (pp. 279–94). One of the forms he takes is the Caribbean itself. Early on in the poem, the name 'Omeros' is dismembered, rejoined and connected to the Antillean language and landscape:

> I said 'Omeros,'
>
> And *O* was the conch-shell's invocation, *mer* was
> both mother and sea in our Antillean patois,
> *os*, a grey bone, and the white surf as it crashes
>
> and spreads its sibilant collar on a lace shore.
> Omeros was the crunch of dry leaves, and the washes
> that echoed from a cave-mouth when the tide has ebbed.
>
> (p. 14)

Helen, too, is both a character in the poem and a place, since St Lucia is known as the Helen of the West Indies (p. 311): 'I thought of Helen / as my island lost in the haze', says the narrator (p. 222).

The various locations mentioned earlier are linked through movement and migration: the swift and Achille connect Africa with the Caribbean; the Plunketts link the Caribbean with Europe (England and Ireland in particular), as does Omeros through his appearance as the London tramp; the narrator makes appearances in London, Lisbon, Boston and the Caribbean. These migrations are connected with another recurring symbol in *Omeros*, the meridian. In the first line of Book 5, the narrator declares, 'I crossed my meridian' (p. 189). These opening pages of Book 5 see the narrator in Lisbon, capital of one of the early imperial powers, Portugal, and the meridian is part of the colonial history of the two Iberian nations. In *Omeros*, Walcott invokes a momentous meridional act in the history of the Americas, Pope Alexander VI's papal bull towards the end of the fifteenth century dividing the spheres of influence and colonization in the New World between Spain and Portugal: 'Once the world's green gourd was split like a calabash / by Pope Alexander's decree' (p. 191), and 'Alexander's meridian / gave half a gourd to Lisbon ... / and half to Imperial Spain' (p. 193).[26] Slightly further on, another imperial capital is also characterized by reference to a meridian, the 'meridian of Greenwich' (p. 196).

The narrator's transgression (etymologically, 'going over') of the meridian of Alexander VI is also a different way of seeing. 'Across the meridian, I try seeing the other side', he says (p. 191), as if the vision were now a different one from the imperial vision. The gourd/meridian that the narrator crosses and joins together echoes a similar image in 'The Muse of History'. In the peroration to this essay Walcott declares:

> I give the strange and bitter and yet ennobling thanks for the mon-umental groaning and soldering of two great worlds, like the halves of a fruit seamed by its own bitter juice, that exiled from your own Edens you have placed me in the wonder of another, and that was my inheritance and your gift.
>
> (p. 64)

Although neither of the words 'meridian' or 'gourd' is used here, clearly the sentence describes the same idea. Crossing the meridian and join-ing the two halves of the bitter gourd, seem, then, to be further images for the vision of the second Adam.

In contrast to the demarcations of imperial and meridional histories, these anti- or post-imperial crossings of history lead to a different kind of world, which is also a different kind of text:

> I followed a sea-swift to both sides of this text;
> her hyphen stitched its seam, like the interlocking
> basins of a globe in which one half fits the next
>
> into an equator, both shores neatly clicking
> into a globe; except that its meridian
> was not North and South but East and West. One, the New
>
> World, made exactly like the Old, halves of one brain,
> or the beat of both hands rowing that bear the two
> vessels of the heart with balance, weight, and design.
>
> Her wing-beat carries these islands to Africa,
> she sewed the Atlantic rift with a needle's line,
> the rift in the soul.
>
> (p. 319)

Many things come together in these lines: text and world, New World and Old World, Africa and the Caribbean, the two hemispheres of the

brain, the divisions of the soul. The hyphen here is an image of both
language and the world: a punctuation mark (the one in 'sea-swift' and
'wing-beat') as well as the physical journey made by the swift in its
migrations. The description of the globe also has a dual reference: to the
actual earth and to a representation of it. But a hyphen simultaneously
joins and separates, and the image (along with the others used here)
suggests that the join is not seamless, that the place of suture is visible,
as the hyphen is, or the place where the stitches have been done, or the
equator joining the two halves of an educational globe.

This visibility is an important aspect of the poem because it indicates
the non-transparency of the link between representation and reality.
More than one critic has commented on *Omeros's* self-reflexiveness, its
emphasis on its own status as artifice.[27] The visibility of the join where
the fragments I described earlier come together is a significant part of
that emphasis, and Walcott indicates this in a variety of ways. In one
of the poem's many self-reflexive moments, mediated here through one
of the characters, Major Plunkett comes to a similar realization about
representation (the 'she' of the second line is, in the context, both the
island of St Lucia, and the character Helen):

> The Major made his own flock of V's, winged comments
> in the margins when he found parallels. If she
> hid in their net of myths, knotted entanglements
>
> of figures and dates, she was not a fantasy
> but a webbed connection

> (p. 95)

A few lines later, he refers to 'the Homeric repetition / of details' (p. 96).
Although she is not a 'fantasy', she is in some way, he realizes, a con-
struction, a network of representations, or, as these lines have it, a 'webbed
connection'. The idea is reiterated briefly in a slightly later reference to
'Homeric coincidence' (p. 100). The 'Homeric repetition / of details', the
'webbed connection': these are descriptions of many of Walcott's own pat-
terns and devices in *Omeros*, such as the vase, the swift, the yellow dress
and the other repeated images mentioned earlier. It is noteworthy that
many of these recurrent motifs have a dual status as both natural object
and the product of human artifice. The dress, for instance, also mutates
into the butterfly and the immortelle; and the swift, too, is both a 'real'
bird and artifice, since it is one of the objects which Maud Plunkett

stitches into the quilt. O-mer-os too is both artefact (a bust, for instance) and natural object (conch shell, mother, sea, bones, surf and dry leaves).

In his stress on the necessary artificiality of art and representation, Walcott also emphasizes that his characters, including the first-person narrator (and indeed all human selves) are fictions. When he first introduces Major Plunkett in chapter 5, he recounts the latter's war experiences and tells us of the wound Plunkett received in the desert:

> This wound I have stitched into Plunkett's character:
> He has to be wounded, affliction is one theme
> of this work, this fiction, since every 'I' is a
>
> fiction finally. Phantom narrator, resume

(p. 28)

In chapter 53, similarly, the narrator depicts his own presence at Maud Plunkett's funeral, but then goes on to tell the reader:

> I was both there and not there. I was attending
> the funeral of a character I'd created;
> the fiction of her life needed a good ending
>
> as much as mine

(p. 266)

The narrator's presence at the fictional funeral of a fictional character inevitably makes him, too, a fiction.

Devices such as the ones I have been discussing inevitably place the act of representation at the forefront. Yet there is unease about representation as well, an unease which takes a number of forms. One is a misgiving that he might simply be using the poor people he writes about as fodder for his art, wallowing in nostalgia or operating as an economically privileged voyeur:

> Didn't I want the poor
> to stay in the same light so that I could transfix
> them in amber, the afterglow of an empire
>
> preferring a shed of palm-thatch with tilted sticks
> to that blue bus-stop?

(p. 227)

He goes on to castigate himself:

> Why hallow that pretence
> of preserving what they left, the hypocrisy
> of loving them from hotels, a biscuit-tin fence
>
> smothered in love-vines, scenes to which I was attached
> as blindly as Plunkett with his remorseful research?
> Art is History's nostalgia, it prefers a thatched
>
> roof to a concrete factory, and the huge church
> above a bleached village.

(p. 228)

Elsewhere, contemplating 'that other Europe / of mausoleum muse-ums', with its fountains and statues and tritons, he concludes:

> Tell that to a slave from the outer regions
> of their fraying empires, what power lay in the work
> of forgiving fountains with naiads and lions.

(p. 205)

At other times, he goes even further, moving beyond this fear that art might be a betrayal of those who suffer into a questioning of the act of representation as such. Immediately after the passage about the 'Homeric repetition' which I discussed earlier, Plunkett has an encounter with Helen which forces on him a realization of the unsatis-factoriness of language. Catching her in the act of trying on a bracelet belonging to his wife, he is unable to do or say anything. Paralysed by Helen's power over him, and experiencing a sudden wave of pleasure and passion, he is aware that 'the passionless books / did not contain smell, eyes, the long black arm' (p. 96).

His own poetry, concludes the narrator at one point, is no different from Plunkett's historical research. Although they use 'opposing stratagems', they are engaged in essentially the same task through the way they represent and magnify Helen. He speculates about an alternative:

> Why not see Helen
>
> as the sun saw her, with no Homeric shadow,
> swinging her plastic sandals on that beach alone,
> as fresh as the sea-wind? Why make the smoke a door?

(p. 271)

Castigating himself for the 'echoes' circulating in his head, the parallels he keeps drawing between what is in front of him and literary precursors, he asks

> when would I not hear the Trojan War
> in two fishermen cursing in Ma Kilman's shop?
> When would my head shake off its echoes like a horse
>
> shaking off a wreath of flies? When would it stop,
> the echo in the throat, insisting, 'Omeros';
> when would I enter that light beyond metaphor?
>
> (p. 271)

Here the wreath, as both poetic laurel and funerary symbol, links poetry with death, possibly implying that poetry kills its subjects through representation; and the word 'echo' further emphasizes the secondariness of art. This idea that the real Helen is being distorted and replaced by her 'shadow' links the narrator with Achille and Hector, since, early in the poem we are told: 'The duel of these fishermen / was over a shadow and its name was Helen' (p. 17).

The desire to see Helen without a 'Homeric shadow', as the sun sees her, to 'enter that light beyond metaphor': this is a desire to be beyond all kinds of symbolization and representation, beyond language – or at least beyond a language that does not inevitably and imperceptibly distort the wholeness or pure being of the object (which all human language does). Some years before *Omeros*, in poem XL of *Midsummer*, Walcott had used the same image of light to depict this place beyond language:

> On a light-angled wall,
> through the clear, soundless pane, one sees a speech
> that calls to us, but is beyond our powers,
> composed of O's from a reflected bridge,
> the language of white, ponderous clouds convening
> over aerials, spires, rooftops, water towers.[28]

The pane of glass here embodies a complex of meanings. It is a channel of perception (it allows him to see the light on the wall), a barrier (it is 'soundless', cutting off the noise of the external world) and, in its clarity as well as its soundlessness (now seen in a different aspect), it may also represent a pure or transparent language that will allow complete comprehension of the object. In this last sense, the soundlessness could also signal the impossibility of the desire for such a language, since no human language can fulfil this desire. Beyond language there is only silence. The clear glass had figured earlier in the poem as well:

> Through the cleaned glass I watch a sparrow perch
> on a black branch with a tattered crimson fringe
> on some tree I can't name, though I am sure
> Sparrow could sing it like a citizen.[29]

Here the glass allows him to perceive the tree physically, but he is simultaneously cut off from it by his inability to give it a name. He is conscious of the imperfection of language (or at least of his language, since the calypsonian Sparrow can 'sing it'): although he cannot name it precisely, he does have some rough words which will encompass at least part of the tree ('a black branch with a tattered crimson fringe'). Rei Terada, who discusses this poem and others from *Midsummer*, comments that 'light is an "untranslatable" language, whereas the poet needs a translatable one'. This, I think, is only part of the picture. Light is in fact translatable – by means of the *word* 'light', for instance – but like all translations and, Walcott is suggesting, all representation, this version is imperfect. In a self-undoing gesture, what Walcott is expressing *in language* is the desire to be beyond language, to arrive at a state, which, as Terada notes, is not possible for us: 'A wordless, imageless suspension would mean oblivion'. The answer to Walcott's question 'Why not see Helen / as the sun saw her?' is that 'we are not the sun'.[30]

These aspects of the poem were pointed out by Walcott himself in his talk 'Reflections on *Omeros*', where he emphasized the way that the poem 'accuses itself of vanity, of the vanity of poetry, of the vanity of the narrator', and argued that 'to get beyond art is the ideal of the artist', describing the end of Dante's *Paradiso* as an example of 'a light that is ... beyond art'.[31] What can the aspiration to this unattainable condition, this undistorting language of light possibly mean? Perhaps it is the vision not of Walcott's second Adam, but of the first one. This Adam's language, which existed before Babel, is imagined as a seamless, transparent connection of word and object. George Steiner, like Walcott, uses the imagery of light and glass to describe it: 'The tongue of Eden was like a flawless glass; a light of total understanding streamed through it.'[32]

It is true that the idea of a single pre-Babel language is a myth unsupported by any empirical evidence, and, as Douglas Robinson argues, can be both 'nostalgic' and 'eschatological', as well as being potentially dangerous.[33] Yet it is a myth which also embodies that aspiration to total understanding which Steiner describes. Walter Benjamin's version of it is the idea of a 'pure language', which I have discussed before in this book. I do not want to go over the same ground here, but there is one striking link with the aspirations that Walcott is depicting in the passages I have quoted, and with 'The Antilles'. In the course of trying to explain what he means by the idea of a pure language beyond the 'constant state of flux' which all existing languages display, Benjamin uses an image which bears a startling resemblance to Walcott's comparison of Caribbean cultures with the reassembled fragments of a broken vase:

> Fragments of a vessel which are to be glued together must match one another in the smallest details, although they need not be like one another. In the same way a translation, instead of resembling the meaning of the original, must lovingly and in detail incorporate the original's mode of signification, thus making both the original and the translation recognizable as fragments of a greater language, just as fragments are part of a vessel.[34]

This seems to imply that the points of suture are visible, otherwise we would not recognize the fragments as fragments. And – reverting for a moment to *Omeros* – one way of making us aware of this, of enhancing the visibility of the fragments is through devices such as those Walcott uses: the multiple layers of narrative, the stress on artifice, the repetition of motifs (together with explicit acts of drawing attention to the notion of 'Homeric repetition' or 'webbed connection'), the insistence on the self as fiction, the positioning of the narrator and so on. These are, surely, ways of incorporating the 'mode of signification' Benjamin refers to here.

Benjamin also precedes Walcott in using the image of light to aspire to a condition beyond this, to a condition of pure transparency: 'A real translation is transparent; it does not cover the original, does not block its light, but allows the pure language, as though reinforced by its own medium, to shine upon the original all the more fully'.[35] It is difficult to see how fragmentariness and transparency can coexist, how a translation (which is a fragment) can in fact be transparent, and not block the light of the original. The 'real translation' Benjamin refers to here can only be an unattainable ideal. Since my aim is not to unravel Benjamin's complex essay but to focus on questions relevant to *Omeros*, I do not want to strive here towards a reconciliation of the two, but to take the tension between fragmentariness and transparency as symptomatic of the same kind of division which appears in Walcott's poem as a contestation between the impurity of actual representation (the visibility of the means of representation, or what I have described as 'sutures') and the aspiration to move beyond those means into transparency. The tension, or even contradiction, between these two positions is, I think, a necessary or inevitable one, which is inherent in the very act of representation.

This contradiction is inevitable because of the nature of language. The much-discussed idea of the wound is one of the recurrent motifs in *Omeros* which I have not referred to so far.[36] It turns up in many different forms, physical, mental and metaphorical. Philoctete's wound, derived from the Homeric source (in *Omeros* it is created by a rusty anchor), is the most prominent of these. The wound is also the wound of slavery and colonialism: Philoctete believes that the 'swelling came from the chained ankles / of his grandfathers' (p. 19). Plunkett, who himself carries a war-wound, is wounded again by his wife's death, and slowly healed (p. 309). Achille's pain at the affair between Helen and Hector is likened to Philoctete's shin wound (p. 40). Yet in *Omeros* the wound is also the cure. The flower from which Ma Kilman makes the concoction that cures Philoctete is a wound, because 'The mulch it / was rooted in carried the smell, when it gangrened, / of Philoctete's cut' (pp. 237–8), an idea repeated a few pages later: 'the wound of the flower, its gangrene, its rage / festering for centuries, reeked with corrupted blood' (p. 244). 'The wound has found her own cure', writes Walcott (p. 248). Similarly, speaking of himself and Philoctete, he says 'we shared the one wound, the same cure' (p. 295), where the apposition suggests again that the wound is the same as the cure.

Ultimately, it is language which is both wound and cure: 'Like Philoctete's wound, this language carries its cure, / its radiant affliction' (p. 323).[37] Earlier, the narrator has referred to 'the wound of a language I'd no wish to remove' (p. 270). Language is a wound partly because the one that Walcott is using is a legacy of colonial history, and a cure because it allows the writer to deal with the pain of the wound. But there is a more general sense in which language is both cure and wound: it simultaneously enables us to see, and, because it is always and inevitably a partial vision, it prevents us from seeing in some complete and unattainable sense, some form of the Adamic vision. As Terada says, 'writing – substituting figuration for presence – marks the site of perpetually abandoned presence'.[38] These different aspects of language as wound and cure return us to the image embodied in the reassembled vase, which both carries the scars of the breakage and is a sign of healing. This image is also, I have argued, an image for the poem itself, which is stitched together and shows its seams.

This is why nothingness is also something, and why amnesia is both scar and opportunity.

This instability of language and text is partly a product of the fragmented nature of Caribbean history, which is why, perhaps, in those words of Benítez-Rojo I quoted at the beginning, 'The Caribbean poem and novel are ... projects that communicate their own turbulence, their own clash, and their own void'. But the instability is also the constant toing and froing between object and representation, the simultaneity of figuration with absence described by Terada. In its turbulence, language is like that pervasive presence in Walcott's poems – the sea. It is no surprise, then, to find that he repeatedly links the sea with writing, not only in *Omeros*, but elsewhere too. In 'The Schooner *Flight*' (*CP*, pp. 345–61), the sailor Shabine is a poet (poet and sailor are also linked in *Omeros* [p. 291]). In 'Sea Grapes' (*CP*, p. 297), which I quoted earlier, 'the great hexameters come / to the conclusions of exhausted surf'. Poem XLVIII of *Midsummer* concludes: 'a scepter / swayed by the surf, the scansion of the sea'.[39] And in another one of those self-reflexive moments which permeate *Omeros*, Walcott describes the sea as 'an epic where every line was erased / yet freshly written in sheets of exploding surf' (p. 296). Paul Breslin notes that while 'a thoroughly erased surface is indistinguishable, to the eye, from one never written upon', nevertheless 'to describe it as erased is to reveal one's awareness of the past', since 'a truly Adamic consciousness would describe an erased surface as blank'.[40] Erasure is therefore a mark of the second Adam, who is able to create new things from the fragmented remnants of the past. In those lines from *Omeros*, the Caribbean, like Nehru's India, is a palimpsestic culture.

Walcott contrasts the way the past is recorded in other cultures (Europe in particular) with the way that it is recorded in the Caribbean, often using the statue or architecture as an emblem for the former, and various aspects of nature, including the sea, for the latter. In Lisbon, for instance, having crossed his meridian, he notices the statue of a 'bronze horseman' and 'the Empire's plazas', but is immediately aware of the way that the Caribbean differs from this:

> For those to whom history is the presence
>
> of ruins, there is a green nothing. No bell tower utters
> its flotilla of swallows memorizing an alphabet,
> no cobbles crawl towards the sea. We think of the past
>
> as better forgotten than fixed with stony regret.
>
> (p. 192)

In cities such as Istanbul and Venice, he realizes that 'what I preferred / was not statues but the bird in the statue's hair' (p. 204).

But the contrast between the fixed statue and the mobile sea is not straightforward, since Walcott complicates it by suggesting elsewhere, in what seems a direct contradiction, that the sea and nature in general cannot erase the past:

> It is not that History is obliterated by this sunrise. It is there in Antillean geography, in the vegetation itself. The sea sighs with the drowned from the Middle Passage, the butchery of its aborigines, Carib and Aruac and Taino, bleeds in the scarlet of the immortelle, and even the actions of surf on sand cannot erase the African memory or the lances of cane as a green prison where indentured Asians, the ancestors of Felicity, are still serving time.
>
> (*A*, p. 81)

The sea is also the location and memory of a deep wound: it was where the slave ships had plied their trade, the surface on which they had, in the etymological sense of the word, 'translated' their victims. In *Omeros*, Achille is brought face to face with this realization, when, diving in search of lost treasure from a wreck which is believed to lie on the sea bed, he realizes that the sea is the repository of Empire and slavery: 'coins with the profiles of Iberian kings', dead bodies 'that had perished in the crossing'. He becomes aware that 'This was not a world meant for the living' (p. 45).

By juxtaposing this meaning of the sea with the idea of it as an epic that is constantly being erased and rewritten, it seems to emerge as yet another image of the wound and the cure being the same, because it is simultaneously the repository and erasure of the past. The erased (or more, strictly, partially erased and fragmented) history has to be acknowledged, since it haunts the present, but to remain entrenched in it is dangerous, since it can lead to what Walcott describes in 'The Muse of History' as the literatures of remorse and revenge. The sea, in Paul Breslin's words, is a 'trope of memory-as-forgetting, hoarding the past in its depths, but erasing, with each surge of generative energy, the marks of human presence on the shore'.[41]

The sea is, finally, a way of focusing that more general wound, that unsatisfactoriness of representation which I discussed earlier, since, like light, it outstrips language. The last line of the poem is given over to it: 'When he left the beach the sea was still going on' (p. 325). This is a reminder that his poem is, and will always be, incomplete, as Walcott has realized a few pages earlier: 'So much left unspoken / by my chirping nib!' (p. 321). This sense of incompletion at the end of the poem returns us to the idea of the poem as artifice and to translation.

On one level, the poem is engaged in straddling meridians, translating or carrying across different cultural fragments in order to make them comprehensible to each other, to the narrator, to the people of the Caribbean, to the reader. On the linguistic level, it is engaged with a different kind of translation. Although I have appeared to shift during the course of this chapter between translation and language (or representation) as such, seemingly passing over differences between them, the two are related in ways that go beyond the widely acknowledged view that a theory of translation must involve a theory of language. For Walcott, as we have seen, there are the human languages that we have, and there is another, unattainable one, which we might call, in the image that he uses, the language of light or the language of the sun. Terada argues that the latter languages are untranslatable. My own contention has been that the language of poetry is a translation of the language of light, but that it is marked by the unsatisfactoriness of all translation. If, as the Italian saying *tradutore, traditore* has it, to translate is to betray, Walcott seems to go a step further. *Omeros* is haunted by the sense that all representation is betrayal; yet it is the only tool available to try and translate ('carry across') the language of light. The poem seems to endorse Octavio Paz's claim that 'language itself, in its very essence, is already a translation – first from the non-verbal world, and then, because each sign and each phrase is a translation of another sign, another phrase'.[42] In oscillating between these two positions, writing a poem which aspires to go, in Walcott's own words, 'beyond art', while at the same time questioning it and emphasizing its artificiality, Walcott finds himself in what I described earlier in this chapter as a 'translational structure', a structure of sameness and difference, the dilemma of all translation, whether cultural or linguistic. Ideally, he should be able to see Helen 'as the sun saw her', to merge perception and what is being perceived, to dissolve the barrier between language and its object (sameness), and yet every attempt to represent her is a symptom of her absence, of what George Steiner calls the 'resistant particularity of the "other"' (difference). Her 'real presence', whatever that might be, will always be elusive. That is why the poem concludes with a final self-undoing, an ending which is not an ending, since the sea is still 'going on', and no poem can ever match that.

Conclusion

It is difficult to reach any conclusions that will apply neatly to the diverse writers and cultures discussed in the previous chapters. Nevertheless, certain recurrent themes have seemed to emerge during the course of writing this book, occasionally taking me in directions that I had not expected when setting out. Some may feel that the term 'translation' has been stretched and pulled beyond the limits of acceptability – even, as in the chapter on Derek Walcott, shading over into representation more generally. This extension of the term has occurred in part because a theory of translation is inseparable from a theory about the nature and workings of language, and in part because of the increasing awareness that interlingual difference is inseparable from cultural difference. Steiner and Schleiermacher, amongst others, have argued that we should think of translation in broad terms as a phenomenon which need not be confined to a process occurring between entirely different languages. These two theorists of translation speak, for instance, of communication between different regions and different classes, or our reading of the past, as requiring translation.

I have taken as a central aspect of translation a particular kind of structure, which, in the previous chapter, I called a 'translational structure', that is to say, something which is marked simultaneously by similarity and difference. The case for this has been made clearly, I think, by Clifford Geertz, who says of the relationship between ourselves (whoever 'we' may be in this case) and those who are culturally distant from us: 'The differences *do* go far deeper than an easy men-are-men humanism permits itself to see, and the similarities *are* far too substantial for an easy other-beasts, other-mores relativism to dissolve.' While this may not, he says, be 'precisely the most comfortable position, nor even a wholly coherent one, it is, I think, the only one that can be effectively defended'.[1] Such a structure creates a dialectic or antinomy, a toing and froing between the two sides, so that no stable resting point is possible.

The further shading over of translation into representation is a product of a sense that the latter of its very nature is a translational structure: even while it depicts something, it simultaneously marks the original's absence. Octavio Paz, whom I quoted briefly in the first and the previous chapters, sees translation as being more or less coextensive with representation, and with what has more recently come to be known as intertextuality (although of course he retains its more restricted sense of a process which involves different languages):

> Thanks to translation, we become aware that our neighbors do not speak and think as we do. On the one hand, the world is presented to us as a collection of similarities; on the other, as a growing heap of texts, each slightly different from the one that came before it: translations of translations of translations. Each text is unique, yet at the same time it is the translation of another text. No text can be completely original because language itself, in its very essence, is already a translation – first from the nonverbal world, and then, because each sign and phrase is a translation of another sign, another phrase. However, the inverse of this reasoning is also entirely valid. All texts are originals because each translation has its own distinctive character. Up to a point, each translation is a creation and thus constitutes a unique text.[2]

Certainly this coextensiveness of translation and representation comes through in *Omeros*, where language is conceived of as an inadequate translation of an elusive reality, a feeling which is rather similar to Benjamin's awareness of the limits of any particular translation or language in relation to the 'pure language'.

One specific aspect of the translational structure is summed up in A. K. Ramanujan's phrase 'reflexive worlds'.[3] An image in a mirror has that combination of similarity to and difference from the object or person reflected. Octavio Paz, again, has expressed some aspects of this doubleness: 'In the mirror the body becomes simultaneously visible and untouchable'.[4] In one sense a mirror enables us to see the body clearly – even things which we would never otherwise see, such as our eyes – and in another sense it makes the body utterly remote; the image in the mirror is not how we experience our own bodies or those of others. This reflexivity came particularly to the fore in the chapter on Ramanujan and in the analysis of Caribbean cultures by

Glissant and Benítez-Rojo outlined at the beginning of the previous chapter. India's different cultures are, in Ramanujan's analysis, things which stand to each other in a relationship partly of similarity and partly of difference; they mirror, distort, parody, resemble and subvert one another. Reflexivity can also be seen as a feature of the various cultures contained in the Caribbean and in Walcott's *Omeros*, where the different fragments coexist not in a synthesis but in a mode which both joins and separates, and where the process of creolization is also a process of mirroring, distorted mirroring, resemblance and subversion of the original cultures. In different forms, and using metaphors other than the visual, the process can be seen in the work of other poets as well. Seamus Heaney's idea of the acoustic, for instance, shifts the phenomenon to the dimension of sound. If reflexivity is a hall of mirrors, 'acoustic' suggests something more like an echo chamber or the well with its reverberating sounds which he depicts in 'Personal Helicon'. Heaney's theorizing as well as his practice position poetry so that 'further language' is always hovering somewhere on the outskirts, setting up resonances for the actual work in front of the reader – as Ireland and the modern world are acoustics for his translation of *Beowulf*. Ireland, again, and Europe in general constitute acoustics for MacNeice's cultural translations of India, while Walcott's Caribbean fragments can also be seen as providing acoustics for each other.

A second theme which recurred as this book developed was the resistance to being translated which marks one of the limits of translation. Another way of putting this point might be that resistance is the embodiment of that difference which clings to even the most successful translations, or perhaps *especially* the most successful translations, as George Steiner claims. These traces of difference can, but need not, be marked by that method which translation theorists such as Lawrence Venuti call 'foreignization'. In the first chapter I drew briefly on Prasenjit Gupta's distinction between 'surface' and 'deep' resistance in translation. The former, he points out, 'has more to do with language itself, with meaning and sound and syntax', and the latter 'more with extra-linguistic, underlying constructs such as manners, relationships, world-views'.[5]

Much of this book has been concerned with various kinds of deep resistance. Judith Wright is particularly aware of the difference in world views between white and Aboriginal Australians. Her attempts to represent Australia are often permeated by a resistance which reduces sound and poetry to fragments or feeble remnants, in a structure that reiterates what the European invasion of Australia did to the Aboriginal cultures in that country. Sometimes, as I have argued in the chapter on her poetry, her sense of difference and her consciousness of the destruction leads her towards an embodiment of the most extreme form of resistance, which is silence. Although, in her own words, 'Silence might be best', something still survives to sing and speak, even if what comes out is a whisper or a 'broken chant'. Les Murray, on the other hand, makes bold claims for the fusion of Australian cultures, and for poetry in general, but we find nevertheless that a poem such as 'The Buladelah-Taree Holiday Song Cycle', which consciously aims at that fusion, still embodies, almost despite itself, the difference between Aboriginal and white Australian cultures. And in his 'Translations from the Natural World', the sense of difference is much more acute. He is aware, as in the concluding poem, 'Possum's Nocturnal Day', that, finally, language cannot translate the flora and fauna he is depicting, and indeed that language is what distinguishes human beings from the creatures. For the latter, language is unnecessary, since, in the words of the possum, 'nothing is apart enough for language'. In the poem which precedes this one, 'From Where We Live on Presence', the beetle speaking the poem claims that 'I translate into segments, laminates, / cachou eyes, pungent chemistry, cusps. But I remain the true word for me.' Its 'language' is its whole being. Or, as it has said earlier in the poem, 'Beetlehood itself was my expression'; and of course no human words can capture that beetlehood, which will always and ultimately evade linguistic representation. Similarly, *Omeros* brings us up against the limits of representation: Helen escapes translation into language, as does the sea, which is 'still going on' when the poems stops.

In Ramanujan's poetry, resistance takes a number of forms. A characteristic feature of his poems, I tried to suggest in my discussion of them, is a structure which resists or fragments meaning in the very act of conveying it (by circling round the subject from a variety of viewpoints, for instance). Ramanujan's notion of 'reflexivity' implies a sense of dialogue rather than silence between traditions and cultures, and, indeed, he sometimes sees Bakhtin's notion of dialogism as an analogue.[6] Yet reflexivity, like dialogism, also implies some form of resistance to translation, since both can involve quarrelsome as well as cooperative relationships. In some cases here perhaps resistance emanates more from the receiving culture than from the providing one. The latter does not pass over into the former unchanged, as Vicente Rafael's account of the reception of Christianity in the Philippines makes clear.[7] In Rafael's analysis, resistance is embodied in the changes wrought upon the hegemonic culture and language even as they pass over into Tagalog. The cultural object or text in question is refracted and 'transcreated', as is the case in India when epics from the hegemonic Sanskrit culture are rendered into the various vernaculars. And in the resulting combination of similarity and difference there is another version of a translational structure. Ramanujan's 'Prayers to Lord Murugan', I have claimed, can be seen as a radical transcreation of an earlier model.

Perhaps another way of putting these points is to reiterate the old truth that while things may be lost in translation – Helen's 'reality' in *Omeros*, the 'true' India in MacNeice, amongst other examples discussed in this book – something can also be found. Of course, translation can be used for reprehensible purposes, as in the American cases Eric Cheyfitz looks at in his *The Poetics of Imperialism*. Yet translation can tell us something about another culture (though never the whole truth) while also telling us something about our own, something we may not have been able to articulate, explore or develop without that process of translation. Clifford Geertz quotes some lines from the American poet James Merrill's beautiful poem 'Lost in Translation' which express eloquently this double sense:

> Lost, is it, buried? One more missing piece?

> But nothing's lost. Or else: all is translation
> And every bit of us is lost in it
> (Or found – I wander through the ruin of S
> Now and then, wondering at the peacefulness)[8]

The poem continues and concludes in a way that shows waste turning into gain, the lost past into a creative memory:

> And in that loss a self-effacing tree,
> Color of context, imperceptibly
> Rustling with its angel, turns the waste
> To shade and fiber, milk and memory.[9]

Notes

Introduction

1. Some of the criticism of these three poets is cited in the chapters on their work. There have also been studies confined within the framework of individual nations, such as works by Bruce King (on India) and Paul Kane (on Australia), which are cited in the chapters on Ramanujan, Wright and Murray and listed in the bibliography. Works which attempt to cross national boundaries include Jahan Ramazani, *The Hybrid Muse: Postcolonial Poetry in English* (Chicago, IL: University of Chicago Press, 2001), Rajeev S. Patke, *Postcolonial Poetry in English* (Oxford: Oxford University Press, 2006) and James Wieland, *The Ensphering Mind: History, Myth and Fiction in the Poetry of Allen Curnow, Nissim Ezekiel, A. D. Hope, A. M. Klein, Christopher Okigbo, and Derek Walcott* (Washington: Three Continents Press, 1988). Patke makes similar points about the place of postcolonial poetry in literary studies (p. vii).
2. My expression 'colonial divide' is a provisional way of speaking, since this whole book is in effect a study of how that divide is constantly being transgressed.
3. Mary Louise Pratt, *Imperial Eyes: Travel Writing and Transculturation* (London: Routledge, 1992), p. 6.
4. Seamus Heaney, *An Open Letter* (Derry: Field Day, 1983). The anthology in question was *The Penguin Anthology of Contemporary British Poetry* (Harmondsworth: Penguin, 1982).
5. Seamus Heaney, 'Through-Other Places, Through-Other Times: The Irish Poet and Britain', in *Finders Keepers: Selected Prose 1971–2001* (London: Faber and Faber, 2002), pp. 364–82 (p. 368).
6. See, for instance, Ngugi's *Decolonising the Mind: The Politics of Language in African Literature* (London: James Currey, 1986).
7. Heaney, 'Through-Other Places', p. 366.
8. Terence Patrick Dolan, *A Dictionary of Hiberno-English: The Irish Use of English* (Dublin: Gill and Macmillan, 1998), p. 271.
9. Heaney, 'Through-Other Places', p. 379.
10. Peter Hulme, 'Including America', *Ariel*, 26. 1 (January 1995), pp. 117–23 (p. 120).
11. Bart Moore-Gilbert, *Postcolonial Theory: Context, Practices, Politics* (London: Verso, 1997), p. 12.
12. See note 3 of chapter 1.

1 Cultural Translation

1. A sample of well-known essays on the term might include Ella Shohat, 'Notes on the "Post-Colonial"', *Social Text*, 31–2 (Spring 1992), pp. 99–113; Arif Dirlik, 'The Postcolonial Aura: Third World Criticism in the Age of Global Capitalism', *Critical Inquiry*, 20 (1993–4), pp. 328–56; Anne McClintock, 'The

Angel of Progress: Pitfalls of the Term "Post-colonialism"', *Social Text*, 31–2 (Spring 1992), pp. 84–98; Aijaz Ahmad, 'The Politics of Literary Postcoloniality', *Race and Class*, 36.3 (January 1995), pp. 1–20; Stuart Hall, 'When Was "The Post-Colonial?" Thinking at the Limit', in *The Post-Colonial Question: Common Skies, Divided Horizons*, ed. Iain Chambers and Lidia Curti (London: Routledge, 1996), pp. 242–60; and Vijay Mishra and Bob Hodge, 'What is Post(-)colonialism?', *Textual Practice*, 5 (1991), pp. 399–414.

2. I have in mind Vicente L. Rafael's *Contracting Colonialism: Translation and Christian Conversion in Tagalog Society under Early Spanish Rule* (1988; Durham, NC: Duke University Press, 1993). A concise discussion of metaphoric uses of translation is Ruth Evans's article 'Metaphor of Translation', in the *Routledge Encyclopedia of Translation Studies*, ed. Mona Baker, assisted by Kirsten Malmkjær (London: Routledge, 1998), pp. 149–53.

3. Homi Bhabha, *The Location of Culture* (London; Routledge, 1994). Essays in which he deals with cultural translation include 'The Commitment to Theory' (pp. 19–39) and 'How Newness Enters the World: Postmodern Space, Postcolonial Times and the Trials of Cultural Translation' (pp. 212–35). As a rough idea of what I mean by 'mainstream' in this context, I would point to the student-oriented text *Beginning Postcolonialism* by John McLeod (Manchester: Manchester University Press, 2000). This is not a criticism of McLeod's helpful book; I intend only to indicate that the topics discussed in it are generally taken to be the central areas of postcolonial theory. Another introductory book, Robert J. C. Young's *Postcolonialism: A Very Short Introduction* (Oxford: Oxford University Press, 2003) does discuss translation (chapter 7), but without really moving beyond the parameters of accounts such as Bhabha's.

4. Ethnographic essays relevant to postcolonialism include those in *Writing Culture: The Poetics and Politics of Ethnography*, ed. James Clifford and George E. Marcus (Berkeley: University of California Press, 1986). Talal Asad's 'The Concept of Cultural Translation in British Social Anthropology' in this book (pp. 141–64) is a well-known example. A convenient and compact guide to postcolonial translation studies is Douglas Robinson, *Translation and Empire: Postcolonial Theories Explained* (Manchester: St Jerome, 1997). In chapter 2 of *Siting Translation: History, Post-Structuralism and the Colonial Context* (Berkeley and Los Angeles: University of California Press, 1992), Tejaswani Niranjana offers a critique of how both translation studies and ethnography have failed to engage with postcolonial asymmetries of power but her primary emphasis falls on post-structuralism. Her book deals mainly with the work of Walter Benjamin, Paul de Man and Jacques Derrida.

5. Chapters 1 and 2 of Robinson, *Translation and Empire* summarize some of the issues involved here.

6. Some criticisms are outlined in Douglas Robinson's article 'Hermeneutic Motion', in *Routledge Encyclopedia of Translation Studies*, ed. Mona Baker, pp. 97–9.

7. George Steiner, *After Babel: Aspects of Language and Translation*, 3rd ed. (Oxford: Oxford University Press, 1998), p. 312.

8. Ibid., pp. 313, 314, 315, 316.

9. Ibid., p. 316.
10. Ibid., p. 317.
11. Ibid., pp. 316, 416.
12. Ibid., p. 318.
13. Ibid., pp. 318, 423.
14. Ibid., p. 121.
15. Ibid., p. 47.
16. Friedrich Schleiermacher, 'On the Different Methods of Translating', trans. Susan Bernofsky, in *The Translation Studies Reader*, 2nd ed., ed. Lawrence Venuti (London: Routledge, 2000), pp. 43–63 (p. 43).
17. Both the epistle and the address to the reader are conveniently reprinted in Douglas Robinson ed. *Western Translation Theory: From Herodotus to Nietzsche* (Manchester: St Jerome, 1997), pp. 131–5. The quotations can be found on pp. 131 and 134 respectively.
18. Schleiermacher, 'Different Methods', p. 49.
19. Walter Benjamin, 'The Task of the Translator: An Introduction to the Translation of Baudelaire's *Tableaux Parisiens*', in *Illuminations*, ed. Hannah Arendt, trans. Harry Zohn (London : Fontana, 1973), pp. 69–82 (p. 80). A full discussion of the two strategies and their implications can be found in Lawrence Venuti's *The Translator's Invisibility: A History of Translation* (London: Routledge, 1995).
20. Venuti, ed., *Translation Studies Reader*, p. 16.
21. Donald Davie, *Poetry in Translation* (Milton Keynes: Open University Press, 1975), p. 13.
22. Schleiermacher, 'Different Methods', p. 53.
23. Lawrence Venuti, Introduction to *Rethinking Translation: Discourse, Subjectivity, Ideology*, ed. Venuti (London: Routledge, 1992), pp. 1–17 (p. 5).
24. Eric Cheyfitz, *The Poetics of Imperialism: Translation and Colonization from* The Tempest *to* Tarzan (New York: Oxford University Press, 1991), p. 59.
25. Anthony Pym, 'Schleiermacher and the Problem of *Blendlinge*', *Translation and Literature*, 4 (1995), pp. 5–30 (p. 7).
26. Robinson, *Translation and Empire*, pp. 110–13, discusses a few other criticisms of a sharp distinction between domestication and foreignization, some of which draw on his earlier review 'Decolonizing Translation', *Translation and Literature*, 2 (1993), pp. 113–24.
27. Davie, *Poetry in Translation*, p. 13.
28. Ibid.
29. Godfrey Lienhardt, 'Modes of Thought', in E. E. Evans-Pritchard et al., *The Institutions of Primitive Society: A Series of Broadcast Talks* (Oxford: Blackwell, 1954), pp. 95–107 (pp. 96–7).
30. Ibid., pp. 97–8.
31. Niranjana, *Siting Translation*, pp. 69–70.
32. Clifford Geertz, 'Found in Translation: On the Social History of the Moral Imagination', in *Local Knowledge: Further Essays in Interpretive Anthropology* (1983; London: Fontana, 1993), pp. 36–54 (p. 44).
33. Clifford Geertz, '"From the Native's Point of View": On the Nature of Anthropological Understanding', in *Local Knowledge*, pp. 55–70 (p. 70).

34. A cogent account of this problem of power is Asad's 'The Concept of Cultural Translation' (see note 4).
35. Samia Mehrez, 'Translation and the Postcolonial Experience: The Francophone North African Text', in Venuti, *Rethinking Translation*, pp. 120–38 (p. 121).
36. Cheyfitz, *Poetics of Imperialism*, pp. 51–2.
37. Robinson, 'Decolonizing Translation', p. 121. This passage is also incorporated into his *Translation and Empire*, p. 108.
38. Octavio Paz, 'Translation: Literature and Letters', trans. Irene del Corral, in *Theories of Translation: An Anthology of Essays from Dryden to Derrida*, ed. Rainer Schulte and John Biguenet (Chicago, IL: University of Chicago Press, 1992), pp. 152–62 (p. 154).
39. This book has recently been retranslated: O. Chandumenon, *Indulekha*, trans. Anitha Devasia (New Delhi: Oxford University Press, 2005). Chandumenon's account of the origins of the novel is given in the 'Preface to the First Edition of *Indulekha*', pp. 237–40.
40. The classic study in English of the development of fiction in Indian languages is Meenakshi Mukherjee's *Realism and Reality: The Novel and Society in India* (Delhi: Oxford University Press, 1985; repr. with corrections, 1994).
41. Robinson, *Translation and Empire*, p. 106.
42. Rafael, *Contracting Colonialism*, p. 211.
43. Helpful discussions of these ideas are Else Ribeiro Pires Vieira, 'Liberating Calibans: Readings of *Antropofagia* and Haroldo de Campos's Poetics of Transcreation', in *Post-colonial Translation: Theory and Practice*, ed. Susan Bassnett and Harish Trivedi (London: Routledge, 1999), pp. 95–114; and Bassnett's *Comparative Literature: A Critical Introduction* (Oxford: Blackwell, 1993), pp. 153–6.
44. The translation is by Mary Ann Caws and Claudia Caliman and can be found in *Exquisite Corpse: A Journal of Letters and Life*, Cyber Issue 11 (Spring/Summer 2002), http://www.corpse.org/issue_11/manifestos/deandrade.html (accessed 3 June 2006).
45. These extracts from de Campos's 'Da tradução como criação e como crítica' are quoted in Vieira, 'Liberating Calibans', p. 103.
46. Quoted by Vieira, 'Liberating Calibans', p. 95.
47. From Vieira's unpublished Ph. D. Thesis, *Por uma teoria pós-moderna da tradução*, quoted in Bassnett, *Comparative Literature*, p. 155.
48. Harish Trivedi, 'Translating Culture vs. Cultural Translation', *91st Meridian* (May 2005), http://www.uiowa.edu/~iwp/91st/may2005/pdfs/trivedi.pdf (accessed June 3 2006), pp. 5, 6 and 7.
49. Steiner, *After Babel*, p. 397.
50. Prasenjit Gupta, introduction to *Indian Errant: Selected Stories of Nirmal Verma*, trans. Gupta (New Delhi: Indialog, 2002), pp. xxxviii, xl. Surface and deep resistance are discussed on pp. xxxv–xlii. The pagination here is that of the bilingual hardback edition. The paperback edition, which prints only the translations of the stories, puts this material in an afterword.

2   Songlines: Judith Wright and Belonging

The following abbreviations are used in the text and notes for works by Judith Wright:

BI   *Because I Was Invited* (Melbourne: Oxford University Press, 1975)
CD   *The Cry for the Dead* (Melbourne: Oxford University Press, 1981)
CP   *Collected Poems 1942–1982* (Manchester: Carcanet, 1994)
GM   *The Generations of Men* (Sydney: Oxford University Press, 1959)
PAP *Preoccupations in Australian Poetry* (Melbourne: Oxford University Press, 1965)

If no abbreviation is given after a quotation, the source will be readily identifiable from the context.

1. Stuart Macintyre, *A Concise History of Australia*, 2nd ed. (Cambridge: Cambridge University Press, 2004), p. 3.
2. This is from 'The Broken Links', originally published in the Tasmanian Wilderness Calendar for 1981 and later reproduced first in 'Darkie Point: New England National Park', *Notes and Furphies*, no. 12 (April 1984), pp. 6–7 and again in Wright's *Born of the Conquerors* (Canberra: Aboriginal Studies Press, 1991), pp. 29–30. The extract cited is on p. 30 of the last. Two of her prose books, *The Cry for the Dead* and *We Call for a Treaty* (Sydney: Fontana, 1985) deal at length with the history of the relationship between white and Aboriginal Australians. The former is a more personal and impassioned approach to the question. The latter deals mainly with the work of the Aboriginal Treaty Committee, of which Wright was a member, but includes considerable historical and legal material in the process.
3. Marcus Clarke, preface to Adam Lindsay Gordon, *Poems* (London: R. A. Thompson, 1905), pp. vii–xi (p. x).
4. Ibid., p. ix.
5. A. D. Hope, *Collected Poems 1930–1970*, rev. ed. (Sydney: Angus and Robertson, 1972), p. 13.
6. Clarke, preface to Gordon, *Poems*, p. xi. Italics added.
7. Ibid., p. ix.
8. See Simon Ryan, *The Cartographic Eye: How Explorers Saw Australia* (Cambridge: Cambridge University Press, 1996), pp. 123–7.
9. See Judith Wright, 'The Upside-down Hut', *Australian Letters*, 3.4 (June 1961), pp. 30–4 (p. 33).
10. Ibid., p. 31.
11. Adam Shoemaker, *Black Words, White Page: Aboriginal Literature, 1929–1988* (St Lucia: University of Queensland Press, 1989), p. 201.
12. Judith Wright, 'Landscape and Dreaming', *Daedalus*, 114.1 (Winter 1985), pp. 29–56 (pp. 31–2).
13. Bob Hodge and Vijay Mishra, *Dark Side of the Dream: Australian Literature and the Postcolonial Mind* (Sydney: Allen and Unwin, 1990), p. 52.
14. Paul Kane, 'Judith Wright and Silence', in *Australian Poetry: Romanticism and Negativity* (Cambridge: Cambridge University Press, 1996), pp. 156–69; David Brooks, 'A Land Without Lendings: Judith Wright, Kenosis and Australian Vision', *Southerly*, 60.2 (2000), pp. 51–64; Kevin Hart, 'Darkness and Lostness: How to Read a Poem by Judith Wright', in *Imagining Australia: Literature and*

Culture in the New World, ed. Judith Ryan and Chris Wallace-Crabbe (Cambridge, MA: Harvard University Committee on Australian Studies, 2004), pp. 305–19.

15. Brooks, 'Land Without Lendings', p. 60.
16. Kane, *Australian Poetry*, p. 159.
17. Amongst other critics who deal with Wright's Romantic inheritance is Shirley Walker, *Flame and Shadow: A Study of Judith Wright's Poetry* (St Lucia: University of Queensland Press, 1991), pp. 9–10.
18. Quoted in Kane, *Australian Poetry*, p. 169.
19. Deborah Bird Rose, *Dingo Makes Us Human: Life and Land in an Australian Aboriginal Culture* (Cambridge: Cambridge University Press, 2000), pp. 12–13.
20. Bruce Chatwin, *The Songlines* (London: Jonathan Cape, 1987). A clear discussion of the mythological tracks can be found in A. P. Elkin, *The Australian Aborigines: How to Understand Them*, 3rd ed. (Sydney: Angus and Robertson, 1954), pp. 143–7. Two particular mythological tracks, one in the Western Desert, the other in northeast Arnhem Land are discussed by R. M. Berndt, 'Territoriality and the Problem of Demarcating Sociocultural Space', in *Tribes and Boundaries in Australia*, ed. Nicolas Peterson (Canberra: Australian Institute of Aboriginal Studies, 1976), pp. 133–61.
21. Mudrooroo Nyoongah, *Aboriginal Mythology* (London: Aquarian, 1994), p. 150. The italics are in the original and indicate a cross-reference to another entry in the book.
22. A sample of Jindyworobak writing, along with positive and negative criticism of their work, can be found in *The Jindyworobaks*, ed. Brian Elliott (St Lucia: University of Queensland Press, 1979). See, for instance, A. D. Hope's review 'Culture Corroboree', pp. 248–52. Wright's views can be found on pp. 268 and 278–80 (the latter is an extract from her essay 'Some Problems of Being An Australian Poet', in *BI*, pp. 49–58).
23. Lynne Hume, *Ancestral Power: The Dreaming, Consciousness and Aboriginal Australians* (Melbourne: Melbourne University Press, 2002), p. 92. Chapter 6 of this book discusses the functions of song in Aboriginal cultures.
24. Ibid., p. 93.
25. Rose, *Dingo Makes Us Human*, p. 44.
26. The allusion to *John* is noted by Walker, *Flame and Shadow*, p. 58, who interprets it as the 'primal creative life-force'.
27. Jonathan White, introduction to *Recasting the World: Writing after Colonialism*, ed. White (Baltimore: Johns Hopkins University Press, 1993), pp. 1–24 (pp. 12, 11, 13).
28. In 'Darkness and Lostness' (e.g., p. 309), Kevin Hart discusses Wright's poem 'The Lost Man' as an *imitatio Christi*.
29. Marian Theobald, 'Classroom Lament, by Judith Wright', *Sydney Morning Herald*, 19 October 1985, quoted by Susan McKernan, *A Question of Commitment: Australian Literature in the Twenty Years after the War* (Sydney: Allen and Unwin, 1989), p. 147.
30. Judith Wright, 'Reading and Nationalism', in *Going on Talking* (Springwood, NSW: Butterfly Books, 1992), pp. 45–7 (p. 47). She also points out here that the 'old man in question was in fact a mild religious maniac'.
31. Kane, *Australian Poetry*, p. 159.
32. The historical background to this poem is described in the article referred to in note 2 above.

33. Les Murray, *New Collected Poems* (Manchester: Carcanet, 2003), p. 93. The connection with the Aboriginal ancestors is pointed out by Murray in his essay 'The Human-Hair Thread', *The Paperbark Tree: Selected Prose* (Manchester: Carcanet, 1992), pp. 71–99 (p. 85). I discuss this poem in more detail in chapter 3.

34. Rose Lucas and Lyn McCredden, 'Through a Web of Language: Landscapes of Perception in the Poetry of Judith Wright', in *Bridgings: Readings in Australian Women's Poetry* (Melbourne: Oxford University Press, 1996), pp. 18–28 (p. 27).

35. The judgement can be found at http://www.austlii.edu.au/au/cases/cth/high_ct/175clr1.html (accessed 18 June 2006). The words quoted are in paragraph 63.

36. Richard White, *Inventing Australia: Images and Identity 1688–1980* (Sydney: Allen and Unwin, 1981), p. 9. The concept of the 'perversity' of Australia is also examined by Ryan, *Cartographic Eye*, pp. 105–12.

37. T. S. Eliot, *Collected Poems 1909–1962* (London: Faber and Faber, 1963), p. 194.

38. Steiner, *After Babel*, 3rd ed. (Oxford: Oxford University Press, 1998) p. 397.

39. Indira Karamcheti, 'Aimé Césaire's Subjective Geographies: Translating Place and the Difference it Makes', in *Between Languages and Cultures: Translation and Cross-Cultural Texts*, ed. Anuradha Dingwaney and Carol Maier (Pittsburgh: University of Pittsburgh Press, 1995), pp. 181–97 (p. 187). Opaque translation is also advocated by James Boyd White's essay 'On the Virtues of Not Understanding' in the same volume (pp. 333–9).

40. Karamcheti, 'Aimé Césaire's Subjective Geographies', pp. 188–9.

41. Steiner, *After Babel*, p. 65.

42. Ibid., p. 66.

43. Ibid., p. 497.

44. Walter Benjamin, 'The Task of the Translator: An Introduction to the Translation of Baudelaire's *Tableaux Parisiens*', in *Illuminations*, ed. Hannah Arendt, trans. Harry Zohn (London : Fontana, 1973), pp. 69–82 (pp. 76–77).

45. Ibid., p. 80.

3   Fusion and Translation: Les Murray's Australia

The following abbreviations are used in the text and notes for works by Les Murray:

NCP   *New Collected Poems* (Manchester: Carcanet, 2003)
PT   *The Paperbark Tree: Selected Prose* (Manchester: Carcanet, 1992)

If no abbreviation is given after a quotation, the source will be readily identifiable from the context.

1. The nature of Murray's relationship to the land is a complex matter, and I can only touch on a few aspects in this chapter. The subject has been discussed by, amongst others, Martin Leer and Lawrence Bourke, as cited later in these notes.

2. This kind of view is found in a number of places. An example is his contribution to *The Media Report*, an Australian Broadcasting Corporation programme, in June 2001. The transcript of this programme can be found on-line at http://www.abc.net.au/rn/mediareport/stories/2001/312656.htm# (accessed 7 June 2006).

3. Paul Kane discusses the genealogies of these views, linking them to Kant, Rudolf Otto and the Romantic tradition in general: 'Les Murray and Poetry's Otherworld', in *Australian Poetry: Romanticism and Negativity* (Cambridge: Cambridge University Press, 1996), pp. 185–202 (esp. pp. 185–91).

4. The word 'relegation' is used, for instance, in *PT*, p. 64, and 'convergence' on p. 96. Both terms are discussed by Paul Kane in 'Les Murray', *International Literature in English: Essays on the Major Writers*, ed. Robert L. Ross (New York: Garland, 1991), pp. 437–46, and in *Australian Poetry*, pp. 194–6.

5. 'The Dialectic of Dreams' (*NCP*, pp. 216–18) is one of the poems in which he also deals with the reason-dream opposition and its fusion.

6. For instance, *PT*, pp. 311–12.

7. In this respect, I would qualify Paul Kane's emphasis on immanence in his interesting discussion of this poem, 'An Absolutely Ordinary Rainbow' and 'The Broad Bean Sermon' (*Australian Poetry*, pp. 191–3).

8. Les Murray, *The Quality of Sprawl: Thoughts about Australia* (Sydney: Duffy and Snellgrove, 1999).

9. The Athens-Boeotia dualism is set out, most prominently, in Murray's essay 'On Sitting Back and Thinking About Porter's Boeotia', *PT*, pp. 56–65. Murray's use of the terms Athens and Boeotia have been widely discussed. See, for instance, Lawrence Bourke, *A Vivid Steady State: Les Murray and Australian Poetry* (Kensington and Strawberry Hills, NSW: New South Wales University Press/New Endeavour Press, 1992), pp. 26–35.

10. Amongst those who have pointed this out are Kevin Hart in his essay '"Interest" in Les A. Murray', *Australian Literary Studies*, 14 (1989), pp. 147–59; Neil Roberts in the chapter on Murray in his book *Narrative and Voice in Postwar Poetry* (Harlow: Longman, 1999), pp. 108–21 (esp. 110–17); and Andrew Taylor in *Reading Australian Poetry* (St Lucia: University of Queensland Press, 1987), pp. 139–55 (esp. 147–8).

11. '*This is my proper ground/Here I shall stay*', *Collected Poems*, ed. Anthony Thwaite (London: Faber and Faber, 1988), p. 99 (italics in the original).

12. Judith Wright, 'Landscape and Dreaming', *Daedalus*, 114.1 (Winter 1985), pp. 29–56 (p. 32).

13. For instance, Dipesh Chakrabarty, 'Postcoloniality and the Artifice of History: Who Speaks for "Indian" Pasts?', *Representations*, 37 (Winter 1992), pp. 1–26; Paul Carter discusses the issue briefly in relation to the Aborigines in his *The Road to Botany Bay: An Essay in Spatial History* (London: Faber and Faber, 1987), pp. 160–1.

14. Judith Wright, *Preoccupations in Australian Poetry* (Melbourne: Oxford University Press, 1965), pp. xii, xix.

15. Murray gives a brief account of this family history in 'The Human-Hair Thread' (*PT*, p. 85). A fuller description can be found in Peter F. Alexander, *Les Murray: A Life in Progress* (Melbourne: Oxford University Press, 2000), pp. 111–12.

16. *The Peasant Mandarin: Prose Pieces* (St Lucia: University of Queensland Press, 1978), p. 98.

17. A personal interview with Les Murray, quoted by Adam Shoemaker, *Black Words, White Page: Aboriginal Literature, 1929–1988* (St Lucia: University of Queensland Press, 1989), p. 199.

18. Hart, 'Interest', p. 148, italics in original.

19. Bob Hodge and Vijay Mishra, *Dark Side of the Dream: Australian Literature and the Postcolonial Mind* (Sydney: Allen and Unwin, 1990), pp. 143–4. Bernard Smith's remark about 'false consciousness' is quoted on p. 143.
20. *The New Oxford Book of Australian Verse*, ed. Les Murray, 3rd ed. (Melbourne: Oxford University Press, 1996), pp. 240–6.
21. Shoemaker, *Black Words, White Page*, p. 87.
22. Berndt's translation was first published in his paper 'A 'Wɔnguri-'Mandʒikai Song Cycle of the Moon-Bone', *Oceania*, 19 (1948–9), pp. 16–50, which also contains an interlinear version, a transliteration, notes and introduction.
23. *New Oxford Book of Australian Verse*, p. 246; *NCP*, p. 146.
24. *New Oxford Book of Australian Verse*, p. 246; Berndt, ''Wɔnguri-'Mandʒikai Song Cycle', p. 48.
25. *New Oxford Book of Australian Verse*, p. 241.
26. Ibid., p. 246.
27. The story of Bingham is told in *PT*, pp. 375–6.
28. Carter, *Road to Botany Bay*, p. 31.
29. Martin Leer, '"This Country Is My Mind": Les Murray's Poetics of Place', in *The Poetry of Les Murray: Critical Essays*, ed. Laurie Hergenhan and Bruce Clunies Ross (St Lucia: University of Queensland Press, 2001), pp. 15–42 (p. 33). This is a special issue of *Australian Literary Studies*, 20. 2.
30. Jack Gilbert, personal interview with Adam Shoemaker, and Kevin Gilbert, 'Black Policies', in *Aboriginal Writing Today* ed. Jack Davis and Bob Hodge (Canberra: Australian Institute of Aboriginal Studies, 1985), both quoted in Shoemaker, *Black Words, White Page*, p. 128.
31. Shoemaker, *Black Words, White Page*, pp. 199, 200, italics in original.
32. Ibid., p. 201.
33. Leer, '"This Country Is My Mind"', p. 36.
34. I owe this formulation of the point to Lyn Innes.
35. First published in book form in *Translations from the Natural World* (Manchester; Carcanet Press, 1993), pp. 13–54. The version in *NCP*, pp. 355–78 omits two poems and includes two new ones.
36. Robert Crawford, 'Les Murray's "Presence Sequence"', in *Counterbalancing Light: Essays on the Poetry of Les Murray*, ed. Carmel Gaffney (Armidale, NSW: Kardoorair Press, 1996), pp. 54–68 (p. 61). In 'Fullness of Being in Les Murray's "Presence: Translations from the Natural World"', *Antipodes*, 8 (December 1994), pp. 123–6, 128, 130, Bert Almon also suggests that 'Aboriginal beliefs are a natural analogue', although he then goes on to argue that the sequence is 'rooted in a Catholic view of being' (p. 123).
37. Quoted in Lynne Hume, *Ancestral Power: The Dreaming, Consciousness and Aboriginal Australians* (Melbourne: Melbourne University Press, 2002), p. 35.
38. Ibid., p. 36.
39. Crawford, 'Les Murray's "Presence Sequence"', p. 66.
40. It originally appeared as a separate poem in an earlier collection, *The Daylight Moon* (Manchester: Carcanet Press, 1987), p. 36.
41. 'Insect Mating Flight' can be found in Murray, *Translations*, p. 18. Almon discusses the poem in 'Fullness of Being', p. 124.
42. Some of the stylistic and grammatical devices used by Murray are illuminatingly discussed by Almon, 'Fullness of Being', pp. 124–5.

43. Crawford, 'Les Murray's "Presence Sequence"', p. 67.

44. Steven Matthews, *Les Murray* (Manchester: Manchester University Press, 2001), p. 125.

45. Crawford, 'Les Murray's "Presence Sequence"', p. 63.

46. Deborah Bird Rose, *Dingo Makes Us Human: Life and Land in an Australian Aboriginal Culture* (Cambridge: Cambridge University Press, 2000), p. 45.

4 Louis MacNeice, Ireland and India

The following abbreviations are used in the text and notes for works by Louis MacNeice:

CP   Louis MacNeice, *Collected Poems* (London: Faber and Faber, 1966; repr. 1979)
SLC *Selected Literary Criticism of Louis MacNeice*, ed. Alan Heuser (Oxford: Clarendon Press, 1987)
SP   *Selected Prose of Louis MacNeice*, ed. Alan Heuser (Oxford: Clarendon Press, 1990)
MP   *Modern Poetry: A Personal Essay* (Oxford: Oxford University Press, 1938)
SF   *The Strings Are False: An Unfinished Autobiography* (London: Faber and Faber, 1965; repr. in paperback, 1982)

If no abbreviation is given after a quotation, the source will be readily identifiable from the context.

1. Derek Mahon, 'MacNeice in England and Ireland', in *Time Was Away: The World of Louis MacNeice*, ed. Terence Brown and Alec Reid (Dublin: Dolmen Press, 1974), pp. 113–22 (p. 113).

2. Tom Paulin, 'The Man from No Part: Louis MacNeice', in *Ireland and the English Crisis* (Newcastle upon Tyne: Bloodaxe, 1984), pp. 75–9 (p. 75).

3. The Francis Scarfe comment is in *Auden and After: The Liberation of Poetry 1930–1941* (London: Routledge, 1942), p. 62, and is quoted by Alan Peacock in his introduction to *Louis MacNeice and His Influence*, ed. Kathleen Devine and Alan J. Peacock (Gerrards Cross: Colin Smythe, 1998), pp. vii–xvi (p. ix). Brief reviews of MacNeice's changing reputation are provided in Peacock's introduction, in Peter McDonald's *Louis MacNeice: The Poet in His Contexts* (Oxford: Clarendon Press, 1991), pp. 1–9, and in his *Mistaken Identities: Poetry and Northern Ireland* (Oxford: Clarendon Press, 1997), pp. 191–2, 208–15.

4. Short accounts can be found in Glen Hooper's introduction to *Irish and Postcolonial Writing: History, Theory, Practice* (Basingstoke: Palgrave Macmillan, 2002), ed. Hooper and Graham, pp. 1–31 (esp. pp. 9–18), and Claire Carroll's 'Introduction: The Nation and Postcolonial Theory', in *Ireland and Postcolonial Theory*, ed. Claire Carroll and Patricia King (Cork: Cork University Press, 2003), pp. 1–15. A number of essays in the latter volume also present perspectives on this debate: Joe Cleary, '"Misplaced Ideas"?: Colonialism, Location, and Dislocation in Irish Studies', pp. 16–45; David Lloyd, 'After History: Historicism and Irish Postcolonial Studies', pp. 46–62; and Edward Said, 'Afterword: Reflections on Ireland and Postcolonialism',

pp. 177–85. Another brief account can also be found in Joe Cleary, 'Postcolonial Ireland', in *Ireland and the British Empire*, ed. Kevin Kenny (Oxford: Oxford University Press, 2004), pp. 251–88.

5. Seamus Heaney, *The Place of Writing* (Atlanta, GA: Scholars Press, 1989), p. 46.

6. Seamus Heaney, *The Redress of Poetry: Oxford Lectures* (London: Faber and Faber, 1995), p. 200.

7. Heather Clark writes that recent Northern Irish poets' 'reluctance to acknowledge MacNeice's Englishness means that they have somewhat revised his legacy': 'Revising MacNeice', *Cambridge Quarterly*, 31 (2002), pp. 77–92 (p. 92). Terence Brown also feels that the 'English MacNeice has been rather neglected' as a result of the recent 'Hiberno-centred' criticism: 'MacNeice and the Puritan Tradition', in Devine and Peacock, eds, *Louis MacNeice and His Influence*, pp. 20–33 (p. 31).

8. Even to list all of these studies would require an unpalatably swollen note. Several are referred to in the course of this chapter.

9. Eamon Grennan, 'In a Topographical Frame: Ireland in the Poetry of Louis MacNeice', in *Facing the Music: Irish Poetry in the Twentieth Century* (Omaha, Nebraska: Creighton Univerisity Press, 1999), pp. 192–207 (p. 193). This was first published in *Studies: An Irish Quarterly Review*, 70 (1981), pp. 145–61.

10. This has been discussed by a number of critics, among them Terence Brown, Peter McDonald and Edna Longley. In chapter one of *Louis MacNeice* (p. 30), McDonald explores how the conflict between 'flux and stasis ... fixity and fluidity, petrifaction and water' runs through MacNeice's volume *Poems* (1935). See also Longley's *Louis MacNeice: A Study* (London: Faber and Faber, 1988), chapter 5 ('Colour and Meaning'). Brown's *Louis MacNeice: Sceptical Vision* (Dublin: Gill and Macmillan, 1975) is a detailed study of how the dualism operates in MacNeice's writing.

11. G. S. Fraser, 'Evasive Honesty: The Poetry of Louis MacNeice', in *Vision and Rhetoric: Studies in Modern Poetry* (London: Faber and Faber, 1959), pp. 179–92 (p. 182).

12. This contrast between flux and what he calls here 'universals' can be found in different forms and using different terminology in a number of other places, such as *SF*, pp. 118–19, 124–5 and *SP*, pp. 232–3.

13. Declan Kiberd, *Inventing Ireland: The Literature of the Modern Nation* (London: Jonathan Cape, 1995), p. 9.

14. These are definitions II. 6, III. 11a, and III. 10a respectively.

15. 'Tendencies in Modern Poetry: Discussion between F. R. Higgins and Louis MacNeice, Broadcast from Northern Ireland', *The Listener*, 27 July 1939, pp. 185–6 (p. 186); Paul Muldoon prints an extract as the 'Prologue' to *The Faber Book of Contemporary Irish Poetry* (London: Faber and Faber, 1986), pp. 17–18.

16. Heaney, *Place of Writing*, p. 43.

17. 'Prologue' was first printed in *The Listener* in 1971, reprinted in *Time Was Away* in 1974 (see note 1) and then in Jon Stallworthy, *Louis MacNeice* (London: Faber and Faber, 1995), pp. 488–91. The passage quoted is on p. 491 of Stallworthy.

18. Stallworthy, *Louis MacNeice*, pp. 490–1.

19. Paulin, 'The Man from No Part', p. 76.

20. Clifford Geertz, 'Found in Translation: On the Social History of the Moral Imagination', in *Local Knowledge: Further Essays in Interpretive Anthropology* (1983: London: Fontana, 1993), pp. 36–54 (p. 44).

21. In a series of notes for a lecture or essay, dating from MacNeice's Oxford period or from the 1930s, he is already proposing such a method. See Peter McDonald, '"With Eyes Turned Down on the Past": MacNeice's Classicism', in Devine and Peacock, eds, *Louis MacNeice and His Influence*, pp. 34–52 (p. 39).

22. Louis MacNeice, *The Poetry of W. B. Yeats* (London: Oxford University Press, 1941), pp. 45, 46.

23. Lionel Trilling, 'Why We Read Jane Austen', *TLS*, 5 March 1976, pp. 250–2 (p. 252). This essay is reprinted in Trilling's *The Moral Obligation to be Intelligent: Selected Essays*, ed. Leon Wieseltier (New York: Farrar, Strauss and Giroux, 2000), pp. 517–35.

24. A descriptive account of MacNeice's first visit to India and of the radio features it gave rise to can be found in Barbara Coulton, *Louis MacNeice in the BBC* (London: Faber and Faber, 1980), pp. 98–104.

25. The scripts of this and other features which came out of the visit are unpublished and can be found in the BBC Written Archives Centre in Reading. This quotation is from p. 2. Further references will be given in the text.

26. Hedli MacNeice, 'The Story of the House that Louis Built', in *Studies on Louis MacNeice*, ed. Jacqueline Genet and Wynne Hellegouarc'h (Caen: Centre de Publications de l'Université de Caen, 1988), pp. 9–10 (p. 9).

27. Heaney, *Redress of Poetry*, pp. 199–200.

28. Letter to his wife Hedli, quoted in Stallworthy, *Louis MacNeice*, p. 360.

29. Quoted by Stallworthy, *Louis MacNeice*, p. 418. Kit Fryatt notes, referring to evidence from both MacNeice's radio features and his BBC correspondence, that 'parallels between India and Ireland were rarely far from his mind when he was compiling these programmes': '"Banyan Riot of Dialectic": Louis MacNeice's India', a paper delivered at the fourth Galway Conference on Colonialism (June 2004). This paper has since been published in *Ireland and India: Colonies, Culture and Empire*, ed. Maureen O'Connor and Tadhg Foley (Dublin: Irish Academic Press, 2006). I have not seen the published version. In the original paper, Fryatt examines MacNeice's experiences in, and writings about, India. The paper deals with a number of the texts discussed in this chapter, particularly 'India at First Sight' and 'Didymus', drawing attention to the image of translation used in the first of these and to the dualism of 'Didymus'. My use of translation is somewhat different, since I link it to the kinds of issues and contexts discussed in the first chapter.

30. Godfrey Lienhardt, 'Modes of Thought', in E. E. Evans-Pritchard et al., *The Institutions of Primitive Society: A Series of Broadcast Talks* (Oxford: Blackwell, 1954), pp. 95–107 (p. 97).

31. Brown, *Louis MacNeice*, p. 157.

32. Fryatt, '"Banyan Riot of Dialectic"'. This paper discusses the dualism of the poem in detail.

33. *The Poetry of W. B. Yeats* (London: Oxford University Press, 1941), pp. 44–5. I am indebted at this point to Peter McDonald's discussion of these passages in *Mistaken Identities*, pp. 38–9.

34. Louis MacNeice, 'The Sideliner', *New Statesman and Nation*, 4 April 1953, p. 402, quoted in McDonald, *Louis MacNeice*, p. 138.
35. Lienhardt, 'Modes of Thought', p. 97.
36. Higgins and MacNeice, 'Tendencies in Modern Poetry', p. 186.

5   Seamus Heaney's Acoustics

The following abbreviations are used in the text and notes for works by Seamus Heaney (all are published by Faber and Faber, London, unless otherwise specified):

B   *Beowulf* (1999)
CT   *The Cure at Troy: A Version of Sophocles' Philoctetes* (1990)
DN   *Death of a Naturalist* (1966)
EL   *Electric Light* (2001)
FK   *Finders Keepers: Selected Prose 1971–2001* (2002)
GT   *The Government of the Tongue: The 1986 T. S. Eliot Memorial Lectures and Other Critical Writings* (1988)
HL   *The Haw Lantern* (1987)
MV   *The Midnight Verdict* (Oldcastle, Co. Meath: Gallery Books, 1993)
N   *North* (1975)
P   *Preoccupations: Selected Prose 1968–1978* (1980)
PW   *The Place of Writing* (Atlanta, GA: Scholars Press, 1989)
RP   *The Redress of Poetry: Oxford Lectures* (1995)
SI   *Station Island* (1984)
SL   *The Spirit Level* (1996)
WO   *Wintering Out* (1972)

If no abbreviation is given after a quotation in the text, the source will be readily identifiable from the context.

1. David Lloyd, '"Pap for the Dispossessed": Seamus Heaney and the Poetics of Identity', in *Anomalous States: Irish Writing and the Postcolonial Moment* (Dublin: Lilliput Press, 1993), pp. 13–40; Elizabeth Butler Cullingford, '"Thinking of Her … as … Ireland": Yeats, Pearse, and Heaney', *Textual Practice*, 4 (Spring 1990), pp. 1–21 (pp. 1–3); Clair Wills, *Improprieties: Politics and Sexuality in Northern Irish Poetry* (Oxford: Clarendon, 1993), pp. 98–101; and Patricia Coughlan, '"Bog Queens": The Representation of Women in the Poetry of John Montague and Seamus Heaney', in *Gender in Irish Writing*, ed. Toni O'Brien Johnson and David Cairns (Milton Keynes: Open University Press, 1991), pp. 89–111.
2. David Kennedy, 'Mound-dwellers and Mummers: Language and Community in Seamus Heaney's *Wintering Out*', *Irish Studies Review*, 10 (2002), pp. 303–13 (p. 305).
3. The same point is made, and the same word used in *RP*, p. 58.
4. Seamus Heaney, 'The Drag of the Golden Chain', *TLS*, 12 November 1999, pp. 14–16 (p. 14).
5. Ibid., p. 16.
6. Helen Vendler, *Seamus Heaney* (London: HarperCollins, 1998), p. 29.
7. Seamus Heaney, 'Correspondences: Emigrants and Inner Exiles', in *Migrations: The Irish At Home and Abroad*, ed. Richard Kearney (Dublin: Wolfhound Press, 1990), pp. 21–31 (p. 29).

8. Ibid., pp. 29, 30.
9. Ibid., p. 24.
10. Seamus Heaney, 'Further Language', *Studies in the Literary Imagination*, 30. 2 (Fall 1997), pp. 7–16 (p. 10); *B*, p. xxv.
11. On this genre, see, for instance, Bernard O'Donoghue, *Seamus Heaney and the Language of Poetry* (Hemel Hempstead: Harvester Wheatsheaf, 1994), pp. 59–60.
12. For the former, see Wills, *Improprieties*, p. 101, and for the latter, Heaney's *Among Schoolchildren: A Lecture Dedicated to the Memory of John Malone* (Belfast: John Malone Memorial Committee, 1983), p. 9.
13. Kennedy, 'Mound-dwellers and Mummers', p. 305.
14. Vendler, *Seamus Heaney*, p. 18; Neil Corcoran, *The Poetry of Seamus Heaney: A Critical Study* (London: Faber and Faber, 1998), p. 45.
15. Corcoran, *Poetry of Seamus Heaney*, p. 46.
16. Heaney, *Among Schoolchildren*, pp. 9–10.
17. George Steiner, *After Babel: Aspects of Language and Translation*, 3rd ed. (Oxford: Oxford University Press, 1998), pp. 242, 243.
18. The dangers of liminality are illuminatingly discussed by Mary Douglas in her *Purity and Danger: An Analysis of the Concepts of Pollution and Taboo* (1966; London: Ark, 1984).
19. Vendler, *Seamus Heaney*, p. 18.
20. Ciaran Carson, 'Escaped from the Massacre?', *The Honest Ulsterman*, 50 (Winter 1975), pp. 183–6 (pp. 184–5).
21. Cullingford, ' "Thinking of Her" ', pp. 2–3.
22. Lloyd, ' "Pap for the Dispossessed" ', p. 28.
23. The 'optative' nature of the poem has been noted by, among others, Sidney Burris, *The Poetry of Resistance: Seamus Heaney and the Pastoral Tradition* (Athens: Ohio University Press, 1990), p. 99 and Michael Molino, *Questioning Tradition, Language and Myth: The Poetry of Seamus Heaney* (Washington DC: Catholic University of America Press, 1994), p. 88.
24. Remarks made by Heaney in a recording of his poems for a Faber poetry cassette, quoted by Michael Parker, *Seamus Heaney: The Making of the Poet* (Basingstoke: Macmillan, 1993), p. 107.
25. The place-name is spelt 'Grabaulle' in *Wintering Out*, but later corrected to 'Grauballe' in Heaney's *Opened Ground: Poems 1966–1996* (London: Faber and Faber, 1998), p. 65.
26. Seamus Heaney, 'The Frontier of Writing', in *Irish Writers and their Creative Process*, ed. Jacqueline Genet and Wynne Hellegouarc'h (Gerards Cross: Colin Smythe, 1996), pp. 3–16 (pp. 5, 6).
27. Seth Lerer, ' "On fagne flor": The Postcolonial *Beowulf*, from Heorot to Heaney', in *Postcolonial Approaches to the European Middle Ages: Translating Cultures*, ed. Ananya Jahanara Kabir and Deanne Williams (Cambridge: Cambridge University Press, 2005), pp. 77–102 (p. 83).
28. Ibid., p. 89.
29. This is the reading given in the text which I believe was printed with the bilingual US edition of Heaney's translation: *Beowulf: With the Finnesburg Fragment*, ed. C. L. Wrenn, rev. W. F. Bolton, 3rd ed. (London: Harrap, 1973), p. 211. The meanings indicated are those given in the glossary to this edition.
30. Lerer, 'On fagne flor', p. 89.

31. For 'Listen!', see *Beowulf: A New Verse Translation*, trans. R. M. Liuzza (Peterborough, Ontario: Broadview Press, 2000), p. 53; for 'Attend!', *Beowulf: A Verse Translation*, trans. Michael Alexander, rev. ed. (London: Penguin, 2001), p. 3; for 'Lo!', *Beowulf : A Metrical Translation into Modern English*, trans. J. R. Clark Hall (Cambridge: Cambridge University Press, 1914), p. 1; and for 'What Ho!', *The Deeds of Beowulf: An English Epic of the Eighth Century Done into Modern Prose*, trans. John Earle (Oxford: Clarendon Press, 1892), p. 3.

32. See Howell Chickering, 'Beowulf and "Heaneywulf"', *Kenyon Review*, 24. 1 (Winter 2002), pp. 160–78 (esp. p. 161).

33. Ibid., pp. 173, 174. Chickering is quoting p. 16 of Heaney's 'Drag of the Golden Chain'.

34. *A Concise Ulster Dictionary*, ed. C. I. Macafee (Oxford: Oxford University Press, 1996), p. 18.

35. Chickering, 'Beowulf and "Heaneywulf"', p. 174.

36. Wrenn and Bolton, *Beowulf*, p. 228.

37. Quoted by C. L. Innes, 'Postcolonial Studies and Ireland', in *Comparing Postcolonial Literatures: Dislocations*, ed. Ashok Bery and Patricia Murray (Basingstoke: Macmillan, 2000), pp. 21–30 (p. 27). In his essay, 'Language and History in Seamus Heaney's *Beowulf*', *English*, 50 (2001), pp. 149–58 (pp. 153–4), Conor McCarthy discusses 'beyond the pale' as an example of connections between Ireland and the Scandinavian setting, but does not comment on this kind of problem with the use of the phrase.

38. Lerer, 'On fagne flor', pp. 87, 96–7.

39. Chickering, 'Beowulf and "Heaneywulf"', p. 175. See also more generally pp. 175–7.

40. J. W. Foster, 'The Landscape of Three Irelands: Hewitt, Murphy and Montague', in *Contemporary Irish Poetry*, ed. Elmer Andrews (Basingstoke: Macmillan, 1992), p. 150, quoted by Elmer Kennedy-Andrews, in 'John Montague: Global Regionalist?', *Cambridge Quarterly* 35 (2006), pp. 31–48 (p. 48).

41. Heaney, 'Drag of the Golden Chain', p. 16.

42. Quoted, ibid.

43. Quoted, ibid.

44. Ibid.

45. Steiner, *After Babel*, pp. 243, 244.

6   Indian Palimpsests: The Poetry of A. K. Ramanujan

The following abbreviations are used in the text and notes for works by Ramanujan:

CE *The Collected Essays of A. K. Ramanujan*, general editor Vinay Dharwadker (New Delhi: Oxford University Press, 1999)

CP *The Collected Poems of A. K. Ramanujan*, ed. Vinay Dharwadker (New Delhi: Oxford University Press, 1995)

If no abbreviation is given after a quotation, the source will be readily identifiable from the context.

1. I have put the word 'medieval' in inverted commas because it is a term from Western historiography and its applicability in the Indian context is debatable.
2. V. S. Naipaul, *India: A Wounded Civilization* (1977; Harmondsworth: Penguin, 1979), p. 18.
3. See Alok Rai, *Hindi Nationalism* (New Delhi: Orient Longman, 2001).
4. Partha Chatterjee, *The Nation and its Fragments: Colonial and Postcolonial Histories* (Princeton, NJ: Princeton University Press, 1993). For a fuller account of these debates, see my essay '"We Have Grown to Look at the Large World As Part of Us": Modernity and the Nation in Two Indian Novels of the 1930s', in *The Political Subject: Essays on the Self from Art, Politics and Science*, ed. Wendy Wheeler (London: Lawrence and Wishart, 2000), pp. 160–78. I have drawn in parts of this chapter.
5. Vinayak Damodar Savarkar, *Essentials of Hindutva: Who is a Hindu?*, 6th ed. (New Delhi: Bharti Sahitya Sadan, 1989), p. 116.
6. Sunil Khilnani, *The Idea of India* (London: Hamish Hamilton, 1997), pp. 153, 169 and 172. The metaphor of the palimpsest comes from Nehru's *The Discovery of India*, quoted by Khilnani on p. 169.
7. Khilnani, *Idea of India*, p. 171 (the last quotation is drawn from Nehru's *Autobiography*).
8. The cover is reproduced by Arvind Krishna Mehrotra in his essay 'Looking for Ramanujan', in *A History of Indian Literature in English*, ed. Mehrotra (London: Hurst and Co., 2003), pp. 295–307 (p. 296). Ramaujan's ambivalence is indicated in the caption, which quotes his son, Krishna Ramanujan.
9. Parts III and IV of Ramanujan's *Collected Essays* deal with these forms.
10. A. K. Ramanujan, *Uncollected Poems and Prose*, ed. Molly Daniels-Ramanujan and Keith Harrison (New Delhi: Oxford University Press, 2001), p. 55.
11. Such navigation is discussed in one of his most memorable prose pieces, 'Is There an Indian Way of Thinking? An Informal Essay' (*CE*, pp. 34–51), where he uses his father as an example of this ability (pp. 35–7).
12. Arvind Krishna Mehrotra, introduction to *The Oxford India Anthology of Twelve Modern Indian Poets* (Delhi: Oxford University Press, 1992), pp. 1–12 (pp. 5–6).
13. Ayyappa Paniker, 'Towards an Indian Theory of Literary Translation', in *Translation: From Periphery to Centrestage*, ed. Tutun Mukherjee (New Delhi: Prestige, 1998), pp. 39–46 (pp. 40–41).
14. Susan Bassnett and Harish Trivedi, 'Introduction: Of Colonies, Cannibals and Vernaculars', in *Post-colonial Translation: Theory and Practice*, ed. Bassnett and Trivedi (London: Routledge, 1999), pp. 1–18 (p. 9).
15. Paniker, 'Towards an Indian Theory', p. 39.
16. K. Satchidanandan, 'The State of Translation', in *Indian Literature: Positions and Propositions* (Delhi: Pencraft International, 1999), pp. 171–7 (p. 172). In 'Three Hundred *Rāmāyaṇas*: Five Examples and Three Thoughts on Translation' (*CE*, pp. 131–60), Ramanujan discusses a number of retellings.
17. G. N. Devy contrasts Indian and Western ideas of translation on this basis: 'Translation Theory: An Indian Perspective', in Mukherjee, ed. *Translation*, pp. 46–65 (p. 48) and 'Translation and Literary History: An Indian View', in Bassnett and Trivedi, eds, *Post-colonial Translation*, pp. 182–8.
18. His numerous transcreations include *The Mahabharata of Vyasa* (many reprints; e.g., New Delhi: Tarang Paperbacks, 1989). He discusses the term in

Transcreation: Seven Essays on the Art of Transcreation (Calcutta: Writers' Workshop, 1996). See also Sujit Mukherjee, 'Transcreating Translation', in his *Translation as Recovery*, ed. Meenakshi Mukherjee (Delhi: Pencraft International, 2004), pp. 43–52. The cannibalist use of the term is mentioned by Else Ribeiro Pires Vieira, 'Liberating Calibans: Readings of *Antropofagia* and Haroldo de Campos' Poetics of Transcreation', in Bassnett and Trivedi, eds, *Post-colonial Translation*, pp. 95–113 (p. 96).

19. *Speaking of Śiva*, trans. A. K. Ramanujan (London: Penguin Books, 1973), p. 13.

20. 'Preface to Ovid's *Epistles*, Translated by Several Hands', in *John Dryden*, ed. Keith Walker, The Oxford Authors (Oxford: Oxford University Press, 1987) pp. 155–64 (p. 160).

21. Contesting views on these topics can be found in Tejaswani Niranjana, *Siting Translation: History, Post-Structuralism and the Colonial Context* (Berkeley and Los Angeles, CA: University of California Press, 1992), pp. 173–86, and Vinay Dharwadker, 'A. K. Ramanujan's Theory and Practice of Translation', in Bassnett and Trivedi, eds, *Post-colonial Translation*, pp. 114–40.

22. Ramanujan, *Speaking of Śiva*, p. 12.

23. *Poems of Love and War: From the Eight Anthologies and the Ten Long Poems of Classical Tamil*, trans. A. K. Ramanujan (New York: Columbia University Press, 1985), p. xv.

24. Vinay Dharwadker describes the poem as a 'national allegory' (*CP*, p. xxx). For a similar view of the poem, see Sudesh Mishra, *Preparing Faces: Modernism and Indian Poetry in English* (Suva, Fiji and Adelaide: The University of the South Pacific and The Centre for Research in the New Literatures in English, Flinders University, 1995), p. 258: 'The house ... becomes a metonymic extension of the assimilatory power of a capacious India'.

25. A fuller discussion of this poem can be found in my essay '"Reflexive Worlds": The Indias of A. K. Ramanujan', which appeared in *Alternative Indias: Writing, Nation and Communalism*, ed. Peter Morey and Alex Tickell (Amsterdam: Rodopi, 2005), pp. 115–39 (pp. 130–3). There is also an extensive discussion in Jahan Ramazani, 'Metaphor and Postcoloniality: The Poetry of A. K. Ramanujan', *Contemporary Literature*, 39 (1998), pp. 27–53 (pp. 36–40). A slightly revised version of this appears as chapter four of Ramazani's *The Hybrid Muse: Postcolonial Poetry in English* (Chicago, IL: University of Chicago Press, 2001).

26. Margaret and James Stutley, *A Dictionary of Hinduism: Its Mythology, Folklore and Development 1500 B. C. – A. D. 1500* (London and Henley: Routledge and Kegan Paul, 1977), pp. 196, 144.

27. His translation can be found in Ramanujan, trans., *Poems of Love and War*, pp. 215–17 and 226–8.

28. Ramazani, 'Metaphor and Postcoloniality', p. 35.

29. Rama Jha, 'A Conversation with A. K. Ramanujan', *The Humanities Review*, 3, no. 1 (January–June 1981), pp. 5–13, quoted by Bruce King, *Modern Indian Poetry in English*, rev. ed. (New Delhi: Oxford University Press, 2001), p. 214.

30. Ramanujan refers to this saying in 'Classics Lost and Found' (*CE*, p. 185).

31. Ramanujan, trans., *Poems of Love and War*, p. 246.

32. *The Upaniṣads*, trans. Valerie J. Roebuck (New Delhi: Penguin, 2000), pp. xvii, 477, 356 n.77 and 337.

33. *Muṇḍaka Upaniṣad*, 1. 1. 7, in Roebuck, trans., *The Upaniṣads*, p. 373. Other translations, Roebuck points out in her note (also p. 373), render the first of the lines quoted as something like 'emits and draws in [its thread]'. See, for instance, *The Upaniṣads*, trans. Patrick Olivelle (Oxford: Oxford University Press, 1996), p. 268.

34. Alternative translations can be found in Roebuck, trans., *The Upaniṣads*, p. 249 and Olivelle, trans., *The Upaniṣads*, p. 285. The image is discussed by Bruce King in *Three Indian Poets: Nissim Ezekiel, A. K. Ramanujan, Dom Moraes* (Madras: Oxford University Press, 1991), pp. 87–8, and the whole idea of circulation in Ramanujan's poetry by Ramazani in 'Metaphor and Postcoloniality', pp. 42–4.

35. Ramanujan, trans., *Poems of Love and War*, pp. 281–2.

36. The most detailed study of Ramanujan's work in relation to modernism can be found in Mishra, *Preparing Faces*, chap. 6. However, Mishra's concern is largely with Ramanujan's use of personae. Bruce King suggests that Ramanujan 'may have been the last major modernist': *Modern Indian Poetry*, p. 300.

37. King, *Modern Indian Poetry*, p. 302. King excludes from this description the poems gathered under the title *The Black Hen*, compiled by an eight-person committee after Ramanujan's death in 1993 (*CP*, pp. 195–277).

7 Fragmentation and Restoration in Derek Walcott's *Omeros*

The following abbreviations are used in the text and notes for works by Derek Walcott:

A   'The Antilles: Fragments of Epic Memory', in *What the Twilight Says: Essays* (London: Faber and Faber, 1998), pp. 65–84

CM 'The Caribbean: Culture or Mimicry?', *Journal of InterAmerican Studies and World Affairs*, 16 (1974), pp. 3–13

CP *Collected Poems 1948–1984* (New York: Farrar, Strauss and Giroux, 1986)

MH 'The Muse of History', in *What the Twilight Says*, pp. 36–64

O   *Omeros* (London: Faber and Faber, 1990)

If no abbreviation is given after a quotation, the source will be readily identifiable from the context.

1. Edward Brathwaite, *The Development of Creole Society in Jamaica 1770–1820* (Oxford: Clarendon Press, 1971), pp. xiii, 307.

2. 'Creolization diffracts whereas some forms of métissage may concentrate once more'. Edouard Glissant, *Poétique de la Relation* (1990), translated and quoted by Kathleen M. Balutansky and Marie-Agnès Sourieau in the introduction to *Caribbean Creolization: Reflections on the Cultural Dynamics of Language, Literature, and Identity* (Gainesville: University Press of Florida, 1998), pp. 1–11 (p. 1); pp. 1–8 this introduction provides a helpful survey of the topic.

3. Antonio Benítez-Rojo, *The Repeating Island: The Caribbean and the Postmodern Perspective*, 2nd ed. (Durham, NC: Duke University Press, 1996), pp. 21, 26.

4. Ibid., pp. 12–16.

5. Ibid., pp. 26–7.

6. Rei Terada discusses Walcott's 'creole poetics' in chapter 3 of *Derek Walcott's Poetry: American Mimicry* (Boston, MA: Northeastern University Press, 1992). A more recent discussion is Laurence A. Breiner, 'Creole Language in the Poetry of Derek Walcott', *Callaloo*, 28 (2005), pp. 29–41.

7. Paul Breslin, *Nobody's Nation: Reading Derek Walcott* (Chicago, IL: University of Chicago Press, 2001), pp. 261–72. In *Derek Walcott's Poetry*, Terada refers to the 'tirelessly figurative surface of his poetry' (p. 37).

8. 'Self-undoing' is a term used by Breslin in *Nobody's Nation*, p. 244.

9. These themes, as well as the Walcott essays I turn to next, have been widely discussed by critics such as John Thieme, Rei Terada, Paula Burnett and Paul Breslin, all of whom are cited elsewhere in these notes.

10. V. S. Naipaul, *The Middle Passage* (1962; Harmondsworth: Penguin, 1969), p. 29. The Froude comment is from *The English in the West Indies: or, the Bow of Ulysses* (London: Longmans, Green and Co., 1888), and is quoted by Walcott in the epigraph to his poem 'Air' (*CP*, pp. 113–14).

11. Edward Brathwaite, *The Arrivants: A New World Trilogy* (Oxford: Oxford University Press, 1973), p. 13.

12. Derek Walcott, 'The Figure of Crusoe' (1965), repr. in *Critical Perspectives on Derek Walcott*, ed. Robert D. Hamner (Boulder: Lynne Rienner, 1997), pp. 33–40 (p. 35). There are many other dimensions to both figures, and these have been extensively discussed in relation to Walcott by critics such as Breslin, *Nobody's Nation*, chap. 4; John Thieme, *Derek Walcott* (Manchester: Manchester University Press, 1999), chap. 4; Paula Burnett, *Derek Walcott: Politics and Poetics* (Gainesville: University Press of Florida, 2000), pp. 112–18 and Terada, *Derek Walcott's Poetry*, pp. 151, 158–62.

13. R. W. B. Lewis, *The American Adam: Innocence, Tragedy and Tradition in the Nineteenth Century* (Chicago, IL: University of Chicago Press, 1955).

14. 'A Colonial's-Eye View of the Empire', *TriQuarterly*, no. 65 (Winter 1986), pp. 73–7 (p. 77).

15. Breslin, *Nobody's Nation*, p. 249.

16. George Steiner, *After Babel: Aspects of Language and Translation*, 3rd ed. (Oxford: Oxford University Press, 1998), pp. 60–1.

17. Ibid., p. 62.

18. Ibid., p. 397.

19. Ibid., p. 228.

20. One of the rare exceptions is 'The Saddhu of Couva' (*CP*, pp. 372–4).

21. Mary Lefkowitz, 'Bringing Him Back Alive', in Hamner, ed., *Critical Perspectives on Derek Walcott*, pp. 400–3.

22. Walcott, 'Reflections on *Omeros*', *South Atlantic Quarterly*, 96 (1997), pp. 229–46 (pp. 235, 240). The relationship between *Omeros* and epic is also discussed in three other essays in the same issue of *South Atlantic Quarterly*: Joseph Farrell, 'Walcott's *Omeros*: The Classical Epic in a Postmodern World' (pp. 247–73); Gregson Davis, '"With No Homeric Shadow": The Disavowal of Epic in Derek Walcott's *Omeros*' (pp. 321–33); and Carol Dougherty, 'Homer after *Omeros*: Reading a H/Omeric Text' (pp. 335–57). Most books on Walcott also discuss or at least touch on the topic.

23. More detailed discussions of the connections between Dante and *Omeros* can be found in Maria Cristina Fumagalli, *The Flight of the Vernacular: Seamus Heaney, Derek Walcott and the Impress of Dante* (Amsterdam: Rodopi, 2001)

chap. 9 and Mark Balfour, 'The Place of the Poet: Dante in Walcott's Narrative Poetry', in *Dante's Modern Afterlife: Reception and Response from Blake to Heaney*, ed. Nick Havely (Basingstoke: Macmillan, 1998), pp. 223–41 (esp. 232–6).

24. Robert D. Hamner, *Epic of the Dispossessed: Derek Walcott's* Omeros (Columbia: University of Missouri Press, 1997), p. 95. See also Breslin, *Nobody's Nation*, pp. 262–4.

25. This is just a very brief sample of a ubiquitous motif.

26. This meridian has played a significant role in Walcott's writing before *Omeros*. In 'The Caribbean: Culture or Mimicry?', for instance, he refers to the 'meridian of Alexander VI' (p. 7).

27. For instance, Thieme, *Derek Walcott*, pp. 186–7 and Joe W. Moffett '"Master, I Was the Freshest of All Your Readers": Derek Walcott's *Omeros* and Homer as Literary Origin', *Literature Interpretation Theory*, 16 (2005), pp. 1–23.

28. Derek Walcott, *Midsummer* (London: Faber and Faber, 1984), p. 53.

29. Ibid.

30. Terada, *Derek Walcott's Poetry*, pp. 145, 141, 195.

31. Walcott, 'Reflections on *Omeros*', pp. 233, 234, italics in original.

32. Steiner, *After Babel*, p. 61.

33. Douglas Robinson, 'Babel, tower of', in *Routledge Encyclopedia of Translation Studies*, ed. Mona Baker, assisted by Kirsten Malmkjær (London: Routledge, 1998), pp. 21–2.

34. Walter Benjamin, 'The Task of the Translator: An Introduction to the Translation of Baudelaire's *Tableaux Parisiens*', in *Illuminations*, ed. Hannah Arendt, trans. Harry Zohn (London: Fontana, 1973), 69–82 (pp. 74, 78). This passage has been applied to Walcott's work by both Terada, *Derek Walcott's Poetry*, pp. 86–7, 174–5 and Burnett, *Derek Walcott*, pp. 26–7. Terada uses it to demonstrate the difficulty of categorizing Walcott's language as 'either English or English Creole' (p. 86) and to argue that '"the original", itself a fragment, ... is obviously *not original*' (p. 174; Terada's italics). For Burnett, who also notes the link with 'The Antilles', the image is a figure for the Caribbean writer's articulation of 'a plural identity' (p. 27).

35. Benjamin, 'Task of the Translator', p. 79.

36. Many discussions of *Omeros* comment on this; for instance, Terada, *Derek Walcott's Poetry*, pp. 198–200 and Jahan Ramazani, 'The Wound of History: Walcott's *Omeros* and the Postcolonial Poetics of Affliction', *PMLA*, 112 (1997), pp. 405–17. A slightly revised version of Ramazani's essay appears as chapter 3 of his *The Hybrid Muse: Postcolonial Poetry in English* (Chicago, IL: University of Chicago Press, 2001).

37. Terada, *Derek Walcott's Poetry*, pp. 199–200, discusses this idea of language as a wound.

38. Ibid., p. 220.

39. *Midsummer*, p. 68.

40. Breslin, *Nobody's Nation*, p. 113.

41. Ibid., p. 261.

42. Octavio Paz, 'Translation: Literature and Letters', trans. Irene del Corral, in *Theories of Translation: An Anthology of Essays from Dryden to Derrida*, ed. Rainer Schulte and John Biguenet (Chicago, IL: University of Chicago Press, 1992), pp. 152–63 (p. 154).

Conclusion

1. Clifford Geertz, 'Found in Translation: On the Social History of the Moral Imagination', in *Local Knowledge: Further Essays in Interpretive Anthropology* (1983; London: Fontana, 1993), pp. 36–54 (p. 41).
2. Octavio Paz, 'Translation: Literature and Letters', trans. Irene del Corral, in *Theories of Translation: An Anthology of Essays from Dryden to Derrida*, ed. Rainer Schulte and John Biguenet (Chicago, IL: University of Chicago Press, 1992), pp. 152–63 (p. 154).
3. 'Towards a Counter-system: Women's Tales', in *The Collected Essays of A. K. Ramanujan*, general editor Vinay Dharwadker (New Delhi: Oxford University Press, 1999), pp. 429–47 (p. 447).
4. Quoted by Mark Strand in *Dark Harbor: A Poem* (New York: Alfred A. Knopf, 1993), pp. 35, 51.
5. Prasenjit Gupta, trans., Introduction to *Indian Errant: Selected Stories of Nirmal Verma*, (New Delhi: Indialog, 2002), pp. i–lxxvi (p. xli).
6. See, for instance, his essay 'Where Mirrors Are Windows: Toward an Anthology of Reflections', in *The Collected Essays of A. K. Ramanujan*, ed. Vinay Dharwadker, pp. 6–33 (p. 26).
7. Vicente L. Rafael, *Contracting Colonialism: Translation and Christian Conversion in Tagalog Society under Early Spanish Rule* (1988; Durham, NC: Duke University Press, 1993).
8. Quoted by Geertz, 'Found in Translation', p. 50.
9. James Merrill, *Collected Poems* (New York: Alfred A. Knopf, 2001), p. 367.

Select Bibliography

Ahmad, Aijaz, 'The Politics of Literary Postcoloniality', *Race and Class*, 36.3 (1995), pp. 1–20.

Alexander, Michael, trans., *Beowulf: A Verse Translation*, rev. ed. (London: Penguin, 2001).

Alexander, Peter F., *Les Murray: A Life in Progress* (Melbourne: Oxford University Press, 2000).

Almon, Bert, 'Fullness of Being in Les Murray's "Presence: Translations from the Natural World"', *Antipodes*, 8 (December 1994), pp. 123–26, 128, 130.

Andrade, Oswald de, 'Cannibal Manifesto', trans. Mary Ann Caws and Claudia Caliman, *Exquisite Corpse: A Journal of Letters and Life*, Cyber Issue 11 (Spring/ Summer 2002), http://www.corpse.org/issue_11/manifestos/deandrade.html (accessed 3 June 2006).

Asad, Talal, 'The Concept of Cultural Translation in British Social Anthropology', in *Writing Culture*, ed. Clifford and Marcus, pp. 141–64.

Baker, Mona, ed., assisted by Kirsten Malmkjær, *Routledge Encyclopedia of Translation Studies* (London: Routledge, 1998).

Balfour, Mark, 'The Place of the Poet: Dante in Walcott's Narrative Poetry', in *Dante's Modern Afterlife: Reception and Response from Blake to Heaney*, ed. Nick Havely (Basingstoke: Macmillan, 1998), pp. 223–41.

Balutansky, Kathleen M. and Marie-Agnès Sourieau, eds, *Caribbean Creolization: Reflections on the Cultural Dynamics of Language, Literature, and Identity* (Gainesville: University Press of Florida, 1998).

Bassnett, Susan, *Comparative Literature: A Critical Introduction* (Oxford: Blackwell, 1993).

Bassnett, Susan and Harish Trivedi, eds, *Post-colonial Translation: Theory and Practice* (London: Routledge, 1999).

Benítez-Rojo, Antonio, *The Repeating Island: The Caribbean and the Postmodern Perspective*, 2nd ed. (Durham, NC: Duke University Press, 1996).

Benjamin, Walter, 'The Task of the Translator: An Introduction to the Translation of Baudelaire's *Tableaux Parisiens*', in *Illuminations*, ed. Hannah Arendt, trans. Harry Zohn (London: Fontana, 1973), pp. 69–82.

Berndt, R. M., 'A 'Wɔnguri-'Mandʒikai Song Cycle of the Moon-Bone', *Oceania*, 19 (1948–9), pp. 16–50.

——, 'Territoriality and the Problem of Demarcating Sociocultural Space', in *Tribes and Boundaries in Australia*, ed. Nicolas Peterson (Canberra: Australian Institute of Aboriginal Studies, 1976) pp. 133–61.

Bery, Ashok, '"Reflexive Worlds": The Indias of A. K. Ramanujan', in *Alternative Indias: Writing, Nation and Communalism*, ed. Peter Morey and Alex Tickell (Amsterdam: Rodopi, 2005), pp. 115–39.

——, '"We Have Grown to Look at the Large World As Part of Us": Modernity and the Nation in Two Indian Novels of the 1930s', in *The Political Subject: Essays on the Self from Art, Politics and Science*, ed. Wendy Wheeler (London: Lawrence and Wishart, 2000), pp. 160–78.

Bhabha, Homi, *The Location of Culture* (London; Routledge, 1994).

Bourke, Lawrence, *A Vivid Steady State: Les Murray and Australian Poetry* (Kensington and Strawberry Hills, NSW: New South Wales University Press/New Endeavour Press, 1992).

Brathwaite, Edward (E. K.), *The Arrivants: A New World Trilogy* (Oxford: Oxford University Press, 1973).

——, *The Development of Creole Society in Jamaica 1770–1820* (Oxford: Clarendon Press, 1971).

Breiner, Laurence A., 'Creole Language in the Poetry of Derek Walcott', *Callaloo*, 28 (2005), pp. 29–41.

Breslin, Paul, *Nobody's Nation: Reading Derek Walcott* (Chicago, IL: University of Chicago Press, 2001).

Brooks, David, 'A Land Without Lendings: Judith Wright, Kenosis and Australian Vision', *Southerly*, 60. 2 (2000), pp. 51–64.

Brown, Terence, *Louis MacNeice: Sceptical Vision* (Dublin: Gill and Macmillan, 1975).

——, 'MacNeice and the Puritan Tradition', in *Louis MacNeice and His Influence*, ed. Devine and Peacock, pp. 20–33.

Burnett, Paula, *Derek Walcott: Politics and Poetics* (Gainesville: University Press of Florida, 2000).

Burris, Sidney, *The Poetry of Resistance: Seamus Heaney and the Pastoral Tradition* (Athens: Ohio University Press, 1990).

Carroll, Claire, 'Introduction: The Nation and Postcolonial Theory', in *Ireland and Postcolonial Theory*, ed. Carroll and King, pp. 1–15.

Carroll, Claire and Patricia King, eds, *Ireland and Postcolonial Theory* (Cork: Cork University Press, 2003).

Carson, Ciaran, 'Escaped from the Massacre?', *The Honest Ulsterman*, 50 (Winter 1975), pp. 183–6.

Carter, Paul, *The Road to Botany Bay: An Essay in Spatial History* (London: Faber and Faber, 1987).

Chakrabarty, Dipesh, 'Postcoloniality and the Artifice of History: Who Speaks for "Indian" Pasts?', *Representations*, 37 (Winter 1992), pp. 1–26.

Chandumenon, O., *Indulekha*, trans. Anitha Devasia (New Delhi: Oxford University Press, 2005).

Chatterjee, Partha, *The Nation and its Fragments: Colonial and Postcolonial Histories* (Princeton, NJ: Princeton University Press, 1993).

Chatwin, Bruce, *The Songlines* (London: Jonathan Cape, 1987).

Cheyfitz, Eric, *The Poetics of Imperialism: Translation and Colonization from* The Tempest *to* Tarzan (New York: Oxford University Press, 1991).

Chickering, Howell, 'Beowulf and "Heaneywulf"', *Kenyon Review*, 24. 1 (Winter 2002), pp. 160–78.

Clark Hall, J. R., trans., *Beowulf: A Metrical Translation into Modern English* (Cambridge: Cambridge University Press, 1914).

Clark, Heather, 'Revising MacNeice', *Cambridge Quarterly*, 31 (2002), pp. 77–92.

Clarke, Marcus, Preface to Adam Lindsay Gordon, *Poems* (London: R. A. Thompson, 1905).

Cleary, Joe, '"Misplaced Ideas"?: Colonialism, Location, and Dislocation in Irish Studies', in *Ireland and Postcolonial Theory*, ed. Carroll and King, pp. 16–45.

——, 'Postcolonial Ireland', in *Ireland and the British Empire*, ed. Kevin Kenny (Oxford: Oxford University Press, 2004), pp. 251–88.

Clifford, James and George E. Marcus, eds, *Writing Culture: The Poetics and Politics of Ethnography* (Berkeley: University of California Press, 1986).

Corcoran, Neil, *The Poetry of Seamus Heaney: A Critical Study* (London: Faber and Faber, 1998).

Coughlan, Patricia, '"Bog Queens": The Representation of Women in the Poetry of John Montague and Seamus Heaney', in *Gender in Irish Writing*, ed. Toni O'Brien Johnson and David Cairns (Milton Keynes: Open University Press, 1991), pp. 89–111.

Coulton, Barbara, *Louis MacNeice in the BBC* (London: Faber and Faber, 1980).

Crawford, Robert, 'Les Murray's "Presence Sequence"', in *Counterbalancing Light*, ed. Carmel Gaffney, pp. 54–68.

Cullingford, Elizabeth Butler, '"Thinking of Her … as … Ireland": Yeats, Pearse, and Heaney', *Textual Practice*, 4 (1990), pp. 1–21.

Davie, Donald, *Poetry in Translation* (Milton Keynes: Open University Press, 1975).

Davis, Gregson, '"With No Homeric Shadow": The Disavowal of Epic in Derek Walcott's *Omeros*', *South Atlantic Quarterly*, 96 (1997), pp. 321–33.

Devine, Kathleen and Alan J. Peacock, eds, *Louis MacNeice and His Influence* (Gerrards Cross: Colin Smythe, 1998).

Devy, G. N., 'Translation and Literary History: An Indian View', in *Post-colonial Translation*, ed. Susan Bassnett and Harish Trivedi, pp. 182–8.

——, 'Translation Theory: An Indian Perspective', in *Translation: From Periphery to Centrestage*, ed. Tutun Mukherjee, pp. 46–65.

Dharwadker, Vinay, 'A. K. Ramanujan's Theory and Practice of Translation', in *Post-colonial Translation*, ed. Susan Bassnett and Harish Trivedi, pp. 114–40.

Dingwaney, Anuradha and Carol Maier, eds, *Between Languages and Cultures: Translation and Cross-Cultural Texts* (Pittsburgh: University of Pittsburgh Press, 1995).

Dirlik, Arif, 'The Postcolonial Aura: Third World Criticism in the Age of Global Capitalism', *Critical Inquiry*, 20 (Winter 1994), pp. 328–56.

Dolan, Terence Patrick, *A Dictionary of Hiberno-English: The Irish Use of English* (Dublin: Gill and Macmillan, 1998), p. 271.

Dougherty, Carol, 'Homer after *Omeros*: Reading a H/Omeric Text', *South Atlantic Quarterly*, 96 (1997), pp. 335–57.

Douglas, Mary, *Purity and Danger: An Analysis of the Concepts of Pollution and Taboo* (1966; London: Ark, 1984).

Dryden, John, 'Preface to Ovid's *Epistles*, Translated by Several Hands', in *John Dryden*, ed. Keith Walker (Oxford: Oxford University Press, 1987) pp. 155–64.

Earle, John, trans., *The Deeds of Beowulf: An English Epic of the Eighth Century Done into Modern Prose* (Oxford: Clarendon Press, 1892).

Eliot, T. S., *Collected Poems 1909–1962* (London: Faber and Faber, 1963).

Elkin, A. P., *The Australian Aborigines: How to Understand Them*, 3rd ed. (Sydney: Angus and Robertson, 1954).

Elliott, Brian, ed., *The Jindyworobaks* (St Lucia: University of Queensland Press, 1979).

Evans, Ruth, 'Metaphor of Translation', in *Routledge Encyclopedia of Translation Studies*, ed. Baker, pp. 149–53.

Farrell, Joseph, 'Walcott's *Omeros*: The Classical Epic in a Postmodern World', *South Atlantic Quarterly*, 96 (1997), pp. 247–73.

Fraser, G. S., 'Evasive Honesty: The Poetry of Louis MacNeice', in *Vision and Rhetoric: Studies in Modern Poetry* (London: Faber and Faber, 1959), pp. 179–92.

Fryatt, Kit, '"Banyan Riot of Dialectic": Louis MacNeice's India', paper presented at the fourth Galway Conference on Colonialism, 2–5 June 2004: in *Ireland and India: Colonies, Culture and Empire*, ed. Maureen O'Connor and Tadhg Foley (Dublin: Irish Academic Press, 2006).

Fumagalli, Maria Cristina, *The Flight of the Vernacular: Seamus Heaney, Derek Walcott and the Impress of Dante* (Amsterdam: Rodopi, 2001).

Gaffney, Carmel, ed., *Counterbalancing Light: Essays on the Poetry of Les Murray* (Armidale, NSW: Kardoorair Press, 1996).

Geertz, Clifford 'Found in Translation: On the Social History of the Moral Imagination', in *Local Knowledge: Further Essays in Interpretive Anthropology*, (1983; London: Fontana, 1993) pp. 36–54.

——, '"From the Native's Point of View": On the Nature of Anthropological Understanding', in *Local Knowledge*, (1983; London: Fontana, 1993) pp. 55–70.

Grennan, Eamon, 'In a Topographical Frame: Ireland in the Poetry of Louis MacNeice', in *Facing the Music: Irish Poetry in the Twentieth Century* (Omaha, Nebraska: Creighton Univerisity Press, 1999), pp. 192–207.

Gupta, Prasenjit, Introduction to *Indian Errant: Selected Stories of Nirmal Verma*, trans. Gupta (New Delhi: Indialog, 2002), pp. i–lxxvi.

Hall, Stuart, 'When Was "The Post-Colonial?" Thinking at the Limit', in *The Post-Colonial Question: Common Skies, Divided Horizons*, ed. Iain Chambers and Lidia Curti (London: Routledge, 1996), pp. 242–60.

Hamner, Robert D., *Epic of the Dispossessed: Derek Walcott's* Omeros (Columbia: University of Missouri Press, 1997).

——, ed., *Critical Perspectives on Derek Walcott* (Boulder: Lynne Rienner, 1997).

Hart, Kevin, 'Darkness and Lostness: How to Read a Poem by Judith Wright', in *Imagining Australia: Literature and Culture in the New World*, ed. Judith Ryan and Chris Wallace-Crabbe (Cambridge, MA: Harvard University Committee on Australian Studies, 2004).

——, '"Interest" in Les A. Murray', *Australian Literary Studies*, 14 (1989), pp. 147–59.

Heaney, Seamus, *Among Schoolchildren: A Lecture Dedicated to the Memory of John Malone* (Belfast: John Malone Memorial Committee, 1983).

——, *An Open Letter* (Derry: Field Day, 1983).

——, trans., *Beowulf* (London: Faber and Faber, 1999).

——, 'Correspondences: Emigrants and Inner Exiles', in *Migrations: The Irish At Home and Abroad*, ed. Richard Kearney (Dublin: Wolfhound Press, 1990), pp. 21–31.

——, *The Cure at Troy: A Version of Sophocles' Philoctetes* (London: Faber and Faber, 1990).

——, *Death of a Naturalist* (London: Faber and Faber, 1966).

——, 'The Drag of the Golden Chain', *TLS*, 12 November 1999, pp. 14–16.

——, *Electric Light* (London: Faber and Faber, 2001).

——, *Finders Keepers: Selected Prose 1971–2001* (London: Faber and Faber, 2002).

——, 'The Frontier of Writing', in *Irish Writers and their Creative Process*, ed. Jacqueline Genet and Wynne Hellegouarc'h (Gerards Cross: Colin Smythe, 1996), pp. 3–16.

——, 'Further Language', *Studies in the Literary Imagination*, 30. 2 (Fall 1997), pp. 7–16.

——, *The Government of the Tongue: The 1986 T. S. Eliot Memorial Lectures and Other Critical Writings* (London: Faber and Faber, 1988).

——, *The Haw Lantern* (London: Faber and Faber, 1987).

——, *The Midnight Verdict* (Oldcastle, Co. Meath: Gallery Books, 1993).

——, *North* (London: Faber and Faber, 1975).

——, *Opened Ground: Poems 1966–1996* (London: Faber and Faber, 1998).

——, *The Place of Writing* (Atlanta, GA: Scholars Press, 1989).

——, *Preoccupations: Selected Prose 1968–1978* (London: Faber and Faber, 1980).

——, *The Redress of Poetry: Oxford Lectures* (London: Faber and Faber, 1995).

——, *The Spirit Level* (London: Faber and Faber, 1996).

——, *Station Island* (London: Faber and Faber, 1984).

——, *Wintering Out* (London: Faber and Faber, 1972).

Hergenhan, Laurie and Bruce Clunies Ross, eds, *The Poetry of Les Murray: Critical Essays* (St Lucia: University of Queensland Press, 2001).

Higgins, F. R. and Louis MacNeice, 'Tendencies in Modern Poetry: Discussion between F. R. Higgins and Louis MacNeice, Broadcast from Northern Ireland', *The Listener*, 27 July 1939, pp. 185–6.

Hodge, Bob and Vijay Mishra, *Dark Side of the Dream: Australian Literature and the Postcolonial Mind* (Sydney: Allen and Unwin, 1990).

Hooper, Glen, Introduction to *Irish and Postcolonial Writing: History, Theory, Practice*, ed. Glen Hooper and Colin Graham (Basingstoke: Palgrave Macmillan, 2002), pp. 1–31.

Hope, A. D., *Collected Poems 1930–1970*, rev. ed. (Sydney: Angus and Robertson, 1972).

——, 'Culture Corroboree', in *The Jindyworobaks*, ed. Elliott, pp. 248–52.

Hulme, Peter, 'Including America', *Ariel*, 26.1 (January 1995), pp. 117–23 (p. 120).

Hume, Lynne, *Ancestral Power: The Dreaming, Consciousness and Aboriginal Australians* (Melbourne: Melbourne University Press, 2002).

Innes, C. L. 'Postcolonial Studies and Ireland', in *Comparing Postcolonial Literatures: Dislocations*, ed. Ashok Bery and Patricia Murray (Basingstoke: Macmillan, 2000), pp. 21–30.

Kane, Paul, *Australian Poetry: Romanticism and Negativity* (Cambridge: Cambridge University Press, 1996).

——, 'Les Murray', in *International Literature in English: Essays on the Major Writers*, ed. Robert L. Ross (New York: Garland, 1991), pp. 437–46.

Karamcheti, Indira, 'Aimé Césaire's Subjective Geographies: Translating Place and the Difference it Makes', in *Between Languages and Cultures*, ed. Dingwaney and Maier, pp. 181–97.

Kennedy, David, 'Mound-dwellers and Mummers: Language and Community in Seamus Heaney's *Wintering Out*', *Irish Studies Review*, 10 (2002), pp. 303–13.

Kennedy-Andrews, Elmer, 'John Montague: Global Regionalist?', *Cambridge Quarterly*, 35 (2006), pp. 31–48.

Khilnani, Sunil, *The Idea of India* (London: Hamish Hamilton, 1997).

Kiberd, Declan, *Inventing Ireland: The Literature of the Modern Nation* (London: Jonathan Cape, 1995).

King, Bruce, *Modern Indian Poetry in English*, rev. ed. (New Delhi: Oxford University Press, 2001).

——, *Three Indian Poets: Nissim Ezekiel, A. K. Ramanujan, Dom Moraes* (Madras: Oxford University Press, 1991).

Lal, P., trans., *The Mahabharata* of Vyasa (New Delhi: Tarang Paperbacks, 1989).

——, *Transcreation: Seven Essays on the Art of Transcreation* (Calcutta: Writers' Workshop, 1996).

Larkin, Philip, *Collected Poems*, ed. Anthony Thwaite (London: Faber and Faber, 1988).

Leer, Martin, '"This Country Is My Mind": Les Murray's Poetics of Place', in *The Poetry of Les Murray*, ed. Laurie Hergenhan and Bruce Clunies Ross, pp. 15–42.

Lefkowitz, Mary, 'Bringing Him Back Alive', in *Critical Perspectives on Derek Walcott*, ed. Robert D. Hamner (Boulder: Lynne Rienner, 1997) pp. 400–3.

Lerer, Seth, '"On fagne flor": The Postcolonial *Beowulf*, from Heorot to Heaney', in *Postcolonial Approaches to the European Middle Ages: Translating Cultures*, ed. Ananya Jahanara Kabir and Deanne Williams (Cambridge: Cambridge University Press, 2005), pp. 77–102.

Lewis, R. W. B., *The American Adam: Innocence, Tragedy and Tradition in the Nineteenth Century* (Chicago, IL: University of Chicago Press, 1955).

Lienhardt, Godfrey, 'Modes of Thought', in E. E. Evans-Pritchard, Raymond Firth, E. R. Leach, J. G. Peristiany, *The Institutions of Primitive Society: A Series of Broadcast Talks*, John Layard, Max Gluckman, Meyer Fortes and Godfrey Lienhardt (Oxford: Blackwell, 1954), pp. 95–107.

Liuzza, R. M., trans., *Beowulf: A New Verse Translation* (Peterborough, Ontario: Broadview Press, 2000).

Lloyd, David, 'After History: Historicism and Irish Postcolonial Studies', in *Ireland and Postcolonial Theory*, ed. Carroll and King, pp. 46–62.

——, '"Pap for the Dispossessed": Seamus Heaney and the Poetics of Identity', in *Anomalous States: Irish Writing and the Postcolonial Moment* (Dublin: Lilliput Press, 1993), pp. 13–40.

Longley, Edna, *Louis MacNeice: A Study* (London: Faber and Faber, 1988).

Lucas, Rose, and Lyn McCredden, 'Through a Web of Language: Landscapes of Perception in the Poetry of Judith Wright', in *Bridgings: Readings in Australian Women's Poetry* (Melbourne: Oxford University Press, 1996), pp. 18–28.

Mabo and Others v. *Queensland* (No. 2) (1992) 175 clr 1 f. c. 92/014, http://www.austlii.edu.au/au/cases/cth/high_ct/175clr1.html (accessed 18 June 2006).

Macafee, C. I., ed., *A Concise Ulster Dictionary* (Oxford: Oxford University Press, 1996).

Macintyre, Stuart, *A Concise History of Australia*, 2nd ed. (Cambridge: Cambridge University Press, 2004).

MacNeice, Hedli, 'The Story of the House that Louis Built', in *Studies on Louis MacNeice*, ed. Jacqueline Genet and Wynne Hellegouarc'h (Caen: Centre de Publications de l'Université de Caen, 1988).

MacNeice, Louis, *Collected Poems* (London: Faber and Faber, 1966; repr. 1979).

——, 'India at First Sight', BBC Written Archives Centre, Reading.

——, *Modern Poetry: A Personal Essay* (Oxford: Oxford University Press, 1938).

——, *The Poetry of W. B. Yeats* (London: Oxford University Press, 1941).

——, 'The Sideliner', *New Statesman and Nation*, 4 April 1953, p. 402, quoted in McDonald, *Louis MacNeice*, p. 138.

——, *Selected Literary Criticism*, ed. Alan Heuser (Oxford: Clarendon Press, 1987).

——, *Selected Prose*, ed. Alan Heuser (Oxford: Clarendon Press, 1990).

——, *The Strings Are False: An Unfinished Autobiography* (London: Faber and Faber, 1965; repr. in paperback, 1982).

Mahon, Derek, 'MacNeice in England and Ireland', in *Time Was Away: The World of Louis MacNeice*, ed. Terence Brown and Alec Reid (Dublin: Dolmen Press, 1974), pp. 113–22.

Matthews, Steven, *Les Murray* (Manchester: Manchester University Press, 2001).

McCarthy, Conor, 'Language and History in Seamus Heaney's *Beowulf*', *English*, 50 (2001), pp. 149–58.

McClintock, Anne, 'The Angel of Progress: Pitfalls of the Term "Post-colonialism"', *Social Text*, 31–2 (Spring 1992), pp. 84–98.

McDonald, Peter, *Louis MacNeice: The Poet in His Contexts* (Oxford: Clarendon Press, 1991).

——, *Mistaken Identities: Poetry and Northern Ireland* (Oxford: Clarendon Press, 1997).

——, '"With Eyes Turned Down on the Past": MacNeice's Classicism', in *Louis MacNeice and His Influence*, ed. Devine and Peacock, pp. 34–52.

McKernan, Susan, *A Question of Commitment: Australian Literature in the Twenty Years after the War* (Sydney: Allen and Unwin, 1989).

McLeod, John, *Beginning Postcolonialism* (Manchester: Manchester University Press, 2000).

Mehrez, Samia 'Translation and the Postcolonial Experience: The Francophone North African Text', in *Rethinking Translation*, ed. Venuti, pp. 120–38.

Mehrotra, Arvind Krishna, Introduction to *The Oxford India Anthology of Twelve Modern Indian Poets* (Delhi: Oxford University Press, 1992), pp. 1–12.

——, 'Looking for Ramanujan', in *A History of Indian Literature in English*, ed. Arvind Krishna Mehrotra (London: Hurst and Co., 2003), pp. 295–307.

Merrill, James, *Collected Poems* (New York: Alfred A. Knopf, 2001).

Mishra, Sudesh, *Preparing Faces: Modernism and Indian Poetry in English* (Suva, Fiji and Adelaide: The University of the South Pacific and The Centre for Research in the New Literatures in English, Flinders University, 1995).

Mishra, Vijay and Bob Hodge, 'What is Post(-)colonialism?', *Textual Practice*, 5 (1991), pp. 399–414.

Moffett, Joe W., '"Master, I Was the Freshest of All Your Readers": Derek Walcott's *Omeros* and Homer as Literary Origin', *Literature Interpretation Theory*, 16 (2005), pp. 1–23.

Molino, Michael, *Questioning Tradition, Language and Myth: The Poetry of Seamus Heaney* (Washington DC: Catholic University of America Press, 1994).

Moore-Gilbert, Bart, *Postcolonial Theory: Context, Practices, Politics* (London: Verso, 1997).

Mukherjee, Meenakshi, *Realism and Reality: The Novel and Society in India* (Delhi: Oxford University Press, 1985; repr. with corrections, 1994).

Mukherjee, Sujit, 'Transcreating Translation', in *Translation as Recovery*, ed. Meenakshi Mukherjee (Delhi: Pencraft International, 2004), pp. 43–52.

Mukherjee, Tutun, ed., *Translation: From Periphery to Centrestage* (New Delhi: Prestige, 1998).

Muldoon, Paul, ed., *The Faber Book of Contemporary Irish Poetry* (London: Faber and Faber, 1986).

Murray, Les, *The Daylight Moon* (Manchester: Carcanet Press, 1987).

——, *New Collected Poems* (Manchester: Carcanet, 2003).

——, ed., *The New Oxford Book of Australian Verse*, 3rd ed. (Melbourne: Oxford University Press, 1996).

——, *The Paperbark Tree: Selected Prose* (Manchester: Carcanet, 1992).

——, *The Peasant Mandarin: Prose Pieces* (St Lucia: University of Queensland Press, 1978).

——, *The Quality of Sprawl: Thoughts about Australia* (Sydney: Duffy and Snellgrove, 1999).

——, *Translations from the Natural World* (Manchester; Carcanet Press, 1993).

Murray, Les, Todd Gitlin and Mick O'Regan, *The Media Report*, Australian Broadcasting Corporation radio programme, 14 June 2001, http://www.abc.net.au/rn/mediareport/stories/2001/312656.htm# (accessed 7 June 2006).

Naipaul, V.S., *India: A Wounded Civilization* (1977; Harmondsworth: Penguin, 1979).

——, *The Middle Passage* (1962; Harmondsworth: Penguin, 1969).

Niranjana, Tejaswani, *Siting Translation: History, Post-Structuralism and the Colonial Context* (Berkeley and Los Angeles: University of California Press, 1992).

Nyoongah, Mudrooroo, *Aboriginal Mythology* (London: Aquarian, 1994).

O'Donoghue, Bernard, *Seamus Heaney and the Language of Poetry* (Hemel Hempstead: Harvester Wheatsheaf, 1994).

Olivelle, Patrick, trans., *The Upaniṣads* (Oxford: Oxford University Press, 1996).

Pandey, Gyanendra, 'In Defense of the Fragment: Writing About Hindu-Muslim Riots in India Today', *Representations*, 37 (Winter 1992), pp. 27–55.

Paniker, Ayyappa, 'Towards an Indian Theory of Literary Translation', in *Translation: From Periphery to Centrestage*, ed. Tutun Mukherjee, pp. 39–46.

Parker, Michael, *Seamus Heaney: The Making of the Poet* (Basingstoke: Macmillan, 1993).

Patke, Rajeev S., *Postcolonial Poetry in English* (Oxford: Oxford University Press, 2006).

Paulin, Tom, 'The Man from No Part: Louis MacNeice', in *Ireland and the English Crisis* (Newcastle upon Tyne: Bloodaxe, 1984), pp. 75–9.

Paz, Octavio, 'Translation: Literature and Letters', trans. Irene del Corral, in *Theories of Translation from Dryden to Derrida*, ed. Rainer Schulte and John Biguenet (Chicago, IL: University of Chicago Press, 1992), pp. 152–62.

Pratt, Mary Louise, *Imperial Eyes: Travel Writing and Transculturation* (London: Routledge, 1992).

Pym, Anthony, 'Schleiermacher and the Problem of *Blendlinge*', *Translation and Literature* 4 (1995), pp. 5–30.

Rafael, Vicente, *Contracting Colonialism: Translation and Christian Conversion in Tagalog Society under Early Spanish Rule* (1988; Durham, NC: Duke University Press, 1993).

Rai, Alok, *Hindi Nationalism* (New Delhi: Orient Longman, 2001).

Ramanujan, A. K., *The Collected Essays of A. K. Ramanujan*, gen. ed. Vinay Dharwadker (New Delhi: Oxford University Press, 1999).

——, *The Collected Poems of A. K. Ramanujan*, ed. Vinay Dharwadker (New Delhi: Oxford University Press, 1995).

——, trans., *Poems of Love and War: From the Eight Anthologies and the Ten Long Poems of Classical Tamil* (New York: Columbia University Press, 1985).

——, trans., *Speaking of Śiva* (London: Penguin Books, 1973).

——, *Uncollected Poems and Prose*, ed. Molly Daniels-Ramanujan and Keith Harrison (New Delhi: Oxford University Press, 2001).

Ramazani, Jahan, *The Hybrid Muse: Postcolonial Poetry in English* (Chicago, IL: University of Chicago Press, 2001).

——, 'Metaphor and Postcoloniality: The Poetry of A. K. Ramanujan', *Contemporary Literature*, 39 (1998), pp. 27–53.

——, 'The Wound of History: Walcott's *Omeros* and the Postcolonial Poetics of Affliction', *PMLA*, 112 (1997), pp. 405–17.

Roberts, Neil, *Narrative and Voice in Postwar Poetry* (Harlow: Longman, 1999).

Robinson, Douglas, 'Babel, tower of', in *Routledge Encyclopedia of Translation Studies*, ed. Baker, pp. 21–2.

——, 'Decolonizing Translation', *Translation and Literature*, 2 (1993), pp. 113–24.

——, 'Hermeneutic Motion', in *Routledge Encyclopedia of Translation Studies*, ed. Baker, pp. 97–9.

——, *Translation and Empire: Postcolonial Theories Explained* (Manchester: St Jerome, 1997).

——, ed., *Western Translation Theory: From Herodotus to Nietzsche* (Manchester: St Jerome, 1997).

Roebuck, Valerie J., trans., *The Upaniṣads* (New Delhi: Penguin, 2000).

Rose, Deborah Bird, *Dingo Makes Us Human: Life and Land in an Australian Aboriginal Culture* (Cambridge: Cambridge University Press, 2000).

Ryan, Simon, *The Cartographic Eye: How Explorers Saw Australia* (Cambridge: Cambridge University Press, 1996).

Sahgal, Nayantara, 'The Schizophrenic Imagination', in *From Commonwealth to Post-Colonial*, ed. Anna Rutherford (Sydney, Mundelstrup and Coventry: Dangaroo Press, 1992), pp. 30–6.

Said, Edward, 'Afterword: Reflections on Ireland and Postcolonialism', in *Ireland and Postcolonial Theory*, ed. Carroll and King, pp. 177–85.

Satchidanandan, K., 'The State of Translation', in *Indian Literature: Positions and Propositions* (Delhi: Pencraft International, 1999), pp. 171–7.

Savarkar, Vinayak Damodar, *Essentials of Hinduism: Who is a Hindu?*, 6th ed. (New Delhi: Bharti Sahitya Sadan, 1989).

Scarfe, Francis, *Auden and After: The Liberation of Poetry 1930–1941* (London: Routledge, 1942).

Schleiermacher, Friedrich, 'On the Different Methods of Translating', trans. Susan Bernofsky, in *Translation Studies Reader*, ed. Venuti, pp. 43–63.

Shoemaker, Adam, *Black Words, White Page: Aboriginal Literature, 1929–1988* (St Lucia: University of Queensland Press, 1989).

Shohat, Ella, 'Notes on the "Post-Colonial"', *Social Text*, 31–2 (Spring 1992), pp. 99–113.

Stallworthy, Jon, *Louis MacNeice* (London: Faber and Faber, 1995).

Steiner, George, *After Babel: Aspects of Language and Translation*, 3rd ed. (Oxford: Oxford University Press, 1998).

Strand, Mark, *Dark Harbor: A Poem* (New York: Alfred A. Knopf, 1993).

Stutley, Margaret and James, *A Dictionary of Hinduism: Its Mythology, Folklore and Development 1500 BC–AD 1500* (London and Henley: Routledge and Kegan Paul, 1977).

Taylor, Andrew, *Reading Australian Poetry* (St Lucia: University of Queensland Press, 1987).

Terada, Rei, *Derek Walcott's Poetry: American Mimicry* (Boston, MA: Northeastern University Press, 1992).

Thieme, John, *Derek Walcott* (Manchester: Manchester University Press, 1999).

Trilling, Lionel, 'Why We Read Jane Austen', *TLS*, 5 March 1976, pp. 250–2.

Trivedi, Harish, 'India and Post-colonial Discourse', in *Interrogating Post-Colonialism: Theory, Text and Context*, ed. Harish Trivedi and Meenakshi Mukherjee (Shimla: Indian Institute of Advanced Study, 1996).

——, 'Translating Culture vs. Cultural Translation', *91st Meridian* (May 2005), http://www.uiowa.edu/~iwp/91st/may2005/pdfs/trivedi.pdf (accessed 3 June 2006).

Vendler, Helen, *Seamus Heaney* (London: HarperCollins, 1998).

Venuti, Lawrence, ed., *Rethinking Translation: Discourse, Subjectivity, Ideology* (London: Routledge, 1992).

——, *The Translator's Invisibility: A History of Translation* (London: Routledge, 1995).

——, ed., *The Translation Studies Reader*, 2nd ed. (London: Routledge, 2000).

Vieira, Else Ribeiro Pires, 'Liberating Calibans: Readings of *Antropofagia* and Haroldo de Campos' Poetics of Transcreation', in *Post-colonial Translation*, ed. Bassnett and Trivedi, pp. 95–113.

Walcott, Derek, 'The Caribbean: Culture or Mimicry?', *Journal of InterAmerican Studies and World Affairs*, 16 (1974), pp. 3–13.

——, *Collected Poems 1948–1984* (New York: Farrar, Strauss and Giroux, 1986).

——, A Colonial's-Eye View of the Empire', *TriQuarterly*, no. 65 (Winter 1986), pp. 73–7.

——, 'The Figure of Crusoe' (1965), in *Critical Perspectives on Derek Walcott*, ed. Hamner, pp. 33–40.

——, *Midsummer* (London: Faber and Faber, 1984).

——, *Omeros* (London: Faber and Faber, 1990).

——, 'Reflections on *Omeros*', *South Atlantic Quarterly*, 96 (1997), pp. 229–46.

——, *What the Twilight Says: Essays* (London: Faber and Faber, 1998).

Walker, Shirley, *Flame and Shadow: A Study of Judith Wright's Poetry* (St Lucia: University of Queensland Press, 1991).

White James Boyd, 'On the Virtues of Not Understanding', in *Between Languages and Cultures*, ed. Dingwaney and Maier, pp. 333–9.

White, Jonathan, Introduction to *Recasting the World: Writing after Colonialism*, ed. Jonathan White (Baltimore: Johns Hopkins University Press, 1993), pp. 1–24.

White, Richard, *Inventing Australia: Images and Identity 1688–1980* (Sydney: Allen and Unwin, 1981).

Wieland, James, *The Ensphering Mind: History, Myth and Fiction in the Poetry of Allen Curnow, Nissim Ezekiel, A. D. Hope, A. M. Klein, Christopher Okigbo, and Derek Walcott* (Washington: Three Continents Press, 1988).

Wills, Clair, *Improprieties: Politics and Sexuality in Northern Irish Poetry* (Oxford: Clarendon, 1993).

Wrenn, C. L., ed., *Beowulf: With the Finnesburg Fragment*, 3rd ed., rev. W. F. Bolton (London: Harrap, 1973).

Wright, Judith, *Because I Was Invited* (Melbourne: Oxford University Press, 1975).

——, *Born of the Conquerors* (Canberra: Aboriginal Studies Press, 1991).

——, 'The Broken Links', in *Born of the Conquerors* (Canberra: Aboriginal Studies Press, 1991), pp. 29–30.

——, *Collected Poems 1942–1982* (Manchester: Carcanet, 1994).

——, *The Cry for the Dead* (Melbourne: Oxford University Press, 1981).

——, *The Generations of Men* (Sydney: Oxford University Press, 1959).

——, 'Landscape and Dreaming', *Daedalus*, 114.1 (Winter 1985), pp. 29–56.

——, *Preoccupations in Australian Poetry* (Melbourne: Oxford University Press, 1965).

——, 'Reading and Nationalism', in *Going on Talking* (Springwood, NSW: Butterfly Books, 1992), pp. 45–7.

——, 'The Upside-down Hut', *Australian Letters*, 3. 4 (June 1961), pp. 30–4.

——, *We Call for a Treaty* (Sydney: Fontana, 1985).

Young, Robert J. C., *Postcolonialism: A Very Short Introduction* (Oxford: Oxford University Press, 2003).

Index